AF478595

Studies in Economic Transition

General Editors: **Jens Hölscher**, Reader in Economics, University of Brighton; and **Horst Tomann**, Professor of Economics, Free University Berlin

This series has been established in response to a growing demand for a greater understanding of the transformation of economic systems. It brings together theoretical and empirical studies on economic transition and economic development. The post-communist transition from planned to market economies is one of the main areas of applied theory because in this field the most dramatic examples of change and economic dynamics can be found. The series aims to contribute to the understanding of specific major economic changes as well as to advance the theory of economic development. The implications of economic policy will be a major point of focus.

Titles include:

Lucian Cernat
EUROPEANIZATION, VARIETIES OF CAPITALISM AND ECONOMIC PERFORMANCE IN CENTRAL AND EASTERN EUROPE

Irwin Collier, Herwig Roggemann, Oliver Scholz and Horst Tomann (*editors*)
WELFARE STATES IN TRANSITION
East and West

Bruno Dallago (*editor*)
TRANSFORMATION AND EUROPEAN INTEGRATION
The Local Dimension

Bruno Dallago and Ichiro Iwasaki (*editors*)
CORPORATE RESTRUCTURING AND GOVERNANCE IN TRANSITION ECONOMIES

Hella Engerer
PRIVATIZATION AND ITS LIMITS IN CENTRAL AND EASTERN EUROPE
Property Rights in Transition

Saul Estrin, Grzegorz W. Kolodko and Milica Uvalic (*editors*)
TRANSITION AND BEYOND

Hubert Gabrisch and Rudiger Pohl (*editors*)
EU ENLARGEMENT AND ITS MACROECONOMIC EFFECTS IN EASTERN EUROPE
Currencies, Prices, Investment and Competitiveness

Oleh Havrylyshyn
DIVERGENT PATHS IN POST-COMMUNIST TRANSFORMATION
Capitalism for All or Capitalism for the Few?

Jens Hölscher (*editor*)
FINANCIAL TURBULENCE AND CAPITAL MARKETS IN TRANSITION COUNTRIES

Jens Hölscher and Anja Hochberg (*editors*)
EAST GERMANY'S ECONOMIC DEVELOPMENT SINCE UNIFICATION
Domestic and Global Aspects

Iraj Hoshi, Paul J.J. Welfens and Anna Wziatek-Kubiak (*editors*)
INDUSTRIAL COMPETITIVENESS AND RESTRUCTURING IN ENLARGED EUROPE
How Accession Countries Catch Up and Integrate in the European Union

Mihaela Keleman and Monika Kostera (*editors*)
CRITICAL MANAGEMENT RESEARCH IN EASTERN EUROPE
Managing the Transition

Emil J. Kirchner (*editor*)
DECENTRALIZATION AND TRANSITION IN THE VISEGRAD
Poland, Hungary, the Czech Republic and Slovakia

David Lane (*editor*)
THE TRANSFORMATION OF STATE SOCIALISM
System Change, Capitalism, or Something Else?

David Lane and Martin Myant (*editors*)
VARIETIES OF CAPITALISM IN POST-COMMUNIST COUNTRIES

Tomasz Mickiewicz
ECONOMIC TRANSITION IN CENTRAL EUROPE AND THE COMMONWEALTH OF
INDEPENDENT STATES

Milan Nikolić
MONETARY POLICY IN TRANSITION
Inflation Nexus Money Supply in Postcommunist Russia

Julie Pellegrin
THE POLITICAL ECONOMY OF COMPETITIVENESS IN AN ENLARGED EUROPE

Stanislav Poloucek (*editor*)
REFORMING THE FINANCIAL SECTOR IN CENTRAL EUROPEAN COUNTRIES

Gregg S. Robins
BANKING TRANSITION
East Germany after Unification

Johannes Stephan
ECONOMIC TRANSITION IN HUNGARY AND EAST GERMANY
Gradualism and Shock Therapy in Catch-up Development

Johannes Stephan (*editor*)
TECHNOLOGY TRANSFER VIA FOREIGN DIRECT INVESTMENT IN CENTRAL
AND EASTERN EUROPE

Horst Tomann
MONETARY INTEGRATION IN EUROPE

Hans van Zon
THE POLITICAL ECONOMY OF INDEPENDENT UKRAINE

Hans van Zon
RUSSIA'S DEVELOPMENT PROBLEM
The Cult of Power

Adalbert Winkler (*editor*)
BANKING AND MONETARY POLICY IN EASTERN EUROPE
The First Ten Years

Studies in Economic Transition
Series Standing Order ISBN 978–0–333–73353–0
(*outside North America only*)

You can receive future titles in this series as they are published by placing a standing order.
Please contact your bookseller or, in case of difficulty, write to us at the address below with
your name and address, the title of the series and the ISBN quoted above.

Customer Services Department, Macmillan Distribution Ltd, Houndmills, Basingstoke,
Hampshire RG21 6XS, England

Russia's Development Problem

The Cult of Power

Hans van Zon
Professor, Department of Geography
Rotterdam University of Applied Sciences
The Netherlands

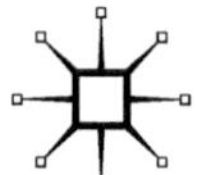

First published 2008 by
PALGRAVE MACMILLAN

Palgrave Macmillan in the UK is an imprint of Macmillan Publishers Limited, registered in England, company number 785998, of Houndmills, Basingstoke, Hampshire RG21 6XS.

Palgrave Macmillan in the US is a division of St Martin's Press LLC, 175 Fifth Avenue, New York, NY 10010.

Palgrave Macmillan is the global academic imprint of the above companies and has companies and representatives throughout the world.

Palgrave® and Macmillan® are registered trademarks in the United States, the United Kingdom, Europe and other countries.

ISBN-13: 978–0–230–54278–5
ISBN-10: 0–230–54278–6

This book is printed on paper suitable for recycling and made from fully managed and sustained forest sources. Logging, pulping and manufacturing processes are expected to conform to the environmental regulations of the country of origin.

A catalogue record for this book is available from the British Library.

Library of Congress Cataloging-in-Publication Data
Zon, Hans van, 1949–
  Russia's development problem : the cult of power / Hans van Zon.
    p. cm. — (Studies in economic transition)
  Includes bibliographical references and index.
  ISBN–13: 978–0–230–54278–5
  ISBN–10: 0–230–54278–6
1. Russia (Federation)—Social conditions—1991–   2. Russia
  (Federation)—Economic conditions—1991–   3. Russia
  (Federation)—Politics and government—1991– I. Title.
HN530.2.A8Z66 2009
306.30947'09049—dc22   2008030650

10 9 8 7 6 5 4 3 2 1
17 16 15 14 13 12 11 10 09 08

Printed and bound in Great Britain by
CPI Antony Rowe, Chippenham and Eastbourne

For Judith, Pauline and Misha

Contents

List of Tables, Schemes, Graphs and Maps

Tables

Schemes

Graphs

Maps

Acknowledgements

I would like to thank Jens Hölscher, Andre Mommen, David Pickup and Igor Egorov for commentating on draft versions of this book. I also would like to thank Alec Dubber and Keith Povey for their help in editing the manuscript.

HANS VAN ZON

Every effort has been made to contact all copyright-holders, but if any have been inadvertently overlooked the publishers will be pleased to make the necessary arrangement at the first opportunity.

Introduction

What development problem does Russia have after almost a decade of robust economic growth? It is maintained here that Russia faces growth without much development. It is reflected in a deteriorating infrastructure, neglected educational and health sectors, lack of innovation in industry, a growing technological gap with the West, enormous spatial imbalances and widespread poverty. These problems can not be seen in isolation from governance problems that are reflected in high levels of corruption, state capture, the inability of government to implement its policy and a parasitic bureaucracy. These governance problems are deeply rooted in a society that has known ages of autocratic rule.

This book is about the social prerequisites for Russian economic development. It focuses upon the way informal practices influenced Russia's recent economic performance. It is not about the realm of freedom but, on the contrary, about the constraints within which politicians and other actors have to act. It is about the path dependence of Russia on the basis of which it is possible to elaborate a successful development strategy.

The book deals with the outcome from below rather than the intention from above. Rather than dealing with the analysis of decision making processes at the top it is about the socio-genesis of the present economic system. Because Russia has known autocracy for most of its history, the ways rulers and ruled interact have been of extreme importance in shaping Russian economic history. It is argued that in Muscovy a mental model emerged that survived into the twenty-first century. It comprises, among others, a preference for personalized rule and an aversion against a regime of rules. It is argued that a cult of power constitutes a major impediment to social and economic development.

Chapter 1 presents circumstantial evidence for the relationship between culture, i.e. the sphere of values and informal social practices, and economic development in Central and Eastern Europe. The fact that good and bad economic performers are clustered geographically suggests that we should look beyond the quality of economic policy in explaining differences in economic performance. Also, the groups of similar economic performance correlate with cultural-behavioural and historic regions. Moreover, patterns of economic backwardness appear to be persistent and since the early nineteenth century Central and Eastern Europe have not managed to catch up with Western Europe.

It seems that catching up involves much more than introducing the market.

In Chapter 2 Soviet Russia's economic history is highlighted from a macro-sociological point of view. It looks at the past in so far as it is relevant for contemporary economic culture. It includes an interpretative history of the Russian state-society nexus. Russia's socialist experiment was one of a series of Russian attempts to catch up with the Western world. They were all state-led. Centuries of autocratic rule created an institutional matrix that was very resistant to change.

Although the October revolution constituted a clear break with tsarism and a centrally planned economy was a new economic system, many elements from the new economy were taken from the pre-socialist period. In many ways the new power built upon the legacy of the tsarist past.

Although informal practices helped people and enterprises to survive in Soviet times, at the same time it constituted a major obstacle to increasing efficiency and lowering transaction costs at all levels. In the last phase of the Soviet Union, informal practices constituted a time bomb for the communist system while at the same time shaping the new socio-economic system.

Chapter 3 shows how post-communist Russia built upon elements of the Soviet and even tsarist past. It is above all in the sphere of informal practices that continuity is prominent. Only in the formal institutional framework does it look as if Western modernity is copied.

Chapter 4 describes the way Russian history is reflected in dominant mental models, i.e., the national character of Russians. The various social practices that influence economic life are interrelated and are mutually re-enforcing. Despite value change since extraction from communism began, continuity in the sphere of values and social practices is prominent especially in the way authority is dealt with (the cult of power). The point of departure held here is the view that there is an interdependence between the structure of society at large and behavioural patterns of individuals.

In Chapter 5 the interrelations between the various elements of the political and economic system are analysed. Bureaucratic rule, the functioning of elite networks and the political process are all considered. Although a hybrid, contemporary Russia is characterized as a neo-patrimonial society with its own logic that is incompatible with Western modernity. Informal practices, hidden under the veneer of 'market economy' and 'parliamentary democracy' are much more important for explaining contemporary Russia than the formal institutional structure. The lack of trust, legal nihilism and the weak rule of law, the existence of closed networks that complicate the entry of new enterprises, parasitic bureaucratic rule and the capture of the state by private interests characterize economic life. The economic system, embedded in a neo-patrimonial polity, is explained from an economic and sociological perspective. It appears that most features of Russian neo-patrimonialism are directly related to the cult of power.

Chapter 6 analyses the case of Ukraine in order to show the strengths and weaknesses of the Russian variety of neo-patrimonialism that is dominant in Southern and Eastern Ukraine. This part of Ukraine belonged to the Soviet heartlands and is heavily russified and sovietized. Just before the Orange Revolution (end 2004) Ukraine drifted in the direction of non-competitive authoritarianism and one clan rule. The clan from Donetsk (eastern Ukraine) became increasingly powerful and many feared that the Donetsk model, very much akin to Russian-type neo-patrimonialism, would prevail in Ukraine. Neo-patrimonial rule was put to the test during the Orange Revolution that led to a re-run of a fraudulent election. When Viktor Yanukovych, who was defeated during the Orange Revolution, came back in 2006 as Prime Minister, the Donetsk model re-asserted itself. After the Orange Revolution the Russian variant of neo-patrimonialism consolidated in Southern and Eastern Ukraine. In a separate section this model is analysed and compared with Russian neo-patrimonialism. In particular the corporatism of Donetsk shows an alternative scenario for Russia.

Chapter 7 addresses the way forward for Russia referring to the global experience in socio-economic development. The chapter not only compares with the experience of Western developed market economies but above all with the experience of other, successful neo-patrimonial societies. The experience of Eastern Asian countries is especially relevant. The chapter proposes path-dependent path creation. It is argued that Russia needs a developmental and strong state and that there is, in principle, no antagonism between the state and the market. The state should create a stable and predictable economic environment. This assumes the curbing of endemic corruption and rent-seeking.

1
Divergence in Post-Socialism: The Role of Culture

In the early 1990s, after the abolishment of communism in Central and Eastern Europe, the dominant mood was that liberal market economy could be imposed in any country in a relatively short time.[1] Many believed that restoring the market meant restoring the natural state of affairs. International institutions like the International Monetary Fund (IMF), Organization for Economic Cooperation and Development (OECD), the World Bank and European Bank for Reconstruction and Development (EBRD) assumed that capitalism could be introduced by decree in Russia and other post-Soviet states. They stated in 1990 that:

> A recovery from the reduced level of output should be able to get underway in two years or so ... further, strong growth of output and rising living standards could be expected for the remainder of the decade and beyond. (IMF *et al.*, 1990, pp. 18–19)

They expected a quick fix that did not require any structural changes. They expected that the market could function as a lever to impose economic rationality upon society and economy. They implicitly assumed the prevalence of *Homo Economicus* who makes rational choices. Soon it became obvious that the post-socialist countries were not only faced with a transformational recession, in which wasteful and value subtracting activities were eliminated, but also with a 'normal' recession, caused by systemic transformation and the collapse of the socialist division of labour. But much more was involved. There is the institutional legacy that comprises ingrained social practices. It was often informal constraints that constituted impediments to the emergence of a more efficient economic system.

The widespread assumption was that Central and Eastern European backwardness was a mere consequence of centrally planned economy and that liberal market economy and market democracy would respond to the deepest aspirations of all people. The task was to quickly remove the barriers for free trade and introduce private property in order to let a liberal capitalism flourish. To that end the institutions of global economic governance elaborated a standardized path of transformation. It was assumed that most Central and East European countries would have good development prospects given the high educational levels, well-developed infrastructure and industrial capacities. The idea was that institutions could be built from scratch so that the tangible potential could be converted in welfare gains. The assumption was also that the past has not left a legacy in the minds of the people concerned in terms of world outlooks, value systems and ingrained social practices.

Later, it appeared that rather than a transition to liberal market economy, a transition to a variety of socio-economic systems took place, often far removed from a liberal market economy but very much shaped by national traditions. Political regimes varied from the Sultanistic autocracies in Central Asia to liberal democracies in Central Europe, from the unreformed dictatorship of Belarus to the oligarchic authoritarianism of Russia. It also appeared that a rapid economic divergence occurred in terms of GDP per capita. In this chapter we analyse divergence in Central and Eastern Europe and focus on the relationship between culture, seen as the collective programming of the mind, politics and economy.

Economic, political and cultural divergence in Central and Eastern Europe

Between 1973 and 1990 a process of economic divergence occurred within Central and Eastern Europe that was accelerated during 1990–1998 (see Maddison, 2001).

Economic performance indicators show clear divides between the countries that became members of the EU in 2004 (two sub-groups, Poland, Slovakia, Czech Republic, Hungary and Slovenia on the one hand and the Baltic states on the other), Bulgaria and Romania (members EU 2007) and lastly, Ukraine, Belarus, Russia and Kazakhstan (Map 1.1, Table 1.1). Notable is that the countries in each group are adjoining and share common histories.

We should take into account the fact that, for example, Russia and Kazakhstan profited enormously from their wealth of natural resources.

Map 1.1   Central and Eastern Europe, country groupings

The same groupings appear if we look at some economic environment indicators such as the perception of corruption and state capture (Table 1.2).[2]

The above mentioned groupings are again pronounced when looking at the correlation between competitiveness, political rights and civil liberties (Table 1.3).

Graph 1.1 shows the performance of selected Central and Eastern European countries with respect to governance indicators (voice and accountability, political stability, government effectiveness, regulatory quality and the rule of law).

They show a clear divide in Central and Eastern Europe between those post-socialist countries that entered the EU in 2004 and the other post-socialist countries.

Table 1.1   Real GDP (2005/1990), GDP per capita (2006) and human development index (2007/8) in Eastern Europe and the CIS

	Real GDP, 2005 (1990 = 100)	GDP per capita, ppp 2006 ($)	Human development index 2007/8 ranking
Poland	168	15,364	37
Slovenia	142	25,769	27
Hungary	137	18,956	36
Slovakia		18,457	42
Czech Republic	124	23,024	32
Estonia	165	19,702	44
Latvia	120	16,198	45
Lithuania	116	16,747	43
Romania	120	11,017	60
Bulgaria	120	10,757	53

	Real GDP/NMP, 2005 (1989 = 100)	GNP per capita, ppp 2006 ($)	Human development index 2007/8 ranking
Belarus	132	8,889	64
Kazakhstan	123	8,837	73
Russia	93	11,957	67
Ukraine	69	7,782	76

Sources: Economic Commission for Europe and Human Development Project

Table 1.2   Central and Eastern Europe: corruption perception index (2007) and state capture index (1999)

	Corruption perception index, 2007	State capture index, 1999
Poland	4.2	0.17
Slovenia	6.6	
Hungary	5.3	0.10
Slovakia	4.9	0.34
Czech Republic	5.2	0.16
Estonia	6.5	0.14
Latvia	4.8	0.22
Lithuania	4.8	0.17
Bulgaria	4.1	0.40
Romania	3.7	0.30
Belarus	2.1	0.12
Kazakhstan	2.1	0.18
Russia	2.3	0.45
Ukraine	2.7	0.45

Sources: Data from Transparency International, World Bank and Havrylyshyn, 2006, p. 192

Table 1.3 Central and Eastern Europe: global competitiveness ranking, political rights and civil liberties ranking

	Global competitiveness ranking 2007/8	Political rights 2005	Civil liberties 2005
Poland	51	1	1
Slovenia	39	1	1
Hungary	47	1	1
Slovakia	41	1	1
Czech Rep.	33	1	1
Estonia	27	1	1
Latvia	45	1	2
Lithuania	38	2	2
Bulgaria	79	1	2
Romania	74	3	2
Belarus		7	6
Kazakhstan	61	6	5
Russia	58	6	5
Ukraine	73	4	3

Sources: Freedom House and World Economic Forum

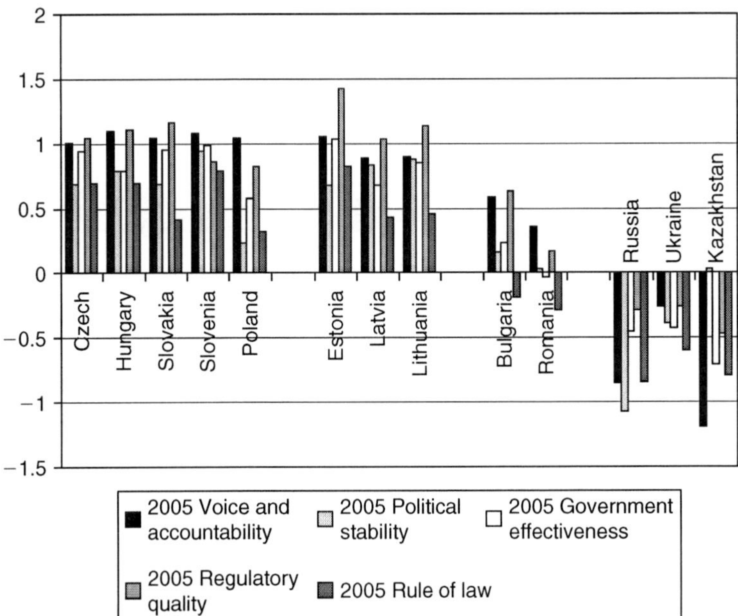

Graph 1.1 Central and Eastern Europe: governance indicators, 2005
Source: World Bank

Also, there is a correlation between the duration of communist rule and the above rankings as there is a correlation between the experience of capitalist development and parliamentary democracy before the introduction of socialism and the rankings. It all suggests that history, especially pre-socialist history, matters very much in present day developments.[3]

The above mentioned relationships between culture, politics and economic performance suggest that in explaining economic performance across Central and Eastern Europe we should go beyond the quality of economic policy. Policy makers operate in an environment in which they socialize and that imposes constraints upon their scope of manoeuvre. Economic development is path dependent and embedded in a culture that is resistant to change.

The age old problem of catching up with Western Europe

Central and Eastern Europe for ages has faced the persistent problem of catching up with Western Europe as Graph 1.2 shows. Even the socialist modernization attempt did not succeed in catching up. This may be surprising because living standards increased dramatically in the

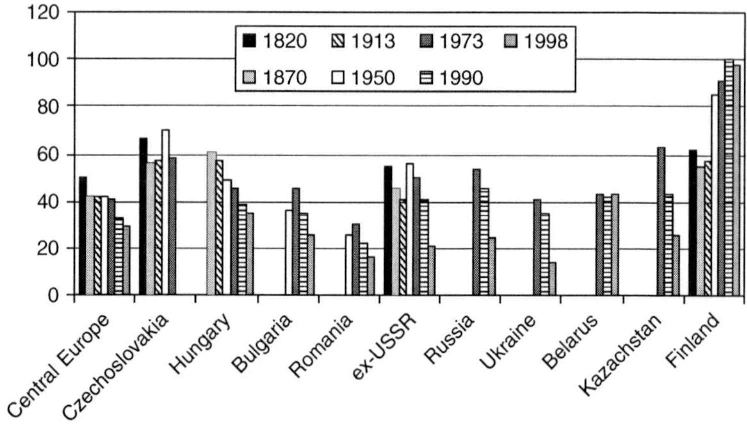

Graph 1.2   Central and Eastern Europe: GDP per capita (in international dollars), as a % of West European* GDP per capita, 1820–1998

Note: *Western Europe is Austria, Belgium, Denmark, Finland, France, Germany, Italy, The Netherlands, Norway, Sweden, Switzerland, UK. Central Europe is the former bloc of European socialist countries minus the countries of the former Soviet Union, but including the countries of the former Yugoslavia. For 1998 the GDP of Slovakia and the Czech Republic are added and divided by their total population.
Source: Maddison, 2001, p. 197

three decades after World War II, especially in the less developed social-ist countries. However, the West European economies also developed dynamically; Western Europe was a moving target.

Berend and Ranki (1982) pointed to the fact that Central and Eastern Europe was faced with several failed attempts to eradicate backwardness. While Western Europe faced the introduction of a decentralized kind of feudalism, Central and Eastern Europe saw, what Berend and Ranki characterize as a backward kind of feudalism (Berend and Ranki, 1982, p. 11). The classical Roman influences were from the start weaker (or totally missing) in what was to become the Central and East European periphery. Central and East European societies in the areas ruled by the Russian and Ottoman empires were static and immobile, centralized and consisting of self-sufficient agrarian communities.

During the eighteenth century, as a reaction to capitalist development in Western Europe, Central Europe re-feudalized. It meant an artificial resurrection of early feudal relations (Berend and Ranki, 1982, p. 18). During the second half of the nineteenth century most of Central and Eastern Europe adopted liberal economic policies and export led indus-trialization. But Central and Eastern Europe remained agricultural and traditional. Although three distinct patterns of reforms can be distin-guished in Central and Eastern Europe during the nineteenth century, they were all executed from above and not the result of revolutions. In the Balkans, the abolishment of feudalism was part of the struggle against the Turks, which started in the early 1820s. Romania, which became independent in 1861, abolished feudal institutions in 1864. At the end of the eighteenth century the Hapsburg monarchy issued laws which limited serfdom and completely abolished it in 1848. Prussia abol-ished serfdom in 1809. During the last third of the nineteenth century, feudalism was abolished in all parts of Central and Eastern Europe.

After World War I, the Central and East European countries introduced strong state-interventionism, various kinds of planning and replaced export-led policies with import substitution through high import tariffs.

According to Berend (2000, p. 48) 'The planned economy of state socialism, in this respect, was only a new, bitter, and extremist version of economic nationalism, or, perhaps more accurately, a modernization dictatorship'. In Russia, the Bolshevik experiment can be seen as the con-tinuation of imposed modernization by the state. Three times, under Ivan IV, Peter I and Catherine the Great, the state-led modernization attempts were initially successful, but ultimately failed.

Berend (2000, p. 50) speaks about the 'peripheral structural crisis' which is destruction without creation. 'Central and Eastern Europe experienced this situation three times from the 1870s to the 1970s–1990s and had only a "backward exit" ' (ibid. p. 50). This suggests that the structural backwardness of Central and Eastern Europe is not just a question of too much state and too little market. Developments since 1989/1991, when an inefficient state socialism was replaced, in most post-socialist countries, by an inefficient capitalism, bear testimony to that. Only in 2007 did Russia attain the per capita GDP level seen at the end of the Soviet period while the core countries of the world economy had moved on during those 17 years.

We can refer here to the work of Gerschenkron (1962) who argued that late-comers and contender states usually follow another development path than the leading nations. The greater the degree of backwardness, the more intervention is required in the market to push capital and entrepreneurial leadership to nascent industries. Also, he argued that relative backwardness creates a tension between the promise of economic development, as achieved elsewhere, and the continuity of stagnation. Such a tension takes political form and motivates institutional innovation, whose product becomes an appropriate substitution for the absent preconditions for growth (see Fishlow, 2003). Mainstream economists and institutions of global economic governance, however, assume that once the economy is liberalized and privatized, the market provides miracles in a similar way irrespective of any historic circumstances. Usually, the scholars who emphasize path dependency are caricaturized and subsequently ignored. A usual criticism of path dependence is that it is 'historical determinism, emasculating the role of any policy choice' (Havrylyshyn, 2006, p. 66). However, the thesis of path dependence does not deny the impact and relevance of policy making. It places policy making in a historical and social context. Transitologists who ignore the issue of path dependence and see the transformation of the post-socialist space as a pre-ordained march towards the market or Anglo-Saxon liberal market economy impose their teleology upon concrete historic processes. The only alternative option in this scenario is that a transition towards liberal market economy is frozen. It denies the option of transformation as an open-ended process.

Cultural-behavioural regions

Many authors have drawn attention to the relationship between culture and economic development.[4] Weber pointed to the influence of Protestantism upon capitalist development, contrasting it with the ethic of Catholicism (Runciman, 1978, pp. 133–74). Landes (1999, p. 66) identifies culture as one of the main factors of economic development. Putnam (1993) traces differences in institutional performance of Italian regions back to prevalent governance patterns during medieval times. Research showed that local government performance in Poland was most strongly affected by their historical location. The Northern and Western parts of Poland which belonged to Germany until World War II performed best. Next was the region which was a part of the German empire before World War I. It was followed by the former Austrian region. The region which was a part of the Russian Empire showed the weakest performance (Katchanovski, 2000, p. 67; Gorzelak, 1998, pp. 124–6).

The case of East Germany, which in the early 1990s had the same institutions as West Germany and received an influx of West German capital and managers, shows how inert attitudes and regional cultures are. Eastern Germany still strongly lags behind Western Germany in terms of productivity and unemployment.

If looking at the interrelationship between culture and economic development in the area of the former Soviet Union, the case of ethnic Germans comes to the fore. They constituted a sizeable group since Tsarina Catherina invited Germans to settle in Russia. They proved to be far more productive than ethnic Russians and managed to preserve their culture and language.

The case of Central Asia is also revealing because there was a non-revolutionary transition from party-state to clan-state. In most cases the former communist leaders stayed in power and transformed into nationalists. The clan structures that thrived below the surface in communist times re-surfaced in 1991.

Also the case of the Baltic States and especially that of Estonia draws attention. After 1995–6 the Baltic countries turned the corner and started to grow dynamically, unlike most other countries of the former Soviet Union. Some would say that the fact that these states managed successfully to restructure their economies while becoming members of the EU in 2004 testifies to the importance of political will in transition and the irrelevance of historic legacies. However, these countries have known Soviet communism only since World War II and have experienced capitalist development and representative democracy during their short period of independence. This may have given them an invaluable experience. Historically, they are a produce of the Hanseatic League. Moreover, when under tsarist rule, these areas always had been atypical; being part of Western Christianity with an important role for the German speaking nobility in that area. Also, under communist rule the Baltic countries

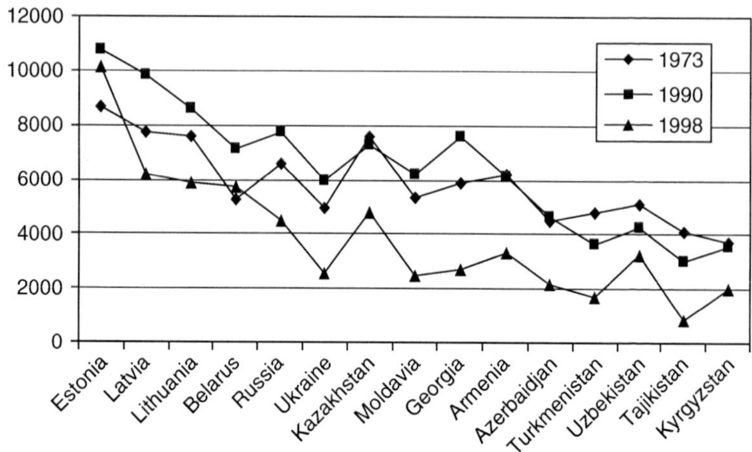

Graph 1.3   GDP per capita of (ex-) republics of the USSR, 1973, 1990 and 1998
Source: Maddison, 2001

had a much higher per capita GDP than other ex-Soviet republics (see Graph 1.3).

Some will say that Finland is a case of rapid extraction from underdevelopment. Since the early nineteenth century, until the October Revolution, Finland was part of Russia (see Map 1.2), and was, in European perspective, a less-developed area (see Graph 1.2). In less than 100 years, Finland has become the most innovative economy in the world with a welfare state that is the envy of the rest of Europe. Again, although part of the Tsarist Empire, this Lutheran country always occupied a special position. Finland has had a tradition of self-government extending back into the Middle Ages. For more than 600 years Finland belonged to the dual Kingdom of Sweden-Finland. Finland became part of the Russian Empire in 1809 but was never fully incorporated into the Empire and retained its own legal system. Finland never knew slavery.[5] Protestantism provided a more favourable atmosphere for free social development than Orthodoxy. Protestantism helped to create internal controls that allowed capitalism to flourish without sacrificing social order. In the nineteenth century, the Finnish diets included not only the standard three estates, but also following the model of the Swedish Riksdag – representatives of a fourth estate: the peasantry.

As part of the Russian Empire, Finland made primary schooling compulsory in 1866. By the beginning of the twentieth century illiteracy was

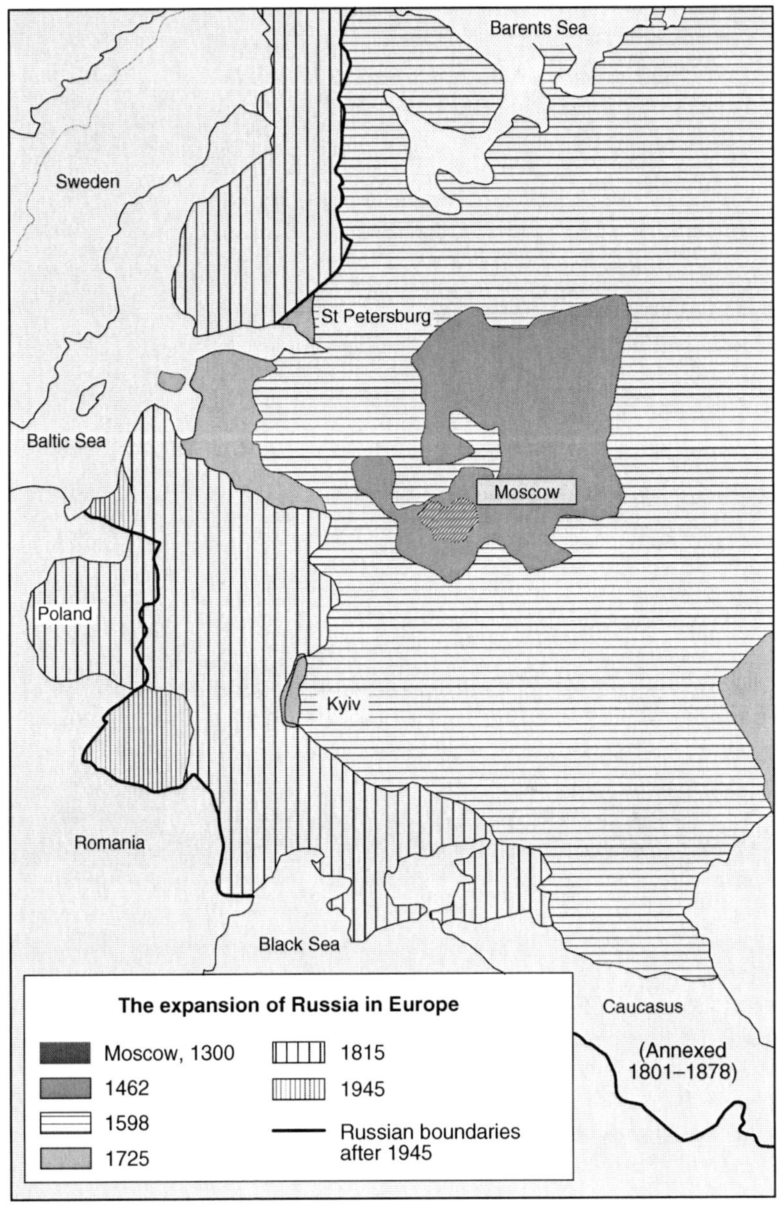

Map 1.2 The expansion of the Russian empire

completely eliminated while in Russia illiteracy reigned supreme (Berend and Ranki, 1982, p. 55). Thus, Finland was far ahead compared to the rest of the Empire and occupied a special position (Billington, 1970, p. 373).

The cases of Finland and the Baltic states support the thesis of a civilizational divide in Europe that is congruent with the divide between Western and Eastern Christianity. Huntington (1993) pointed to this divide in his seminal article in *Foreign Affairs*. Developments since then confirmed his thesis; the regions of Western Christianity followed another path than the regions of Eastern Christianity. Although Bulgaria and Romania, both Orthodox nations, joined the EU in 2007, they are both mired in economic mismanagement and corruption and are far from being success stories. All transition success stories are transition states that belong to Western Christianity. Is this a coincidence? Katchanovski (2000) showed that the percentage of Catholics and Protestants in the population (Western culture index) was the strongest direct determinant of growth in post-communist countries.

On the basis of the World Values Survey a map of personal values has been constructed. When individual responses within a country are averaged, mean country positions can be placed on a map defined by two axes, one contrasting traditional and secular-rational authority while the other contrasts survival and self-expression. The values-mapping shows clusters which correspond to conventional cultural-religious regions: Catholic; Protestant; Orthodox; East Asian, plus implicit Muslim; African animist; and South Asian Hindu areas. According to Sandholtz and Taagepera (2005, p. 112):

> comparatively homogeneous cultural-behavioral regions are formed that can survive even the abolition of the traditional religion, as attempted by communists across Christian, Muslim and East Asian lands.[6]

According to Sandholtz and Taagepera (2005) cultural factors, as measured by the two dimensions of values identified by the American sociologist Inglehart, explain 75 per cent of the variation in the corruption perception index. A strong survival orientation contributes twice as much as a strong 'traditional' orientation to higher levels of corruption.

> When controlling for these cultural variables, communism and post-communism increase the levels of corruption even further, both directly and by contributing to heavier emphasis on survival values (Sandholtz and Taagepera 2005, p. 109).

> The ex-communist countries, as a group have markedly higher levels of perceived corruption than do non-communist countries in the same geographic and cultural regions. (Ibid., p. 109)

This is related to both cultural inertia and structural opportunity (see also Chapter 5). Other surveys confirm above mentioned regional groupings. Whereas in Central Europe strong majorities (usually over 60 per cent) have approved the way the multiparty system works, the overall percentage in the post-Soviet area (excluding Baltic States) has never been much more than a third (Meyer, 2006, p. 81). More than two-thirds of these post-Soviet publics look back favourably on the old communist regimes (ibid.).[7]

The case of Ukraine is interesting in this respect. The civilizational divide of Western and Eastern Christianity passes through Ukraine and reflects the traditional orientation towards Western Europe of some Central and Western Ukrainian provinces. These sparsely populated provinces were incorporated in the Russian empire rather late. Kyiv was incorporated in 1725 while Galicia only in 1945 (see Chapter 6).

Belarus is an example of a country in which there was no sharp break with the communist legacy. Belarus' President Lukashenko led the country in an authoritarian way and no opposition was tolerated.[8] Nevertheless, there is evidence to support the claim that he has strong popular support.[9] This is related, among others to the fact that living standards are much higher than in neighbouring Russia and Ukraine, inequality less pronounced and services on a higher level.[10] As Table 1.1 shows, Belarus is doing rather well in GDP growth despite the fact that Belarus has hardly any natural resources and has a less well-developed industrial base compared to Ukraine and Russia. Belarus has had the second smallest decline in GDP in the area of the former SU, after Uzbekistan that is a major oil exporter.[11] According to the 2006 Human Development Report, Belarus is ahead of most other CIS counties (rank 67, Russia 65, Ukraine 77, Kazakhstan 79) (Ioffe, 2004, p. 99). According to a World Bank study in 2002, compared to other countries of the former Soviet Union, Belarus has by far the lowest percentage of people living in absolute poverty and also much lower than Poland, Bulgaria and Romania (World Bank, 2005b, p. 5). But Belarus still has a largely state-dominated economy while economic life is highly regulated.[12] In Belarus oligarchs do not exist, neither does capital flight, unlike in Ukraine and Russia. Importantly, corruption is relatively minor compared to the other states of the Community of Independent States (Belarus was listed in position 74 on the World Corruption Perception Index 2005, together with Gabon and Jamaica, while Russia was positioned 90 and Ukraine far lower down the list at 122).

The circumstantial evidence shown above suggests a strong link between economic performance and historical legacies that are reflected in culture. Cultural-behavioural regions coincide with country groupings of similar economic performance. Also, the persistence of the economic gap between Central and Eastern Europe with regard to the leading countries in Western Europe and reproduction of pre-socialist patterns of regional inequality suggests that we should look beyond the state-market paradigm when explaining economic performance.[13]

Often, economic systems are conceived as the system of institutions coordinating economic relations that can be studied away from history and independent of its social and economic context. But, as Peter Murrell (1993, p. 220) maintains,

> Socio-economic mechanisms are information-processing devices ... a society's stock of personal knowledge [that] is acquired through a long historical process shaped by the institutions and organizations of that particular society.

In Chapters 2 and 3 the history of Russian society and economy will be presented from a sociological perspective. It is above all about the way rulers and ruled interacted. It will be shown that although major changes occurred in social habitus, synchronous with major social change, elements of continuity are prominent.[14]

2
Soviet Russia: Revolution and Continuity

This chapter is an account of the disintegration of Soviet socialism and the emergence within its womb of the new socio-economic system that revealed itself in the 1990s. It shows that rather than a *tabula rasa* in which liberal market economy could be imposed, the Russia of 1991 was recomposing itself on the basis of elements it inherited from the Soviet and even tsarist past. Although there was radical change in Russia during the twentieth century, e.g. the introduction of the party state and centrally planned economy and the subsequent abolishment of state socialism, elements of continuity are prominent. It is mainly in the sphere of social practices, attitudes and world outlooks, that this continuity reveals itself. Our account of history deals with the substratum of history that is usually overlooked by historians. The focus here is on authority patterns and the changes in the state-society nexus, on all levels. There is a focus on informal social practices that shaped the interaction between rulers and ruled.

Usually in historical accounts, the focus is on the level of decision making whereas here the level of analysis is that of the relations of production at the most rudimentary level. Whereas Chapter 5 gives insight into the mode of operation of post-Soviet Russian neo-patrimonialism, the focus of this chapter and Chapter 3 is on its historical origins.

Russia on the eve of the October Revolution

The Bolsheviks promised a radical break with the past. What kind of country did they find as the subject for their revolutionary experiment?

The overwhelming majority of Russians were peasants, who were freed from serfdom in 1861. In that year, 49.5 million Russians out of 60 million were peasants. The liberation of serfs was incomplete as many remained dependent, through debts, on their former landlords. Only since the middle of the nineteenth century, with the spread of a railway network across the country, has the countryside slowly started to transform. Social mobility increased and a group of relatively wealthy peasants emerged.

The 1897 census had revealed that the literacy rate for the general population was 28.4 per cent, the lowest of any European state.[1] Until the seventeenth century Russia had been cut off from the advances of Western Europe. Universities were unknown and virtually all printed material was sacred orthodox texts. In 1797 the literacy rate was only 6.9 per cent. While in Central and Western Europe the tendency since the thirteenth and fourteenth century was to limit autocratic rule, the trend, in what was to become Russia, was towards unlimited autocratic power.

Unlike in West European feudalism, the tsar in Russia owned all land.[2] There was a complete fusion of sovereign and property. In Russia a property owning class never emerged that could constitute a counterweight to the autocratic tsar.[3] The greatest problem for Muscovite merchants was not 'how to get rich', but 'how to remain rich'. In 1729 the Russian government even deemed it necessary to establish a Chancery of Confiscation (Hedlund, 2005, p. 195). There were no restraints on autocracy.

The boyars constituted a service nobility (the duty of lifelong service to the tsar) that was introduced during the fifteenth century and extended to the whole nobility during the sixteenth century. They managed estates that they could exploit as they liked. It was the system of *kormlenie* (literally feeding, i.e. the right to levy tribute on a specific territory) that very much favoured corruption and patron-client relations. The boyars were autocratic rulers on their own estates but they maintained slave-like bonds with the tsar. They could not move, like the peasants, and they had the obligation to serve the tsar unconditionally. Boyars received their estates conditionally and in the early times of Muscovy there was a circulation of estates among boyars. The nobility had no rights whatsoever and the humiliation of nobles was a regular part of court ceremonies. A sense of honour went along with service in the court. The mentality of the service nobility would be maintained after it was formally abolished (1762).

According to Pipes (1974, p. 185),

> the political philosophy of the mass of the dvoryanstvo was not at all that different from the peasantry's; both preferred unlimited autocracy to a constitutional arrangement, seeing behind the latter manipulations of private interests acting for their own benefit.

Unlike in European feudalism, a reciprocity between 'lord and vassals' was absent. The concept of 'resistance to unjust authority', as it developed in medieval Europe, never emerged in Russia. In Western Europe the power of the king was restrained by the Church, the nobility and the towns.

The lack of reform in Russia, and therewith persistent underdevelopment, was not only related to a lack of will to reform on the part of autocratic authorities. Even in times when the autocrat was willing to reform and a window of opportunity emerged for the nobility to demand rights, they seldom did so. There was what Hedlund (2005, p. 162) called a revealed institutional preference for patrimonial rule and an ingrained fear of a regime of rules. There was a lack of solidarity and a lack of sense of society. This was partly related to the obligation of all subjects to report any criticism of the tsar and his family. Organized distrust was institutionalized. The only way to advance was to cultivate good relations with the court. Mental models emerged in which it was not imaginable for individual nobles to think that a better individual strategy was to act collectively for rights and the rule of law. The lack of solidarity was highlighted in purges among the nobility, for instance during the time of Ivan the Terrible. They were executed without any protest or resistance. Solidarity was made difficult by the system of common responsibility (*krugovaya poruka*). If one member of the group deserted, others could be punished. So, half-hearted reforms that left the core of autocracy intact, combined with the lack of ambitions of groups that could challenge autocracy, led to a cyclical pattern of long periods of immobility alternated with short periods of attempts at reform. There is also a pattern of initially liberal tsars who gradually turned into despots. Also under reform-minded tsars the state established its policies without taking into account possible resistance from society. This lack of countervailing power proved to be a receipt for ill conceived policies. Russia was locked into a permanent inferior equilibrium. Muscovy produced, during the fourteenth to sixteenth centuries, an institutional arrangement that proved to be very persistent.

Strict autocratic rule and legal nihilism created strategies of rule evasion. Rule evasion in turn created a control mania in the state machinery. Muscovite ideology was inimical to commercial culture. It was also rigid and Manichean. It was 'us' against 'them'. A siege mentality was cultivated that furthered xenophobia. This went together with intolerance.

In Muscovy an institutional lock-in emerged in which exit strategies from autocracy proved to be extremely difficult. For those who stepped out, for instance by becoming a free peasant, artisan or merchant, life was often made so difficult that they voluntary opted for re-entry into serfdom (Hedlund, 2005, p. 217).

The system of autocratic rule permeated all aspects of society. The tsars refined autocratic rule by transforming the Orthodox Church into an instrument of power. Peter the Great effectively incorporated the Church into the state. Secular and religious power merged in a system of caesaro-papism in which the tsar was God's representative on earth. The very legitimacy of the state came to rest on essential religious notions (Hedlund, 2005, p. 104). The law was exclusively used in a punitive sense and as an instrument of autocratic power.

Even reforming autocrats who opened a window to the West, did so while maintaining autocratic rule. As Piirainen (1997) noticed, the modernization 'from above' could even bring forth tendencies that contributed to the continuation rather than the dissolution of the non-modern features of Russian society. According to Krasilshchikov:

> Because colossal resources were required if the modernization was to be carried out, the modernization projects were necessarily accompanied, first, by an extreme centralization of the administration, and second, by an intensified exploitation of the people, the latter evoking public anger and discontent. This, in turn, required the building of a strengthened and more repressive police apparatus. A massive bureaucratic machinery was created, a machinery that corresponded to the vast dimensions of the empire. The repression of rights and the cruel exploitation led to a further impoverishment of the people. As a consequence, the society was eventually deprived of all impulses to spontaneous development, because every initiative 'from below' was systematically suppressed by the administration and the landowners, even if such initiatives might accidentally have received support from the Emperor, as it happened sometimes during the reign of Peter Alekseyevitch. The 'imperious model' of modernization produced a peculiar coexistence of the most advanced form in the sphere of science and technology and the most backward and archaic in the spheres of economy and everyday life. The most exquisite cultural life could coexist with scandalous ignorance and vulgarity. Progress and realization of courageous technical and architectural projects went hand in hand with an astonishing disdainful attitude towards human life and with total disregard towards the individuality of man. (Quoted in Piirainen, 1997, p. 68)

The Petrine command economy was based on forced resource extraction. According to Raef (quoted in Hedlund, 2005, p. 178):

> Not only did the government provide most of the purchasing power and investment capital, but it also set rigid standards of production, dictated methods of manufacturing, and made available a good part of the labour force by attaching serfs to mines and factories.

Peter the Great remained focused on central control and would not accept any initiative from below. If Russian entrepreneurs did not perform well, they could be dispossessed. Peter continued to rely on the ancient instruments of Muscovy's autocracy. The political police force introduced by Peter became known for its ruthlessness.

The history of Muscovy provides a very good example for the general observation of Douglass North that 'the increasing returns characteristic for an initial set of institutions that provide disincentives to productive activity will create organizations and interest groups with a stake in the existing constraints' (North, 1990, p. 99). In Muscovy, for any ambitious man there was no other option than to invest in skills that would make him a better pirate.

Only from the middle of the nineteenth century did developments move in the direction of genuine extraction from autocracy. In 1861 serfdom was abolished (introduced 1649) and in 1870 cities became self-governing.

However, the modernization that occurred after the abolition of serfdom was rather shallow. Industrialization was at levels far below those attained in Western Europe and mainly supported by foreigners.[4] In Russia the old order incubated a nascent capitalism although the state remained patrimonial and dominated by the landowning class and nobility, not by merchants and industrialists. Economic transformation was also state led. Interaction with foreigners was very limited and if Russian citizens played an important role in the industrialization process, it was mainly by some ethnic minorities such as Baltic Germans, Jews and Poles. The cultural borrowing from other countries remained very limited as tsarist Russia remained a closed society. Very few Russians travelled abroad.[5] It was cultural borrowing that allowed the most developed countries to attain their wealth (see Sowell, 1998). Tsarist Russia was to a large extent a self-contained civilization, despite it being closely linked with European culture that is reflected in its outstanding contribution in the arts and sciences. The problem is that cultural cross-fertilization hardly affected the economy and social texture of society. Interaction with the outside world led to hardly any social and political change.

In the early twentieth century two very different Russias coexisted that hardly communicated. Lewin (2005, p. 295) noticed a lack of cohesion between the various social strata who geographically inhabited the same territory, but who did not live in the same century economically, socially or culturally.[6]

The first Russia was that of the Russia of ordinary people whose culture differed greatly from that of the upper class, i.e. the second Russia. The Russia of ordinary people, as seen from Western Europe and the Russian upper class, was another planet.

In the upper class, at first sight, behavioural patterns did not differ very much from those to be found in the same class elsewhere in Europe. The culture of the upper class hardly spread outside the largest urban centres and barely touched the Russian countryside, partly related to the fact that a mediating middle class hardly existed. The industrialization process that began in Russia during the 19th century was initiated by the state and enabled by foreign capital and know-how.[7] No endogenous industrial bourgeoisie developed with the consequence that within the upper class (a 'leisure class'– see Veblen, 1998) no value change conducive to a productive capitalism developed. In particular the nobility in the provinces had retreated into complete idleness. Generally, one can observe in former slave societies counterproductive attitudes towards work, among both the former slaves and their descendants and the non-slave members and their descendants (see Sowell, 1994, p. 215).

According to Berdyaev (1937, pp. 21–3), the mass of the Russian nobility and official class was uncultivated, illiterate and led an unreflecting life. The members of the leisure class left it to the bureaucracy to run the country. They also left it to their serfs to run their estates and other enterprises. The merchant class was very different from the West European bourgeoisie. According to Pipes, 'native entrepreneurship (in late-nineteenth century) once again showed little inclination to commit itself' (1974, p. 189). According to Owen (1981, p. 9), Moscow merchants

> were essentially nothing but trading muzhiks (peasants) ... The constant influx of enterprising peasants into the merchant estate naturally contributed to the persistence of many features of peasant life within the merchant milieu.

Cheating was endemic in economic life.[8] In Russia, the merchant class was more interested in commerce than in manufacturing; more anxious to gain government support than to limit government interference.

Within the elites in the developed capitalist countries, a gradual cultural transformation took place, allowing a culture of citizenship and the rule of law to develop. The advance of an industrial bourgeoisie transformed the value system within the elite. A crucial element was the spread of individualism. In Russia, 'sobornost', the merging of the individual in the collectivity, was a core value, emphasized by the Orthodox Church and the patrimonial state, i.e. the state in which the monarch was sovereign and proprietor at the same time. Although Western thought very much influenced the Russian intelligentsia, the dominant mode of thinking within the ruling elite and state bureaucracy was patrimonial and based on 'sobornost'. Moreover, despite the fact that Western literature circulated widely in the tsarist Russia of the nineteenth century and the aristocracy used to travel abroad, Russian Orthodox thought had a profound influence upon the Russian elite and the overwhelming majority adjusted to and accepted the autocratic despotism of the tsar. In the nobility the service mentality persisted. Russians of the upper class used to serve in the army or the court. The business class was treated as *déclassé* or *nouveau riche*.

It seemed, at first sight, that the modernization drive that started in the nineteenth century could, eventually, lead the country out of Russian autocratic path dependence. However, there was economic growth without much genuine development. It was instant modernization (Hedlund, 2005, p. 225). 'The powerhouse of positive change was made up of a small circle of liberal policy makers and a small stratum of merchants and industrialists' (Hedlund, 2005, p. 236). There was also a group of lawyers and bureaucrats that were interested in reform. Gradually, the micro-foundations of society changed and mental models of specific groups within the elite also changed. The autocratic system was gradually undermined but still intact.

The impact of the Bolshevik Revolution

In one of the most backward societies in Europe, the Bolsheviks started their huge experiment in social engineering. Against the background of poverty and misery they wanted to create a new society and a new man.

What was the impact of the Bolshevik revolution upon the social milieu of people? How could the forced modernization of the country affect behavioural patterns and life of citizens?

In order to reconstruct historic events from the perspective of Soviet man a short sociological account of the Bolshevik experiment is given.

The Bolsheviks never constituted a real mass movement. In 1917, the Bolshevik party numbered only about 20,000 members. When the Bolsheviks were faced, after the civil war, with the task of holding power and implementing their policy agenda, they saw a country that was hostile to their revolutionary project. The working class, the presumed social base for the revolution, had almost vanished, while the peasantry did not support the Bolsheviks. There was no clear idea how to proceed and with respect to a positive programme, the Bolsheviks looked above all at existing state-led development models. Apart from that of Germany it was above all the Russian experiences with state-led development that provided an example.

Before the introduction of a formal institutional framework for the new state, informal networks created in the Bolshevik party and the underground struggle provided the informal infrastructure for power. Powerful central patrons in Russia's regions created networks that allowed access to scarce material and organizational resources as Easter (2000) has shown. During the 1920s Russia was an infra-structurally weak state and regionally based networks could attain a significant degree of autonomy from the centre. As Easter (2000) argues, 'in the early post-revolutionary state a "patrimonial" system was favoured over a "bureaucratic" system as the means to strengthen the infrastructural powers of the new state (p. 163).

The New Economic Policy constituted an attempt to move forward in an evolutionary way. However, from the late 1920s onwards Stalin embarked upon forced industrialization and, later, forced collectivization of agriculture. It meant social warfare against the peasantry and the peasant way of life. It also meant the re-submission of the peasantry into *de facto* slavery. They had a service obligation to the state (very badly paid *kolkhoz* work during normal working hours) while most did not get an internal passport so that leaving the *kolkhoz* was very difficult. Like Peter the Great before him, Stalin started to draft the whole population into one vast labour army. While labour ethos was low, coercive methods were deemed important.

With brutal violence the Bolsheviks intended to eradicate backwardness. They pushed a large part of the intelligentsia and upper class into emigration. Those remaining were severely persecuted and decimated. Under Stalin's rule the old culture of the upper class and intelligentsia was virtually destroyed. Bolsheviks opposed their culture and promoted what they saw as the culture of the proletariat. However, the proletariat represented only a tiny part of the population and the 'older' proletariat suffered disproportionately during Stalinist repression. After the Stalinist purges, the Communist Party consisted mainly of people with a peasant background. Lewin (2005, p. 289) argued that because the October Revolution was oriented towards the poor peasantry, soldiers and workers, this revolution could not be socialist but a distant relative of the same: a 'plebeian' revolution.[9]

The state had to impose the communist revolution, propelled by the party-state apparatus. According to Lewin (1977, p. 118), 'instead of serving its basis, the state bureaucracy, using its powerful means at its disposal, was able to press the social body into service under its own diktat'. The Communist Party created its own social base in the form of a dependent bureaucracy. Stalin sought to destroy the regional networks with its purges and imposed a despotic bureaucratic regime. Here, power was allocated on the basis of who was in favour in Stalin's court. According to Easter (2000, p. 165):

> Although bureaucratic lines of command in the state were more clearly defined than at any time in the previous two decades, central leaders still did not abandon the practice of employing a 'patrimonial' system of infrastructural power.

Stalin did not destroy intra-party cliques but sought to control and use these by a balance of power policy and a rotation policy in which officials were regularly moved to other places. Also, the system of reward and advancement for regional elites remained personalized (Easter, 2000, p. 167).

It was mainly bureaucrats, often in the guise of party officials that constituted the social base of the revolution. The culture of the Soviet bureaucracy had an enormous impact upon Soviet culture in general, as the whole of Soviet society became bureaucratized from above. It makes therefore sense to have a closer look at the social background of the Soviet bureaucracy, the social components of which have been little studied.

The party-state bureaucracy as the social base of the revolution

Usually, bureaucrats in Stalin's times were poorly educated and often semi-literate. The stupidity, rudeness and inefficiency of Soviet bureaucrats became a main target for political authorities and popular jokes.

Because the state wanted to impose modernization upon a backward society, it became a tireless regulator of life. The state bureaucracy demanded an endless stream of documents without which even the simplest operations of daily life were not possible. According to Lewin (1977, p. 120):

> The mass of culturally low-key officialdom was certainly a proper milieu – or even a social base, to some extent, for the flourishing of the

'personality cult' ... in a situation of absolutist rule, the dependence of the servants of the state on the arbitrary rule from above finds an indispensable counterpart in the absolutist and arbitrary rule of officials over people below them, or people tout court. Under Stalin, to sum up this point, the network of bosses (nachalstvo) allowed and asked to be authoritarian and rude towards subordinates and the masses in order to discipline them, acquired a dual character, or a Janus-like double face: the one looking down, of a despot; the other looking up, of a serf.

Within the bureaucracy, as Lewin noticed, gradually a hierarchy and rituals appeared that reminds one of practices in tsarist times. Familiar practices of vigilance and control were omnipresent in the Soviet bureaucracy. Denunciation was an obligation, as in tsarist times.

The rank order within the Nomenklature reminds one very much of the Table of Ranks that Peter the Great introduced in 1722. Like Peter, Stalin demanded absolute loyalty to the autocratic power (compare with the service obligation of the nobility).

According to Easter (2000, pp. 173–4):

the Soviet Russian state was a virtual labyrinth of bureaucratic structures, but it was a far cry from a rational-legal bureaucratic state. Beneath the formal façade of the monolithic party and the planned economy existed an informal world of cliques, factions, networks and druzhina. Power and status within the state elite derived as much from the workings of these informal groupings as they did from the formal lines of command... The Soviet Russian case was an early model of a process in which personalistic patterns of political authority and organization were adapted to new formal-legalistic structures within the institutional framework of hastily constructed post-colonial state.

Peasant roots of Soviet-Russian culture

The cultural roots of the Soviet party-state bureaucracy are to be found both in the peasant culture and tsarist bureaucratic culture. Voslensky (1980, p. 119) pointed to the very high percentage of rural born among the higher echelons of the Soviet leaders. In Minsk oblast in 1946, 709 out of 855 leaders were former peasants and only 58 had a working class background.

As in the pre-revolutionary countryside, obligations of personal obedience tend to be essentially unlimited. Lewin characterized Stalinist rule as agrarian despotism and described social change in terms of 'archaization of society' (Lewin, 2005, p. 297). The Bolshevists took over the Manichean world view from the Muscovite ideology ('us' against 'them'). They also took over the messianic view of Russia as the Third Rome, in its secular form of Russia as leader of the world revolution.

Another feature that built upon the peasant legacy was the attempt to abolish the private sphere. The communists invaded the private sphere in many ways like the nobility and tsarist police used to do with the peasantry. Privacy was considered to be 'petty bourgeois'. Enterprises and party bosses were entitled to interfere in affairs that are considered in other societies as private. An extended network of spies reported about activities in the private sphere. Anonymous letters were sufficient ground to persecute people. All this was common in tsarist times as well.

Another element of peasant culture is the deification of the state that was reinforced under communist rule. Communist ideology built upon the superstitious cult of the state and the tsar as prevalent in rural tsarist Russia.

On the other hand, Russian communists did not only demolish the peasantry as a class, but tried as well to demolish their culture while only building upon those elements that could support communist rule.

Berdyaev attributed communism's most essential features to Russia's oriental affinities, not to Marxism. 'Whereas the latter had come to the source of communism, the former provides human capital susceptible to social engineering and made it possible to master the energy of the entire nation'.[10]

It can be said that Soviet Russia transformed into an urbanized and industrialized peasant society. Some spoke about the sociological phenomenon of the 'urban peasantry' because the culture remained in many ways rooted in Russian peasant traditions.[11] Only in the early 1960s did the majority of people in the Soviet Union come to live in towns. In the late 1980s not more than 17 per cent of those under 60 years old were born in towns. Only in the group aged 22 and under were more than half born in towns (Wischnewskij, 1998, p. 9). According to Visnevskii (2005, p. 65), during the 1980s the first generation of *Homo Sovieticus* left the scene being replaced by mutants, better educated and accustomed to more comfort.

Also, the growth of towns was not accompanied by the spread of a fully fledged urban milieu because of the lack of a genuine urban infrastructure and because of the fact that in many ways the links to the villages from which the urbanites originated were maintained. During the period 1961 to 1966 29 million people arrived in towns while 24.2 million moved to other towns (Lewin, 2005, p. 204). It is an indication of the scale of migration and social shock that accompanied urbanization.

Industrialization without proper social foundations

While Soviet society moved forward in economic terms, in many other respects there were moves backwards as the social texture of society was not developed but largely destroyed. The state replaced all autonomous institutions that in other societies constitute civil society. While in Asian 'despotic societies' power was unchecked it did not operate everywhere and firm control was maintained only in those areas that were deemed strategically important. Soviet power, however, extended its control over all areas of life (see Wittfogel, 1957, p. 112). It looked as if the Soviet Union erected the façade of a modern industrial society but neglected the social preconditions of modern economic development. Mental and organizational patterns, or, social habitus, lagged behind economic development.

However, the overwhelming majority of the population was faced, during the Stalinist industrialization drive, with a dramatic change in social roles. This has meant a drastic change in ambitions, world outlook and opportunities for individual development. Massive social dislocations occurred in which old values and habits were discredited. For a longer period, Soviet society was in a kind of flux, in which most people faced major changes in social status: from peasant to factory worker, from factory worker to bureaucrat etc. The sudden appearance of high social mobility was a new phenomenon. The result was that many people, often with a peasant mentality, were put in jobs for which they were not competent.

The Bolshevik revolution had the aim of creating a socialist society and a new man. In order to attain the second goal, the communists were involved in active social engineering. Numerous measures were taken to actively shape the 'new man'.

The characteristics of the new man, *Homo Sovieticus*, are extensively described in Soviet literature.[12] He is rude to the class enemy, a private life does not exist and loyalty to the party has precedence over other loyalties. Famous is the story of Pavel Morozov, the boy who, in 1932 when aged 13, accused his father of anti-Soviet activities. The father was executed and the boy became a hero.

Generally, value generating institutions, such as the church and institutions of civil society, were abolished under communism or brought under state control. They were replaced by the communist state as the sole value generator. The aim of schools was, apart from transferring technical knowledge, to morally educate the pupils. A special role was fulfilled by the youth organizations, Pioneers and Komsomol. The overwhelming majority of the youth became members of these organizations.

The only remaining more or less autonomous bastion of value generation was the family, although the state also invaded this domain. Parents could not speak freely anymore with their children.

The fact that the party-state got such an overwhelming role in educating its citizens had an enormous impact upon the mental programming of the Soviet population. A whole army of 'ideological workers' came into being. Intellectuals constituted the core of this army.

Especially in Stalin's time, it seemed that intellectuals were often more susceptible to communist propaganda than workers. The workers were closer to everyday life. Intellectuals were better placed to give a rationalization of the Soviet order. Arthur Koestler brilliantly described in his *Darkness at Noon* how the hero, an imprisoned leading Bolshevik intellectual, to very the end goes on to defend Stalin and legitimize the dictum that the end justifies all means.[13] In his *Captive Mind* Czeslaw Milosz provided an impressive account of the subjugation of intellectuals in socialist countries.

Although the classical intelligentsia had been eradicated by Stalinist terror, there are striking similarities between the social position of nineteenth century Russian intelligentsia and intellectuals in the Soviet Union.[14]

More than the moral lessons of communists, the realities of Soviet life have had their impact on the mental programming of the population. Stalinist terror disciplined the population and adjusted the peasants, who went in great numbers to the towns, to the new realities of factory work. Huge penalties were imposed on arriving late to work and on disobedience. Low labour ethos was met with coercion. The socialist experiment was aimed at modernization, urbanization, industrialization and mass education. The communist morality laid emphasis on the public good and hard work.

The Soviet communists created a mobilization society. The communist totalitarian project was enabled by the permanent mobilization of the population, pointing to the threat of war, the enemy within and the goal of building socialism. The latter attracted many and was a source of motivation for a larger part of the population. The population could see progress as they saw the fast increasing number of factories, houses, tractors, machines and a number of public services, above all schools and hospitals. The country modernized and within one generation, mass literacy was introduced. It was the combination of terror (fear) and mobilization (legitimacy) that kept the Stalinist experiment moving.

The question emerges how so many could actively participate in the Stalinist terror campaigns. Grossman (1995) wrote in *Life and Fate* referring to the German and Soviet terror campaigns, that 'experience showed that such campaigns made the majority of the population obey every order of the authorities as though hypnotized' (p. 213).

About the German campaigns he wrote:

> When people are to be slaughtered en masse, the local population is not immediately gripped by a bloodthirsty hatred of the old men, women and children who are to be destroyed. It is necessary to stir up feelings of real hatred and revulsion. It was in such an atmosphere that the Germans carried out the extermination of the Ukrainian and Byelorussian Jews. And at an earlier date, in the same regions, Stalin himself had mobilized the fury of the masses, whipping it up to the point of frenzy during the campaigns to liquidate the kulaks as a class and during the extermination of Trotskyist-Bukharinist degenerates and saboteurs. (Ibid.)

Elsewhere Grossman (quoted in Lewin, 2005, p. 528) writes about the Stalinist terror campaigns:

> Fear alone cannot achieve all this. It was the revolutionary cause itself that freed people from morality in the name of morality, that justified today's Pharisees, hypocrites and writers of denunciations in the name of the future.

To give an indication of the scale of the terror: in January 1953 5.2 million people were imprisoned.

Stalin built upon the tsarist experience with mass terror. For example, in the early sixteenth century there was the obligation to report immediately under threat of execution any serious criticism of the Sovereign (Billington, 1970, p. 64). The rule of collective responsibility (*krugovaya poruka*) was introduced; if someone was found guilty, family members could be punished as well.[15] During the Second World War some members of ethnic minorities were under suspicion of collaboration. As a result whole ethnic groups were deported. Stalin's purges of the 1930s can be compared with the unbridled terror of Ivan the Terrible among the boyars in the period 1565 to 1572.

To what extent did the churches provide a bastion against mass terror and moral degeneration? The Russian church always has been subordinated to worldly power and sanctioned the role of the tsar as the proprietor of the nation. According to the Orthodox Church, politics was the responsibility of the secular authorities and it provided no norms that would define 'the good king' as did Western church fathers (Pipes, 2004, p. 12).[16] After a cruel oppression of the Orthodox Church, Stalin succeeded in suppressing the church. During World War II the Orthodox Church actively supported the war efforts.

Population in a state of shock

With the death of Stalin (1953), the population was in a kind of shock, in several ways. Despite Stalinist terror, the masses mourned as if a close relative had died. It reflected the widespread semi-religious beliefs in the leader.

There was shock in another, more structural meaning. Since the outbreak of World War I, the Soviet people had been exposed to many hardships that fundamentally changed and shaped their world outlook: World War I; civil war; Stalinist repression; World War II; and a new wave of Stalinist repression after World War II. The population was continuously exposed to fear and terror, the man-made famine of the 1930s caused 5 to 7 million deaths, mainly in Ukraine (Merridale, 2000, p. 198). Current estimates for World War II losses generally exceed 25 million. Many millions died in Stalin's camps. Forty years of continuous exposure to major shocks caused deep traumas. People began to feel themselves survivors.[17] There was a collective memory of innocent deaths and the moral obligations to them.

The shock of the Great Patriotic War, with its huge sacrifices, had a particularly long-lasting impact on the collective memory of the people as this experience was exploited by the communists as a means to further the cohesion of Soviet society.

The social memory was highly selective, given the heavy interference of the state in the mechanisms that usually constitute collective memory.[18] Although the state could prevent historic experiences being transmitted openly to new generations – people were afraid to do so – the transmission of emotions and typical behavioural patterns could not be prevented.

From 1953 to the middle of the 1970s: fear without mass terror

Under party leader Khrushchev (1957–64) mass terror was replaced by more subtle forms of repression, e.g. civilized violence (Shalin, 1996, p. 237). However, state power remained overwhelming, even when the forms of oppression were less visible. Although a thaw appeared in art, a general relaxation of the intellectual atmosphere only appeared from 1958/1960 onwards because in the first phase of the reign of Khrushchev many were still paralyzed by the fear of Stalinist repression. The army of spies continued to do their work, while the Communist Party tried to uphold the mobilization spirit by emphasizing the external threat.

Many authors have described the change from state terror cum mobilization to disciplinization through subtler means. Some have analysed this in terms of a kind of social contract: the regime bought the population's cooperation with economic welfare. The surrender of individual rights was bought with consumer goods and social security. From the early 1950s to the early 1980s there was a growth in living standards although this growth slowed down from the middle of the 1970s. Many people got their own flats, refrigerators and TVs. Higher education became attainable for all layers of the population. Russian people became more affluent than ever before. People felt material progress in all spheres. The Soviet Union transformed into an urbanized society.

The private sphere expanded somewhat as mass terror disappeared. The fact that gradually more people moved from Kommunalkas to their own flats contributed to the spread of privacy. However, double-think, and above all, double-talk, became more widespread and more pronounced.

The universalistic claims of ideology gradually became more hollow, especially given the process of feudalization of socialist rule that undermined its credibility. The social contract proved to be non-sustainable because the relaxation of Soviet political life brought about a weakening of administrative control in the workplace. Also, the prevalence of criteria of political compliance over meritocratic criteria contributed to disincentives to work.

A major innovation was that the cadres became more secure. Under party leader Khrushchev the Nomenklatura began its transformation into a ruling caste. The regional elites and factions on the central level attained more leverage. After securing physical guarantees they began to push for social and economic privileges that they got particularly under the rule of Leonid Brezhnev (1964 onwards). The cadres rotation policy was also softened. This meant the gradual spread of 'family circles' that Stalin had sought to destroy. Enhanced security spread the way for corruption and bribery. Members of the Nomenklatura did not have any rights, as everybody else in Soviet society, but they could profit from an ever expanding set of services and goods provided by the state. Elite schools spread. It became increasingly difficult for outsiders to penetrate the Nomenklatura. Gradually, the Nomenklatura's way of governing became reminiscent of tsarist rule. Clientelism spread. Loyalty to a patron gradually became more important than personal performance. Dynasties began to appear, especially under party leader Brezhnev, on the national, regional and local level. It happened above all in the less developed republics. The Soviet polity transformed from an autocracy into a form of bureaucratic absolutism.

1975–85: cynicism, apathy and stagnation

In the middle of the 1970s a period of 'stagnation' began. The growth of living standards slowed down and, more importantly, most people began to feel a deadlock situation in all spheres of life. All kinds of escapism attained epidemic proportions while the personality cult around party leader Brezhnev (1964–82) was at its height. However, Soviet power felt more secure than ever because it had attained parity with the USA and projected its influence all over the world. High energy prices since the early 1970s allowed, for approximately a decade, relatively high import levels, disguising declining economic performance. While Soviet leaders were enjoying expanding Soviet influence across the world, Soviet power was undermined from within.

From the middle of the 1950s remuneration of workers became less linked to performance while loyalty gained importance. People gradually developed a mentality that allowed them to ignore public interests and to absorb themselves in private and illegal activity. This applies especially for the Nomenklatura. Soviet society increasingly resembled an archipelago of networks whose members were wheeling and dealing with each other at the expense of outsiders.

Egalitarianism increased, the wage differences between various professional groupings decreased, and the economic incentive structure weakened.[19] Repeatedly the Soviet leadership sought to address the problem of a lack of incentives by rewarding good performing enterprises and workers. However, the incentives were so meagre that it hardly had results.

It was only during the early 1980s that Soviet sociologists began to notice that a new class of Soviet workers had emerged with deeply ingrained negative attitudes to work. Tatyana Zaslavskaya (1984: see Shlapentokh, 1989) was the first, in the early 1980s, to point to the phenomenon:

> A low level of labour and production discipline, indifferent attitudes toward the work being done, low quality of work, social inertia, low importance of work as a means of self-realization, and a low level of

morality are traits common to many workers, which have been shaped during recent five-year plans. It is enough to recall the broad scale of the activities of the so-called 'pilferers', the spread of all sort of 'shady' dealings at the public expense, the development of illicit 'enterprises' and figures-finagling, and the 'worming out' of wages regardless of the result of work.[20]

Sociological research showed that the number of 'bad workers' had increased gradually since the early 1960s. Surveys by Iadov (see Shlapentokh, 1989) among young workers, in 1962 and 1976, revealed a lowering of labour ethos. During the late Brezhnev period, social scientists converged on their estimates of 30–40 per cent as the share of workers whose discipline was very low, even by Brezhnev's standards (Shlapentokh, 1989, p. 47). Increasing labour shortage contributed to low labour ethos and discipline. A worker, dismissed for malfunctioning, could easily find a job elsewhere, sometimes with a higher salary.

The operating mode of the typical Soviet enterprise was very different from a typical Western company. The function was the fulfilment of the wishes of the central planners, to satisfy all material requirements of the workforce, including housing, holidays and health care, as well as the provision of basic goods. Enterprise organization was very paternalistic and enterprise management could even interfere in the private affairs of employees.

However, since the death of Stalin internal discipline in the enterprises gradually diminished. Also, from the late 1950s, there was a gradual loss of the state's authority. The gradual privatization of the state, that was accelerated under the reign of Brezhnev and that encompassed the use of public functions for private purposes, led to the undermining of the economic and political system. Allowing corruption to flourish can also be seen as a substitute for reform. Corrupted officials created a constituency against reform.

Increasingly, people experienced the public sphere, including the workplace, as hostile to their interests. Since the 1960s the shadow economy continuously expanded. It was not so much the precursor of a modern market economy, but rather that of a pre-modern economy, based on primary groups and kinship relations. The shadow economy was at once indispensable and parasitic. Gradually it underpinned the process of feudalization of Soviet society and prepared the ground for the post-socialist transition. Also, the growing shadow economy was increasingly penetrated by organized crime that sought to impose its own order in this sphere. This was especially the case in the Central

Asian republics. Under Brezhnev the system of 'despotic' power became more routinized and checked (Easter, 2000, p. 169). The infrastructural capabilities of the state were weakened by the change in the structure of network ties (Easter, 2000, p. 169). Under Brezhnev 'the career patterns of regional leaders displayed a marked decrease in vertical and horizontal movements' (ibid.). It meant a strengthening and deepening of regional networks. This was different to the early phase of state building in the 1920s when regional network ties exhibited an outward structure through relocation of officials to other regions and the centre. It also meant a gradual diffusion of power away from the centre along informal lines (Easter, 2000, p. 170). The informal networks also created mechanisms for mutual cover-up that fostered misinformation, opportunism and other pathologies.

The planning system encompassed all state production entities and collective farms. Not covered were a plethora of legal, grey and black activities. There was the growing of food on private plots and its sale in *kolkhoz* markets. In much of the Soviet period these plots provided about a quarter of Soviet food consumption. There was the grey area of spare time repair work by skilled workers or tuition by teachers. In the arts several activities were conducted on a freelance basis. Then there was the outright black economy, from the sale of stolen goods, the running of prostitutes, the illegal distilling of vodka and other criminal activities. In the 1970s and 1980s the value added of the private sector (legal, semi-legal and illegal) may have amounted to around 10 per cent of Soviet GDP (Hanson, 2003, p. 13). In particular the black economy expanded in size.

The perceived gap between Soviet ideology and Soviet reality became greater as society stopped 'moving' as under Stalin. The 'mobilization ideology' was not compatible with the reality of late Brezhnevist rule that was extremely conservative. Brezhnevism meant anti-change and anti-innovation. Spreading corruption undermined the legitimacy of the regime that was based on the appearance of being non-corrupt, efficient and promoting social justice. Etkind and Gozmann (1992) write about a psychological crisis that gripped Soviet society from the early 1970s. Also, the dissolution of totalitarian structures spurred the differentiation between public and private spheres.

For many decades, Soviet economic and social life was a highly institutionalized inefficiency. As Kon noted (1996, p.199), 'productive social activity was being gradually eliminated and replaced by bureaucratic simulation and meaningless rituals'. The predominant and ever growing feeling in the 1970s and 1980s was social apathy. This situation taught the individual 'learned helplessness'.

According to Ken Jowitt, the Communist Party traded *de facto* privatization in non-priority areas for active party control and penetration of priority areas. 'This became particularly true for the Brezhnev period, when the private egoism, *personalism* not individualism, became the major socio-cultural reality.' (Jowitt, 1992, p. 228, original italicization).

Soviet citizens were obliged to compromise with the system which meant being involved in amoral behaviour, such as spying and lying. The moral conflicts that accompanied this collaboration with the system had a lasting psychological impact. It was in the late 1980s and early 1990s, in a more open climate that a public debate developed about the 'ecology of the soul'. Double-talk and spreading cynicism contributed to a feeling of general depression into which at least the Soviet intelligentsia was gradually plunged under Brezhnev.

Heller and Nekrich (1986, p. 731) described the consolidation of Soviet power as follows:

> A new human community has come into existence in which no one has rights, but each possesses a tiny share of power: he can work poorly; mock the customer if he is a sales clerk; denounce his neighbour; and be arrogant towards little people if he is a civil servant. He can steal, and give and take bribes. This bit of power is always gained by an abuse or infraction of official legislation, to which the state closes its eye.[21]

Conspicuous in the Soviet system was the large number of laws and decrees that were often contradictory, often not published and comprising all aspects of life. Almost everyone could be accused of violating the law. It made people very cautious and caused them to act according to the principle of 'everything is prohibited, unless it is explicitly allowed'.

Alexander Yakovlev, member of Politburo (from 1985), has argued that the systematic persecution of persons who showed initiative and independent behaviour led to the mass lumpenization of society which in turn spawned incompetence and irresponsibility (Millar and Wolchik, 1994, p. 215). One can even speak about institutionalized irresponsibility. Under Brezhnev, the adage became: 'just try to do your job properly, and do not care for anything else'. People withdrew into their private lives. The army of spies and informers caused loss of mutual trust and led to the atomization of society.

The attitude of hierarchical egalitarianism became under Brezhnev even more pronounced. The typical Russian 'community spirit' gradually faded away as first generation urbanites became a minority and atomization of society broke traditional bonds.

During the Brezhnev era, ideological indoctrination became even farther removed from the reality that people experienced in their daily lives. However, most people thought, that the basic parameters of the official image of Soviet life were correct.[22] Shlapentokh noticed that the people 'possessed a dual mentality, typical of people living in totalitarian societies'. 'It combined a pragmatic and realistic approach to the issues of everyday life with most of the official dogmas' (Shlapentokh, 1998, p. 33). All this did not mean that popular support for socialism diminished.[23]

Especially under Brezhnev it seemed as if history came to a standstill as people continued to get more of the same. History was petrified, as was personal life. The party-state took care of people from cradle to grave.

Power in the Soviet Union meant the ability not to listen and not to learn. This meant, especially in the Brezhnev era, a pervasive resistance to change and innovation. All feedback mechanisms were blocked which resulted in increased inefficiency at all levels.

The crisis of society was reflected in increasing mortality, especially male and infant mortality. From 1965 onwards life expectancy started to decline gradually. Deviant behaviour such as prostitution, gang membership, drug and alcohol abuse spread. This was particularly the case with juvenile crime which had started to increase in the late Brezhnev period.

The crisis of society was also reflected in the army where *dedovshchina*, i.e., the abuse by senior soldiers (*dedy*, i.e. grandfathers) spread and undermined the discipline and morale in the army. After 1945 the army had been the pride of the country. It also had been a success story in terms of integration of ethnic minorities (see Hosking, 2006, p. 336). By the 1970s it had 'deteriorated into an Aguas stable of alcoholism, drug abuse, and vice, and an arena for interethnic feuds' (ibid.).

Perestroika: the Nomenklatura transforms into a rentier-bourgeoisie

When Michael Gorbachev became secretary general of the Communist Party (1985), there was in the upper echelons of the party-state no feeling of urgency with respect to a fundamental remake of the economic and political system. Economic growth had slowed and there was a general feeling that the Soviet Union could not match the US arms build-up.

Therefore, economic 'acceleration' was needed by inserting some market elements in the economic system. There was a consensus in the highest levels of the Nomenklatura that the Soviet system was inefficient but stable. Calmness and inertia were prevalent. This was partly related to the fact that up to the highest level politicians and bureaucrats were not fully informed about the real economic situation. Everybody knew, of course, that the official statistics were biased but no one was ready to risk his career in order to reveal the real situation (see the account of Khanin in Ellman and Kontorovich, 1998). According to Khanin, who published an alternative assessment of Soviet economic growth, the Soviet leadership failed to recognize the general social crisis in the country.[24] Not that the Soviet people were dissatisfied with their living standards. Personal consumption had grown during the period 1975 to 1985. Most Russians opposed radical changes in the economic order. However, there was growing discontent about increasing levels of corruption and dishonesty and a decline in moral standards.

When Gorbachev came to power the primacy of politics over economics (the belief that political will was more important than economic constraints, that political will transcended common sense) continued. With his anti-alcohol campaign, launched in 1985, Gorbachev caused economic disruption and a huge fall in government income because of the loss of sales of alcoholic beverages (Ellman and Kontorovich, 1998, p. 74).[25] Although alcohol consumption may have diminished, the production of dangerous and illegally produced vodka soared. The drop in world oil prices in the early 1980s had a large negative impact on the Soviet economy. Soon the revelation of the true extent of the military burden on the Soviet economy (some assess that about one-third of GDP was spent on the military),[26] and the conviction that without a reduction of the military expenditures it would not be possible to solve urgent socio-economic problems, led to a change in the military doctrine (Ellman and Kontorovich, 1998, p. 96). However, the disorganized way in which a reduction in military spending was accomplished added further to the economic crisis.

The (often young and academic) reformers that came to the fore were ignorant both about the workings of the centrally planned economy and market economy. The dominant idea was that the economic system is malleable to such an extent that any mixture of plan and market is feasible and the question is how to attain the optimal mixture. The dominant idea was that changes in the economic system would not lead to initial decline in growth rates. As reforms did not immediately give the desired results in terms of output growth, other young and inexperienced reformers were called in to implement new reforms which were badly and inconsistently applied. This was also related to the authoritarian way in which they were prepared and implemented. There were no proper feedback mechanisms. This vacillating economic policy was disastrous for enterprises that could not develop and implement a coherent economic strategy. Reforms started to cause serious disruptions as central control over enterprises loosened. With the 1987 enterprise reforms the state lost leverage potential over enterprises that increasingly started to ignore central orders. The enterprises were to be commercialized based on market relations among them. Centralized resource distribution was to be replaced by wholesale trade. Enterprise directors started to be appointed by the working collective and were more difficult to fire. Enterprise directors did encounter fewer restrictions on their behaviour. This was facilitated by a withdrawal of the party from the economy.

The removal of party control over economic management caused an institutional vacuum which resulted in a serious disorganization of the economy. Previously, the coercive role of the party forced managers to implement orders from higher levels. From 1987 onwards commands did not reach those who were supposed to execute them, and if they did, were not fulfilled (Ellman and Kontorovich, 1998, p. 24). The local and regional committees of the CPSU ceased to function as a regional coordinator, but the need for coordination did not disappear. Enterprises had to find new ways of enforcing delivery agreements and contractual agreements.

When in 1989 the government tried to roll back earlier reforms it failed because it had already given away the instruments to impose government decisions.

Until late 1991 local and regional Soviets remained responsible for executing government policy while being without any instruments to steer economic activities. According to Kondratenko, chairman of the Krasnodar krai Soviet, speaking in the summer of 1991:

A manager is becoming more and more independent. He is told 'to keep on trading'. You applaud this in Moscow, and do not see that this is bad, because it is me, the head of the regional government, not the manager, who bears the entire responsibility... If Gorbachev and Yeltsin are such supporters of the market, they should declare that local Soviets are no longer responsible for providing the population with foodstuffs, since the market will take care of it. (Ellman and Kontorovich, 1998, p. 199)

According to Rafikova, in 1991:

> the ineffectiveness of the state machinery in ensuring protection of private rights and contract enforcement caused the assumption of these functions by the legal and illegal coercive bodies, such as 'the mafia' (organized crime), registered security and law firms, police and other official armed agencies providing protection. (Quoted in Ellman and Kontorovich, 1998, p. 201)

Earlier it has been observed how under the rule of Brezhnev a process of feudalization undermined the effectiveness of governance and the strengthening of regional fiefdoms. Gorbachev tried to uproot this patrimonial system while introducing modern bureaucratic rule. Among others, he introduced elections and removed the party bureaucracy from the policy process. This undermined patrimonialism but he failed to introduce modern bureaucratic methods. Moreover, the basic parameters of patrimonial rule were even strengthened in most Soviet regions, except the Baltic republics as the regional elites tried to shield themselves from democratic reform while enriching themselves with the economic reforms. The informal regional networks that had come into being since the rule of Khrushchev provided the context for the seizure of state assets that accelerated under the rule of Gorbachev.

As Easter (2000, p. 173) observed:

> As the formal structures of power collapsed or were dismantled, informal personal networks were left standing. Members of these personal networks were placed in an advantageous position in the ensuing competition over political and economic resources.

The reforms undermined the Soviet order. But it was striking how little resistance the reforms that undermined core elements of the Soviet system encountered. For example, when the monopoly on foreign trade was abolished there was no resistance from the side of the ministry of foreign trade (Ellman and Kontorovich, 1998, p. 22). One could argue that this could be expected because leading bureaucrats from this ministry would gain by using their previous contacts for conducting their private foreign transactions. But also when Gosplan was dismantled, this met with hardly any resistance. The lack of resistance is partly related to the fact that at the highest level many had ceased to believe in the fundamentals of Marxism-Leninism and Soviet socialism. According to Alexander Tsipko, who worked for the Central Committee, 'even prior to Perestroika, a significant part of the CC apparat regarded communism as a façade... In practice since 1988 the CC apparat was actually more anti-communist, at least potentially, than the opposition formed from the ranks of the intelligentsia' (Ellman and Kontorovich, 1998, p. 186).[27]

The gradual dismantling of the Soviet centrally planned system greatly enhanced the power of the managerial class and the bureaucracy because they were the gate keepers to economic opportunities.

It became increasingly clear that the Soviet economy was built upon a fundamental contradiction. It was built upon the command and control system that struggled with the recalcitrant body of imperfect human material whose imperfections surfaced in a shadow economy symbiotically embedded into the first, official, economy, but at the same time having the potential of undermining it. With Gorbachev's reforms it was not a market economy that came to the fore but the shadow economy, an economy of favours, a semi-feudal system in which the right contacts meant everything.

The policies under Gorbachev can be compared to navigating without a compass. The loosening of control over the flow of funds sparked inflation. Scarcities of all kind of basic commodities became more pronounced. In a centrally planned economy the most important source of economic stability is the balance between monetary flow and the stability of product flow. In the course of a few years the mechanisms to ensure stability in these spheres were taken away.

It was the inadequate policies of the political leadership that accelerated the decay of the old economic system that with minor changes could have functioned for further decades. Growth figures had slowed but until the late 1980s there was still growth. According to Moisei Eydelman, who worked in the Central Statistical Administration of the USSR, the per capita growth rate during 1975–1990 was under 1 per cent per annum (Ellman and Kontorovich, 1998, p. 76); this is very close to Maddison's estimate (see Table 2.1).

In 1990 GDP fell by 2 per cent and in 1991 by 15 per cent. The increase of the money supply led to massive price hikes and during the first half of 1990 food prices increased by 18 per cent.

There was a huge gap between Secretary General Gorbachev's (1985–1991) talk about positive change and deteriorating socio-economic circumstances. Perestroika paved the way for the Nomenklatura and criminal elements to enrich themselves. Therefore, Perestroika was encountered with huge scepticism. For many Perestroika and Glasnost meant the acceleration of the decay of Soviet power rather than a 'renewal of socialism'. Those who were in the centre of the distribution

Table 2.1   USSR: rates of economic growth, 1961–90

Period	Official data	Seliunin and Khanin	CIA estimates	Maddison (2001)
7th Five Year Plan 1961–5	6.5	4.4	4.8	1961–70: 3.5%
8th FYP 1966–70	7.8	4.1	5.0	
9th FYP 1971–4	5.6	3.2	3.1	1971–80: 1.5%
10th FYP 1975–80	4.3	1.0	2.2	
11th FYP 1981–5	3.2	0.6	1.8	1981–90: 0.8%
12th FYP 1986–9	2.7		1.4	

Sources: Spulber, 2003, p. 279; Economic Survey of Europe, 2000, 1, p. 179; and Maddison, 2001

system or those who could dispose the most freely with employees' time, were the ones who profited most from the new situation. Parasitic attitudes became even more rewarded. Senior ranks of the bureaucracy began to appropriate state property. The 1987 law on enterprises and the 1988 law on cooperatives allowed enterprise managers and traders to gradually appropriate non-fixed assets of enterprises. According to Yasin:

> The cooperatives were like parasitic fungi preying upon the state economy and decomposing it. This became another front in the struggle between planning and market, where planning suffered total defeat' (in Ellman and Kontorovich, 1998, p. 151).

The new laws enabled destructive entrepreneurship to emerge, siphoning money and goods from the state wherever possible.

Youth centres of scientific technical crafts were established under the aegis of the Komsomol in 1987 and 1988. These centres became the first commercial structures in the Soviet Union. They were allowed to use liquidity stored in enterprises and got big fees in financial mediation. This allowed Komsomol functionaries, first in Moscow and later across the country, to start businesses in tourism and show business, to establish banks and construction and real estate companies. According to Olga Kryshtanovskaya (*Vremya*, 18 January 2002) between 1987 and 1992, the ratio of ex-functionaries in the business elite grew from 38 per cent to 61 per cent (ibid.). The 'golden youth' that emerged in the business elite was in most cases backed up by state structures.

The bureaucracy got increasingly out of control. According to Lewin (2005, p. 369) a crystallization of a proto-capitalism within the state-owned economy took place. An economy of favours developed that furthered personal power and patrimonial relations. Together with the spread of cooperatives organized crime proliferated. This was visible in the racketeers, often sportsmen, controlling local markets.[28] Organized crime often merged with bureaucratic structures.

Tolkachi, i.e. 'pushers' who arranged, in informal ways, supplies for enterprises, became increasingly important. They bridged the gap between the formal rules and the informal workings of the system (Ledeneva, 2006, p. 177).

Most Western Sovietologists looked at the Soviet Union from a decision maker perspective and noticed the break of Gorbachev and co. with Stalinist ideology and the accompanying revolution in ideas and ideals. They failed to understand to what extent Gorbachev was out of touch with Soviet reality and how the numerous policy initiatives proved to be counter-productive (at least from the perspective of official government objectives). Western Sovietologists hardly paid attention to developments in the shadow economy and the process of (hidden) privatization of the state by part of the bureaucracy. They largely ignored the underworld of personalistic relations.

By 1989 the economy was out of control and Gorbachev and his close advisers became convinced that a radical break with centrally planned economy would be necessary. But the more government liberalized, the more chaos appeared.

There was also the decision that the Soviet Union could and should not any more support the communist parties in power in Central Europe. It led to the disintegration of the Soviet empire on its fringes, first in Hungary and Poland where in August and October 1989 noncommunist governments came to power. Together with the fall of the Berlin wall, in November 1989, it meant a radical blow to the future of communism.

In August 1990 Yeltsin and Gorbachev gave the economists Shatalin and Gaidar the task to elaborate a plan for the transition to market economy. Subsequently they presented a plan to introduce market economy in 500 days.[29] The plan was not accepted by the government but reflected the mood of the reformers very well.

The decision for a market economy was not made under pressure of a broad popular movement that demanded an end to communism but it was a political decision at the top of the party-state based on the belief that the centrally planned economy and party-state did not have a future.

Until 1989, it was a revolution from above. From then onwards, forces had been released that could not be contained any longer. The democratization process and the loss of party control enabled actors, above all enterprise managers and bureaucrats, to pursue their own agendas.

The population was not informed about many aspects of the policy changes in the Kremlin, despite increased openness (*glasnost*). But they did become well informed about many negative aspects of communism and Soviet history.

Glasnost reduced the effectiveness of power. The official dismantling of numerous myths was seen by many people as a weakness, not as a strength, the more so as no improvement in everyday life was discernible. On the micro-level, the collapse of formal controls had exacerbated the collapse of social controls and helped to spur the explosion of deviant behaviour and massive theft.[30] Opinion polls reveal that support for socialism and a centrally planned economy dropped quickly from 1989 to 1991.

Although there was an avalanche of publications re-evaluating Soviet history, most people did not come to terms with the past of their country and, to a certain extent, their individual histories. The upsurge of civic activism occurred mainly in the Western part of the Soviet Union, i.e. the Western Ukraine and the Baltic republics (see Fleron, 1998, p. 62).[31]

The impetus for the rapid systemic change that started with Perestroika was the result of elite actions, on the highest level and not induced by massive popular discontent. It seems that the farther from the centre, the lesser the social and economic change (except for some of the Western fringes where a popular movement emerged). Most of the republics, regions and enterprises continued to be governed in the old ways. The systemic change was most pronounced in the centre. Perestroika can be compared with a computer in which the operating system is being removed before installing a new one. The command and control mechanisms were removed at the centre without being replaced with other coordination mechanisms. It was assumed that enterprises who previously accessed their suppliers and customers from the centre would suddenly find suppliers and markets through an imaginary channel. The unintended consequences of the reforms were shortages and disruption of production everywhere. At the end of the 1980s informal practices shifted from the phase of 'benign aid' to 'corrupting' and potentially 'system-threatening' (Ledeneva, 2006, p. 15).

3
Post-Soviet Russia: Captured by the Past?

In this chapter it will be established to what extent the development of post-communist Russia has been path-dependent and the result of a reconfiguration of elements from the past. Two distinct periods crystallize. First the Russia under President Yeltsin when centrifugal tendencies predominated and society and economy faced a deep crisis. Then the period after 1999 in which President Putin (2000–8) restored some order while building on Russian legacies.[1]

The Yeltsin era: things fall apart

From 1989 the Soviet republics became actors. First, inspired by developments in Central Europe and under the pressure of a growing mass movement the Baltic republics sought sovereignty. In November 1988 Estonia had already declared itself a sovereignty and in January 1989 the Estonian government accepted an economic autonomy plan and asserted the primacy of Estonian over Soviet law. Lithuania declared itself independent and in April 1991 Georgia followed. In February 1988 the Azerbaijanis launched pogroms against ethnic Armenians and in April 1989 Soviet troops killed 20 when breaking up a demonstration for Georgian independence in Tblisi.

On 29 May 1990 Boris Yeltsin was elected as President of Russia. This was followed by the Russian parliament declaring the supremacy of Russian laws on Russian territory on 12 June 1990. Russia also ruled what state property within Russia the Union government could control. This happened after the adoption of a Union level law stating that the Soviet Union would be based on the multiplicity of ownership forms whereby each ownership form would be, in principle, equal within the law. This paved the way for the privatization of state property. Boris

Yeltsin in 1990 stimulated enterprises to switch tax payments from the federal to the republic level and Russia started to ask political favours in exchange for tax payments to the federal level. Other republics followed suit. A series of actions were undertaken in various republics to enhance autonomy with regard to the centre. Generally, republics started to hoard goods.

Hanson (2003) observed that there was a strong economic logic to the Soviet break-up, but it sprang from political conflict. In 1991 the emission of rubles was something for which the Soviet central bank was responsible. But government spending was no longer controlled by the centre resulting in spendthrift republics siphoning resources from the prudent republics. 'So long as the republic leaderships were not prepared to cooperate for the long-term benefit of ruble stabilization for the whole federation, this monetary union was doomed. Yeltsin, for one, was not prepared to cooperate' (Hanson, 2003, p. 235). With uncoordinated fiscal policies and a single currency, the attraction of free-riding for each republic would prevent macro-stabilization.

As a result of increasing economic chaos, food shortages spread. In 1990 the government was forced to introduce food rationing in Leningrad. Lithuania and Kazakhstan had cut off grain supplies and milk and meat were scarce.

The foreign debt attained $120 billion in 1992 (Gabrisch and Hoelscher, 2006, p. 171). The Soviet Union declared a default on its foreign debt in December 1991.

In view of these disintegrative tendencies and just before a new treaty regulating the relations between the republics of the USSR would be signed, conservative elements staged a coup (August 1991). The coup was so badly prepared, during which President Gorbachev was kept hostage in his weekend house in Crimea, that it was a relatively easy task for Boris Yeltsin to take the initiative and defeat the plotters. The centre of political gravity shifted to the republics and the federal government became increasingly disempowered. The Soviet Union transformed into a union of sovereign states.

The coup also showed how weak and badly organized the conservative elements in the upper-party echelons were. The main political struggles in 1990 and 1991 were, however, not about alternative economic programmes (see Barnes, 2006, p. 51); they were mainly about power. Russian President Yeltsin gave the final blow to the Soviet Union in his quest for power. In December 1991 the leaders of Russia, Kazakhstan, Ukraine and Belarus decided to destroy the Soviet state as they perceived that their interests and that of the Nomenklatura they represented were better served with the creation of 15 successor states. This had enormous consequences not only for the population of what used to be the Soviet Union, but for the world as a whole. In terms of territory, Russia shrank behind the borders it had attained at the end of the seventeenth century (see Maps 1.2 and 3.1). In terms of population it became smaller than Bangladesh and in terms of GDP, smaller than Mexico.

In Russia government declared that the country would chose the path of parliamentary democracy and market economy.

Instead, what has happened in Russia since 1991 has been the decomposition of the structure of Soviet society, state and economy. According to Strobe Talbott, advisor to US President Clinton, the values of the Clinton administration (1992–2000) and Yeltsin (1991–1999) collided, and therefore 'it was a common demolition project. And that is the story of that period'.[2] In Spring 1991, Washington shifted support from Gorbachev, who had a social democratic conception of the future of the Soviet Union, to Yeltsin, who fully embraced the market.

On the surface it seemed for many, above all in the liberal intelligentsia, that Russia was moving in the direction of liberal market economy. Apart from the emerging oligarchs and the West, the liberal intelligentsia constituted the third pillar of support for Yeltsin. Yeltsin recruited many of the intelligentsia in government. Never since 1917 had the intelligentsia played such an important role in government. Boris Yeltsin's advisors were often ex-scientists of the Academy of Sciences. Yeltsin appointed the young and inexperienced Gaidar, Glaziev, Khakamada, Generalov and other academics to the government. However, under Yeltsin support for science and culture dwindled.[3]

The intelligentsia did not constitute a lobby. The lobby that was in the ascendancy was the group that had access to export receipts. The influence of those industries that mainly relied on subsidies declined fast although they managed to remove some radical liberals from government.

Under President Yeltsin Russia was faced with a meltdown of the state. At least one-third of firms did not pay taxes while only 17 per cent of citizens paid taxes (Mohacsi, 2000, p. 15). As a result, in real terms, tax revenues dropped by an accumulative 45 per cent during 1992–1997 and expenditures dropped by a cumulative 54 per cent in the same period. However, this did not go hand in hand with a reform of the state and the provision of public goods. The entitlement system did not change. The fiscal deficit between 1993 and 1998 was between 6 and 8 per cent of GDP and contributed to inflation (Mohacsi, 2000, p. 35). Real interest rates remained very high, contributing to disinvestment.

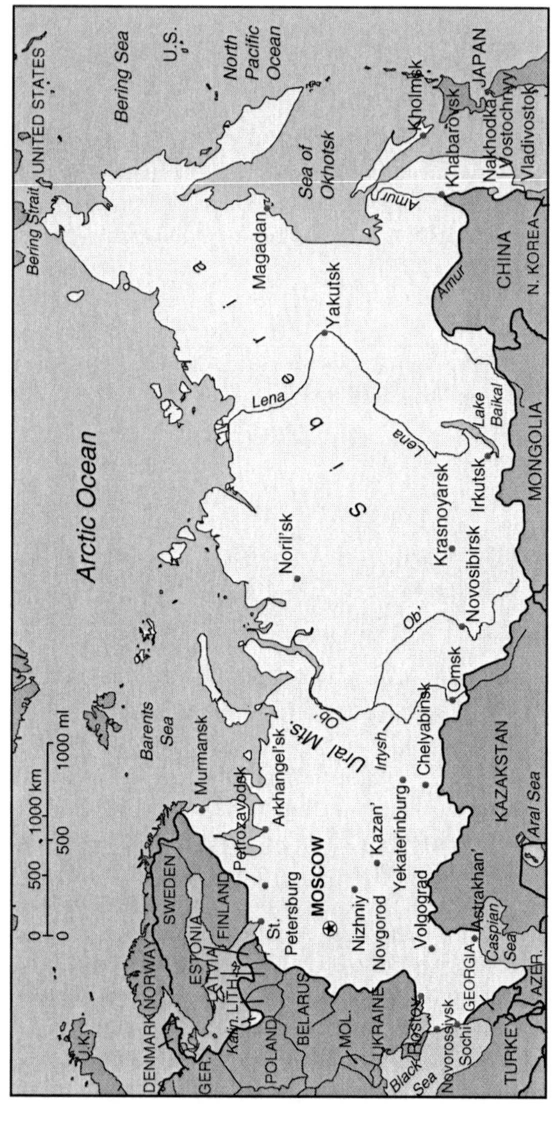

Map 3.1 Russia post-1991

Much progress was made with privatization. While in 1990, 5 per cent of the Russian economy was in private hands, by the middle of 1998 this figure had reached 70 per cent (Mohacsi, 2000, p. 13). But the build-up of institutions that could underpin market economy, such as an adequate financial infrastructure and the rule of law, was very slow. Moreover, 75 per cent of Russia's 6000 most basic goods were supplied by a single producer meaning that privatization would lead to monopoly abuse. This is one of the main reasons price liberalization led to hyper-inflation (26 fold increase in 1992). Price liberalization was incomplete. For example, price controls on some strategic goods like oil and gas remained. Oil could be bought for 1 per cent of the world market price. Therefore, oil trade profits of $24 billion were made, in 1992 alone, depriving the state of much needed funds (Hedlund, 2005, p. 279). Most profits were channelled abroad. The liberalization of international capital transactions was one of the biggest policy mistakes as it drained resources from Russia. The Chinese did not make this mistake.

Increasingly, the state institutions were captured by corporate interests, especially since the privatization of large enterprises started, that created a group of super-rich tycoons that could buy influence in the Kremlin.

Liberalization of imports led to the unnecessary destruction of many Russian enterprises. By 1995, imports comprised as much as 70 per cent of the goods sold in some of Russia's largest cities (Goldman, 2003, p. 57).

In the process of marketization of the Russian economy a crucial role was fulfilled by shadow traders (*tolkachi*). With the reforms of 1987–1988 their role was legalized. At the same time the enterprise directors obtained the power to deal with supplies and produce goods as they liked. As money was in short supply the new trading mechanisms involved a lot of barter. Enterprise products were sold to traders very cheaply in return for goods that the enterprise needed for production. In this process kickbacks were paid to the enterprise directors. The fact that these deals made most enterprises loss making was less important. In this way huge amounts of money got accumulated in the commercial firms in which often enterprise directors had a stake.

This process spread over the whole of the Russian economy during the early 1990s. It meant that in the process of transition most enterprise directors squeezed their enterprises. The new Russian businessmen were not builders, they were typically squeezers. The traders often belonged to ethnic minorities. In Soviet times, Russians and communists looked down at the *tolkachi*.

Enterprises developed sophisticated financial schemes in order to protect against the predatory behaviour of the state but also in order to further the private interests of their directors. Enterprises 'constructed reality, thus documenting properly something that never happened. Instead of over-reporting to satisfy plan targets one now finds under-reporting of profits for tax purposes' (Ledeneva, 2006, p. 117). Barter schemes were used to avoid taxation but also to channel profits to private accounts – 'To evade or, rather, to avoid taxes, a company has to simulate arrears' (Ledeneva, 2006, p. 155), as one director observed 'we first decide how much tax we want to pay … and then adjust the books accordingly' (Ledeneva, 2006, p. 132). Often foreign firms and foreign accounts were used to secure enterprise resources and channel money abroad.

Financial schemes were above all used for barter. Ledeneva (2006, p. 136) quotes an enterprise director:

> For producing oil and gas equipment I need metal forms from KMZ, which has a monopoly. The director of that plant can dictate his terms. He gives me a list of their priorities: say, payments for energy, for timber, for metal, or supplies of aluminium – perhaps twenty of his problems. I decide which ones I can solve, choose three or four areas, and start building schemes around them. It is understood between us, permanent partners, that we cannot change direction every time. They know the problems I solve: I can pay their electric energy expenses, I can pay for their gas or supply gas for their heating and technological needs, I can arrange aluminium supplies – these are my four areas. On top of this I pay their transport expenses, since it so happens that the railway owes me as a result of another barter chain.

It is obvious that these barter schemes, although they helped to navigate the Russian economy through the 1990s, were very costly. In summer 1994 in some regions barter accounted for more than 75 per cent of payments (Ledeneva, 2006, p. 119). In 1992 barter accounted for about 40 per cent in foreign trade (Ledeneva, 2006, p. 121). Barter also put at a disadvantage whole industrial sectors. In barter trade goods were accepted that could easily be sold like oil and gas, and eventually food. But furniture and cloth were difficult to sell in the short term. This contributed to the extremely rapid decline of light industry during the 1990s (see Table 3.1).

Barter is typical for closed networks, it aids the insiders and excludes the outsiders. It also involves high risk. Financial fraud seems to be a

Table 3.1   Production index by economic activity, 2000 and 2006

Economic activity	2000	2006
*Mining and quarrying**	74.3	101.3
Mining and quarrying of energy producing materials	80.9	114.2
Mining and quarrying, except of energy producing materials	60.0	62.7
*Manufacturing**	51.0	70.8
Food products, including beverages and tobacco	54.5	77.6
Textile and textile products	23.4	25.2
Leather and leather products	15.5	24.7
Wood and wood products	37.5	47.6
Pulp, paper and paper products; publishing and printing	81.2	113.0
Coke, refined petroleum products and nuclear fuel	60.1	75.6
Chemicals, chemical products and man-made fibres	69.8	82.3
Rubber and plastic products	52.5	75.3
Other non-metallic mineral products	40.3	56.4
Basic metals and fabricated metal products	66.8	94.2
Machinery and equipment n.e.c.	32.3	46.8
Electrical, electronic and optical equipment	45.3	99.6
Transport equipment	53.1	53.9
*Electricity, gas and water supply**	76.9	90.1

Notes: 1991 = 100; *Data given with the account of adjustment for informal activities
Source: Federal State Statistics Service (www.gsk.ru)

feature that is, from top to bottom, characteristic of a high risk environment. In big companies everything is centralized because they do not trust people on the ground. They often prefer to buy equipment abroad not because it is better but because it is easier to organize broker fees and keep these on foreign accounts.

Because the state could not provide protection, organized crime (*krishi*, i.e., roofs) imposed themselves upon enterprises. The big enterprises organized their own security. A survey of 50 shops in Moscow in 1996 revealed that 76 per cent needed mafia protection compared to only 6 per cent of the 55 shops surveyed in Warsaw (Goldman, 2003, p. 69). In 1993, Russian organized crime was said to dominate over 50 per cent of the country's enterprises (Goldman, 2003, p. 75).

Although organized crime, as a rule, imposed themselves upon enterprises, their services often helped to keep the taxman at bay. While during the 1990s taxes approached 80 per cent of profits, racketeers usually asked 20–30 per cent of profits (Volkov, 2005a, pp. 154, 157). In 1996, 40 per cent of retail traders found dealing with racketeers less of a problem than with officials and the taxman (Volkov, 2005a, p. 141).

In the first phase of organized crime, the racketeers just asked for money while subsequently (during 1992–1995) they aimed to control 'their' enterprises, through a stake in the enterprise or control over specific functions such as book-keeping (Volkov, 2005a, p. 146). Organized crime recruited heavily from the official power structures like secret services. It is telling that during the 1990s each year about a quarter of personnel (approximately 25,000 persons each year) were expelled from the law enforcement agencies due to law violations. According to Volkov (2005a, p. 149) during the 1990s each year 15,000 law enforcement agents were recruited by organized crime.

Russian organized crime became omni-present and constituted a major barrier to entry for new firms. It led to the monopolization-cum-criminalization of major sectors and regions of Russia. It contributed to the disintegration of the Russian state. A state is defined by the ability to exercise the monopoly of violence and a monopoly of tax raising on its territory but it was these functions that were undermined by organized crime.

Under Yeltsin it wasn't the corruption that was new, (this was characteristic for Russia) but the violence associated with it. It was, along with other factors, reflected in the explosion of violent deaths during the 1990s. While in 1985 there were 15,000 in the whole of the Soviet Union, in 2000 there were 31,829 for Russia alone. It was difficult to distinguish between organized crime and state bureaucracy.

Russian privatization occurred in four phases (see Volkov, 2005a, pp. 324–33). The first phase, between 1988 and 1991, was that of hidden privatization when enterprise directors created cooperatives through which they acquired enterprise assets. The second phase, from 1992 to 1995, was that of voucher privatization in which all small and medium sized enterprises were privatized. The state maintained 30 per cent of the shares while 60 per cent of shares went to workers' collectives and management and 10 per cent to external investors. In many cases these state shares were bought by outsiders who could often use their leverage to capture the privatized firms. The third phase occurred during 1996 and 1997 when many big enterprises, above all in the sphere of natural resources, were privatized and given, for small amounts, to people close to the presidential administration. The fourth phase started in 1998 when a wave of raids, usually with the help of state agencies like the secret services, changed the ownership of many thousands of enterprises and led to the creation of vertically integrated holdings, often exercising monopoly control in sectors or territories.

In the early phase of transition, it was mainly insiders, i.e., senior management that got control over the enterprises. In this period big enterprises that were part of a single production chain were often unbundled into separate economic entities (see Avdasheva, 2005, p. 304). During the second half of the 1990s state intervention took property away from the enterprise directors who understood industry and gave it to oligarchs well connected with the political authorities. This process was supported by the West (see Fleron, 1998, p. 65). Leading oligarchs managed to gain control over a substantial part of the Russian economy (see Chapter 5). They hardly paid for their acquisitions. Privatization proceeds for government amounted during 1992 to 1998 to only 1 per cent of GDP (Primakov, 2001, p. 270). Privatization was not preceded by genuine commercialization of the economy. Most markets were monopolies, dominated by big industrial enterprises.[4] Ledeneva observed that the state was in many ways paid by big business 'while businessmen benefit from the sanctioned process of monopolization as this also increases the "manageability" of the economy for the state' (Ledeneva, 2006, p. 187).

Squeezing of enterprises was most pronounced in extractive industries. The history of privatization and corporate governance during the 1990s showed a number of institutional traps that were the consequence of the ignorance of policy makers in designing the blueprints of reforms. These traps include barter, payment arrears, tax evasion and corruption. All enterprises were embedded in a production chain, which made their separate privatization harmful:

> The deeper the enterprises are located in a production chain, the fewer alternative choices they have with respect to alternative suppliers and buyers. As a result, the enterprises in the middle of the chain are transformed into the hostages of those that are located at its fringes. The separate privatization of the links in the same chain has led to the appropriation of a 'rent' by the owners of the enterprise lying closer to its start (extraction) and end (sale to final customers). (Oleinik, 2005, pp. vii, viii)

There is no evidence to show that privatization has made Russian industry more efficient.[5] Incentives to restructure privatized enterprises were swamped by self-dealing among managers, a punitive tax system, corruption and organized crime.

In many sectors monopolies, with the help of the state bureaucracy, erected high barriers to entry for new enterprises. That is the reason why the sector of small and medium sized enterprises is so small in Russia (see Chapter 7).

Instead of the market, the wheeling and dealing of the old enterprise directors, added with *tolkachi* and officials, became the main coordination mechanism in the economy. Gradually the set of rules of the new capitalists, which conflicted with the Soviet style network coordination, became more important. The new capitalists often used legislation to enforce ownership rights while the old directors initially hardly paid attention to questions of legal ownership. The two different sets of rules that were operating during the 1990s created much uncertainty. Increasingly, the new rules undermined the informal network rules of Soviet times.

President Boris Yeltsin became very unpopular and he only managed to get re-elected in 1996 with the massive support of the mass media that were to a large extent controlled by the oligarchs.[6] They rallied behind Yeltsin in fear that their wealth would be confiscated by an eventual victory of the communist presidential candidate Zyuganov. Part of the strategy was to make sure Zyuganov would go to the second round rather than a more popular politician. It was believed that the bogeyman of communism would rally people around Yeltsin.

Yeltsin was despised because he was held responsible for the freefall of the Russian economy and the emergence of robber capitalism in Russia.[7] Some have described the Russian transition to capitalism as the greatest plunder of modern times. This happened under the banner of the introduction of market economy, herewith supported by the institutions of global economic governance, such as the IMF and World Bank, and Western governments.[8] It can be said that Western institutions had during the 1990s major leverage on Russian government policies. Western institutions believed that the market would produce democracy and transparency. It was assumed that from under the veneer of cultural differences *Homo Economicus* would appear.

Yeltsin and his advisers assumed that the Soviet legacy was just a burden and the share of the state in GDP and employment should be reduced. Only market transactions, price stabilization and the private ownership of assets were important while a rule governed environment was deemed less important.

The Western press seemed to report developments in Russia through the lenses of wishful thinking and portrayed Yeltsin as a democrat and the political process as 'democratization'. Although Yeltsin was the first democratically elected leader of Russia, he soon turned out to be an authoritarian leader. Already in October 1991 he secured the right to govern by decree. When the Russian parliament disagreed with Yeltsin's economic policies, he dismissed it. When the constitutional court proclaimed his move unconstitutional, Yeltsin suspended it. When the parliament refused to obey and rebelled, he sent tanks to it (1993). The shelling of parliament and the way in which the presidential elections of 1996 were organized evoked hardly any criticism in the West. Media freedom under Yeltsin was interpreted in Russia as giving away the media to media tycoons who manipulated their assets for their own benefit. Yeltsin's presidency was characterized by arbitrariness and short-termism.

Yeltsin initiated personalistic and patrimonial rule. It was mainly the small coterie of politicians and businessmen around Yeltsin that profited from 'transition'. 'Liberals' like Anatoly Chubais and Egor Gaidar presented themselves very well as proponents of liberal market economy in the West although they were seen very differently in Russia. The rule of the oligarchs around Yeltsin has been described in Russia as Semiboyarchina, that means a kind of feudal regime with a weak king, referring to early seventeenth century Russia.

The reforms under President Yeltsin were badly prepared and the Russian 'market bolshevists' did not take into account Russian starting conditions and traditions.[9] They opted for the Washington Consensus: a minimal state; free exchange rates; monetary stability; opening for foreign competition; and the introduction of markets for goods, labour and capital. As happened before in Russian history, the reformers accepted Western ideas in their most extreme form.[10] As a result Russian GDP continuously decreased during 1990–9. According to the Russian secret service capital flight attained 1.5 to 2 billion dollars a month during 1998 (Primakov, 2001, p. 354). By the middle of 1998 more than half of the food consumed in Russia originated from abroad (Primakov, 2001, p. 273). Only the financial crisis of 1998 that caused a decline of 25 per cent in the population's real incomes brought about a change in government policies, with a move away from IMF recommendations and with more state intervention although The Family continued its predatory policies (see Primakov, 2001, pp. 250–333).

Yevgeni Primakov (Prime Minister, 1998–1999) quoted a report from the secret service according to which the most profitable sectors of the economy were shared between various financial and industrial groups, closely linked to organized crime; on the basis of growing corruption of state officials and local groups, as well as a considerable part of the judiciary and police (Primakov, 2001, p. 355).

Russia has been a prime example of a destructive revolution. Here a comparison with China is instructive. The Chinese leaders learned from the destructive impact of Mao's adventurism and voluntarism. They pointed to the Chinese proverb that while crossing the river one should grope for the stepping stones rather than jumping over the chasm in one 'great leap forward'.

The political regime transformed into a modern clan system that was much less ascriptive than the Nomenklatura system. A strong democratic counter culture did not develop.

The 1990s meant for most Russians one of the most traumatic periods in their lives. The revolution of the 1990s, like the one of 1917, issued a challenge to personal and social identity. There was a changeover from a completely planned individual life, in which no personal initiative was required, into total existential uncertainty in which initiative is crucial for survival. Russian GDP was in 2000 only 67 per cent of the 1991 level while investment levels collapsed (see Table 3.2). Living standards dropped dramatically and by the turn of the millennium almost half of Russians were living under the official poverty line.[11]

Many people, especially in the older generation, became desperate as the salary in their official job was not enough to live on. During the 1990s the methods used to satisfy the family's basic needs became less market oriented than in the Soviet era. According to a survey in early 1998 (Rose, 1998, p. 27), 56 per cent of 2002 people interviewed had resorted to defensive portfolios in which they prioritized: a) earnings

Table 3.2   Russian GDP by utilization, 1991–2000

	1992	1993	1994	1995	1996	1997	1998	1999	2000
GDP	85.5	78.1	68.1	65.3	60.9	61.5	58.9	61.3	67
Personal consumption	69.6	70.4	71.3	69.3	66.0	69.6	67.9	65.6	71
State consumption	72.3	67.7	65.7	66.4	66.9	65.3	65.7	66.1	67
Gross fixed capital investment	88.7	65.8	48.7	45.0	36.4	34.3	30.9	32.4	37

Note: 1991 = 100
Source: Federal State Statistics Service (www.gks.ru)

from regular jobs, benefits at place of work or pension; and b) growing food, using free connections, repairing their house or helping friends and relatives as the two most important activities.

Society became fragmented, and the interests of the large masses of the population ceased to be represented at the political level. Extreme collectivism, in which the individual is crushed under the weight of the omnipresent state that penetrates all spheres of life, had been gradually replaced by jungle individualism. This was expressed in an aggressive greed and recklessness of the ruling elite, and criminalization of society as a whole.

It was the falling away of the Communist Party that removed the last obstacles for the plunder of the nation's assets. Paradoxically, the Communist Party did not only fulfil the role of transmission belt for the Soviet leaders, it also fulfilled a role to further social cohesion, to resolve conflicts at the local level and to coordinate economic relations at the regional level. It provided some degree of protection for citizens. For example, if there were problems in the neighbourhood with respect to leakages or other inconveniences, the local party cell could often help. The same applied for problems in enterprises.

One of the means to socialize the Soviet youth, apart from educational establishments, had been the Pioneers and Komsomol organizations. In Western publications the repressive aspects have been emphasized, but these organizations played an important positive role in socializing and integrating Soviet youth. This became apparent once these organizations disappeared after the collapse of communism. This was not only reflected in the numerous derelict youth camps, playgrounds and sport complexes, but also in rising youth delinquency and drug abuse.

The context of family life changed fundamentally. As parents had to work more hours in order to make ends meet, children got less attention. Childcare provisions, like kindergarten, worsened and grand-mothers (*babushka*) who previously cared for grandchildren often had to work in order to survive as pensions were not sufficient to survive. Divorce became more frequent with 80 per cent of marriages failing (RIA Novosti, 9 December 2004). This all led to a generation of neglected and sometimes abandoned children. As Ellerman (2003, p. 15) noticed:

> most Russians encountered the market not as something that strengthened their capabilities and empowered them to do more but something that took away what they were capable of doing and left them in a position where the rational choice was to grab what they could in the face of a very uncertain and uncontrollable future.

The state of depression that became generalized in the late Brezhnev period deepened, resulting in a general feeling of despair throughout the 1990s. This was reflected in the spread of escapist behaviour like suicides, alcohol and drug abuse[12] and an increase in the number of mental disorders.[13] Between 1991 and 1994 life expectancy for males in Russia had fallen by over six years (from 63.8 to 57.5 years).[14] In 1950, Russia was among the leading countries with respect to longevity (a life expectancy of 65, the world average was 45); by 1999 Russia was lagging behind with a life expectancy of 67 (world average 67) (Maddison, 2001, p. 30).

The Putin era

President Yeltsin nominated as his successor the former head of the FSB (the former KGB) Vladimir Putin who was elected in 2000 as President after the second war against Chechnya commenced.[15] The most important task President Putin faced was damage limitation. Under President Putin some order in state affairs was restored that was largely absent in the chaotic years under President Yeltsin that some characterized as 'anarcho-liberalism'. In 1999 a large part of the national wealth was held by seven oligarchs.

It also meant the gradual restoring of the primacy of politics and the disciplining of the political opposition.

In February 2000 Putin stated that big business should keep out of politics while several months later media magnate Gusinsky was jailed and shortly afterwards allowed to leave the country. Late in 2000 Berezovsky, who owned a vast media empire and who had been one of the most influential oligarchs in the Kremlin during the late Yeltsin years, fled Russia. Since then most private media outlets have gradually become under the control of the Kremlin or Kremlin friendly owners.

Putin made clear: businessmen should not meddle in politics; the state accepted the results of privatization; the state lowers taxes; and business will pay these taxes (*New York Times*, 25 March 2004).

It did not mean that the owners of big business suffered. They could go on with the old ways of doing business as long as they did not challenge the new rules of the game. This was reflected in the astronomic rise of wealth of the richest Russians. Under President Putin, Moscow became the world's leading city with respect to the number of billionaires and Russia in 2007 occupied second place, after the USA, in the total number of billionaires, registering 87 as compared to 52 in 2006 (*Forbes*, 5 March 2008). Nevertheless, a redistribution of property took place in which above all the environment of President Putin profited.[16] This often happened by raising the stakes of the state in enterprises or the state getting a majority stake, especially in strategic industries. The state officials placed on the boards of these enterprises could easily enrich themselves. State corporations expanded their influence and often managed to gain favourable treatment by the tax office. On the other hand, small and medium sized business continued to be faced with bureaucratic harassment (see Chapter 7).

Putin gradually established a new symbiosis of money and power. Remarkable was that only six out of the twenty seven board members of the Russian Union of Industrialists and Entrepreneurs, in which all oligarchs were represented and claimed to represent 60 per cent of GDP, spoke out against the arrest of Khodorkovsky (Hanson and Teague, 2005, p. 663).

The Duma was transformed into a rubber stamping institution from which no genuine opposition emerged. Under President Putin Russia was developing in the direction of a moderate authoritarian 'managed democracy'. Nevertheless, massive fraud did not seem to have occurred during national elections under President Putin in which United Russia, 'the party of power', consolidated its grip on power. In this process, 'administrative resources' were often used. 'United Russia' attained 1 million members early 2006 (*RIA Novosti*, 6 March 2006). The party of power sought to exert monopoly power over parliament, civil society, the media and the economy. Fake opposition parties were established to create the appearance of opposition. Real opposition parties were criminalized and broken (see Wilson, 2005). Political technologists helped to create disinformation campaigns.

Buying of mandates became more common. According to *Moskovskii Komsomolets*, (17 May 2006) by 2006 the going price for a seat in the senate was between 3.5 and 5 million dollars. Of the Duma members 20 had a capital worth more than 150 million dollars and 19 of them were members of the United Russia faction (*Trud*, 3 October 2007).

It is telling that, in 2004, 25 per cent of the people in the higher echelons of power were officers and generals, compared to 11 per cent in 1993 (Shlapentokh, 2004). Olga Kryshtanovskaya, director of the Moscow based Centre for the Study of Elites, analysed the biographies of 1,016 leading political figures, departmental heads of the presidential administration, all members of the government, all deputies of both houses of parliament, the heads of federal units and the heads of regional executive and legislative branches. She found that 26 per cent had reported serving in the KGB or its successor agencies (*Washington Post*, 12 December 2006).

Examining unexplained gaps in curriculum vitaes, unlikely career paths or service in organizations affiliated with the KGB suggests the startling figure of 78 per cent representation (ibid.). Under President Gorbachev, only 5 per cent of the upper echelons of the government bureaucracy were from the secret services (Anderson, 2007).

However, some Western researchers, like Bettina Renz (2006), point to the fact that the *siloviki*, i.e. the network of former and current state-security officers, do not dominate in the business section of the elite. Renz also concludes that it was not a deliberate strategy of Putin to aim at a more authoritarian regime. She points out that in the presidential administration only 9 out of 47 leading positions have a background in the force structures. Bremmer and Charap (2006–7) argue that the label 'siloviki' is misleading because it does not cover one coherent Kremlin faction. The number of these factions number from two to ten. The *siloviki* control many government agencies, not only force structures but also, for instance, energy and customs. The general outlook of the *siloviki* faction can be characterized as statist and nationalist. Other factions are, according to Bremmer and Charap, the free market liberals (German Gref and Alexei Kudrin) and the 'technocrats' (the future president Dmitry Medvedev and Alexei Miller). Belkovsky (*Gazeta.ru*, 27 February 2008) argues that Russia is *de facto* governed by approximately 15 influential groups that own a large part of the Russian economy, 'each has its own siloviki, liberal economists, legal experts, and officials on all levels, including governors and the mayors of big cities'. He points out that in inter-group conflicts closeness to the President was not crucial and that there were many cases where the president's men lost conflicts. More important is financial clout.

About two-thirds of employees of the secret services are involved in private businesses, mainly private security services that often work in close cooperation with businessmen and organized crime.[17] Organized crime was not defeated but incorporated. According to Goldman (2003, p.193) there are 'more and more instances where organized crime in Russia is controlled by a government syndicate' that is made up of officials from the Ministry of the Interior and the FSB (KGB) and non-governmental security forces, all working with the Mafia. Organized crime groups shifted their activities from racketeering to more complex power-partnerships with enterprises. President Putin also began to tackle organized crime that worked 'in the old ways'. For example, law enforcement agencies acted against mafia groups in Moscow and St Petersburg (Volkov, 2005a, p. 313). Also, private security agencies were brought under stricter control.[18]

Despite the strengthening of the 'vertical of power', crime rates have increased since Putin came to power. According to Rashid Nurgaliyev, Russia's most senior police officer, one-tenth of Russia is under control of organized crime (*The Independent*, 15 March 2007). Criminal groups employ approximately 300,000 people. Since 2002 reported crime went up continuously from about 2,500,000 in 2002 to more than 3,500,000 in 2005 (ibid.). However, according to the Interior Ministry, contract killings went down from an average of 600–800 during the 1990s to 70 in 2002, (Eurasianhome.org, 10 April 2007).

Under President Putin courts started to be used for economic conflict regulation. Until 2000 the *krishi* (roofs), i.e. protection provided by mafia/private security services and violence were used to settle conflicts. During the 1990s 70 per cent of conflicts were regulated outside the courts. As the governors became more powerful, judges and police became more important power instruments. The new liberal bankruptcy law of 1998 gave local bureaucrats more power over enterprises, not only to enforce tax payment but also to appropriate enterprises. It is telling that 79 per cent of bankruptcy cases in 2001 were initiated by the state, not by private debtors (Volkov, 2005b). From 1998 onwards influential business groups were formed which, together with local bureaucrats, judges and the governor, took over many enterprises. Only those businessmen who invested in bureaucratic structures obtained stakes in enterprises. Often, law enforcement agencies and secret services were hired in the raiding of enterprises with the help of the bankruptcy law (Volkov, 2005a, p. 329). During his election campaign Dmitry Medvedev prioritized the fight against corporate raids and in connection to this the independence of the judiciary (RosbusinessConsulting, 15 February 2008).

The weak rule of law is also exemplified by the fact that in 2006 about 200,000 apartment owners started to organize themselves because their apartments had been defrauded and illegitimately appropriated by building associations. Judiciary authorities have not done anything about this (*Moscow News*, 27 April 2007).

It was no surprise also that under President Putin public trust in law enforcement agencies remained on a dangerously low level and were lower than in 1990 (Lapin, 2007, p. 6; see also Chapter 5).[19]

Under President Putin a centralization of power on all levels took place. Under President Yeltsin the regions gradually got more autonomy and were usually ruled like feudal fiefdoms. They often had their own laws that contradicted federal law. At the regional level law enforcement agencies, politicians, officials, businessmen and the criminal elements frequently performed their function with their own business interests as a priority.

President Putin restored the vertical power structures, making, among other things, the regions more dependent on the centre. Regions were forbidden from introducing regulations and decrees that contravened federal legislation.

President Putin abolished regional executive elections in 2004. He started to appoint governors. One of the major reasons was to undermine the position of certain regional clans. However, between February 2005 and March 2008 only 12 regional governors out of 67 left office. According to Aleksandr Kynev, most of the leaders who had been seen by the public as the main violators of federal legislation in the regions kept their posts. The governors who lost their titles did so for completely different reasons, primarily membership of an opposition party, criticism of the federal regime or a bad relationship with federal leaders (*Gazeta.ru*, 17 March 2008). Putin was very cautious about upsetting local clans. Elected regional assemblies continued to function and increased their strength in the political process. A survey of 32 regions showed that the Party of Power, i.e. United Russia, began to constitute a counterweight for the regional clans that usually acted in accordance with personal business interests (*Argumenty i Fakty*, 18 April 2007; see also Raspopov, 2006). Putin transferred a large portion of tax receipts from the regions to the centre,[20] but the social obligations, on the contrary, fell on the regions (*Vremya Novosti*, July 10, 2005).[21] Regions are only responsible for those areas that the government does not want to fund.

De facto, many regions continued to be ruled as fiefdoms where local barons could rule with impunity. In 2005 Putin singled out regions in Southern Russia where 'local markets are monopolized by local clans' and 'where administrative intervention is out of proportion' (*Izvestia*, 22 September 2005). In July 2006 Putin again addressed the problem of local monopolies and corruption in the regions (*RIA Novosti*, 21 July 2006). According to Turovskiy:

> The principle of the bureaucratic hierarchy, on which elites have been formed since Soviet times, is operating obedience to any new master means the possibility of keeping your own political autonomy and preserving your own sphere of influence. This includes shadows spheres that usually exist and are protected most of all. (*Nezavisimaya Gazeta*, 29 March 2007)

In her survey of regional elites Stoner-Weiss (2006, pp. 18, 24) concluded that on the regional level economic and political elites often collude, and are certainly much more influential on each other than the federal authorities are on either of them. According to her, despite his centralization, Putin has not really gained control of the provinces. It is authoritarianism without authority.

Extreme regional disparities have not diminished but increased. The City of Moscow, the province of Moscow, St Petersburg and Tyumen account together for almost half of the national gross product (Wood, 2007). The majority (70 per cent) of Russia's 88 regions receive subsidies from the federal budget. Regarding the human development index that takes into account educational attainment and health indicators, in Moscow it is at a similar level to the Czech Republic, in St Petersburg it is at the same level as Bulgaria but in Ingushetia and Tyva the index is the same as in Guatemala (Unger and Chan, 2007). It shows how unbalanced economic development in the Russia under Putin has become.

President Putin also increased state control over strategic industries, especially in the sphere of natural resources. He also diminished the influence of the IMF over Russian politics by reducing foreign debt while making it manageable. It fits into a strategy of establishing a state-led capitalism with an emphasis on national sovereignty.

Russian society under President Putin can be characterized as a diffused state of fragmented, cartelized sovereignty. *De facto*, power in Russia under Putin was still very much dissipated, although less than under President Yeltsin. Apart from the regional and local power centres there are also the oligarchs who control whole sectors of the economy, particularly the most profitable ones. With their fortunes they can buy political influence. Therefore we can not speak about an emerging autocracy under Putin. However, power sharing was not institutionalized and all lines of command led towards Putin's court, i.e. the Presidential Administration.

Putin's economic policy contrasted that of Yeltsin. A prudent macroeconomic policy led to lower inflation falling from 84 per cent in 1998 to 10–12 per cent in the period 2004 to 2006. Putin introduced a flat income tax of 13 per cent and a cut in corporate tax from 35 to 24 per cent. At the same time tax payment discipline improved and as a result tax receipts were significantly increased.[22] Although the shadow economy shrank, its size remained considerable. For example, in 2006 small entrepreneurs constituted 38.3 per cent of the shadow economy against 44.6 per cent in 2002 (Yasin, 2007, p. 54).

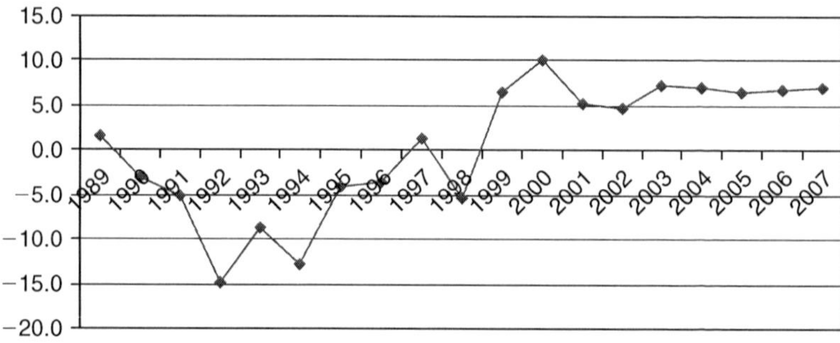

Graph 3.1   Russia GDP growth, annual % change, 1989–2007*
Note: *2007 estimate
Source: European Bank for Reconstruction and Development

Payments for all kind of communal services and public transport were enhanced significantly while privileges in kind for deprived groups such as pensioners were largely cancelled.[23] This was not accompanied with a drastic reform of social policy – according to a World Bank study, only about 20 per cent of the total sum spent on social assistance is targeted on Russian poorest (World Bank, 2007a).

Economic policies contributed to robust economic growth from 1999. However it wasn't until 2007 that Russian GDP regained its 1989 level (see Graph 3.1).

The result was, among others, that during 1998 and 2004 the average real income grew by 12 per cent per year and salaries were more often paid on time.[24] Unemployment (ILO standard) stabilized around 8 per cent (6.3 per cent in 2007, 7.6 per cent in 2004, 11.9 per cent in 1998). However, regional variations were high. The unemployment rate in 2004 in Dagestan was 27 per cent and in Ingushia 46 per cent.

Factors affecting growth included the decline of barter, which in 1998 accounted for 51 per cent of all industrial transactions. This decline resulted in a shift of activities from the shadow to the legal sphere. Another factor was the devaluation of the ruble, which encouraged low-cost import substitution, giving a boost to home industries where, during 1996–97, industrial productive capacity utilization stood at only 54 per cent of the level considered normal by enterprises (Menshikov, 2005, p. 357).

The recovery was to a significant extent fuelled by booming exports. During 2001–4 natural resources accounted for one-third of GDP growth but for 70 per cent of growth in industrial output (Ahrend, 1996, p. 12). Oil, natural gas, metals, precious metals and chemicals account

Table 3.3 Average export prices for the main export commodities, 1995, 2000 and 2006 (US$ per ton)

	1995	2000	2006
Iron ore and concentrates	23.1	15.8	39.3
Crude oil	107	175	411
Petroleum products	105	174	431
Natural gas, for 1000 cu. m	63.1	85.9	216
Electric power, for 1 mln. kWh	23,580	16,855	34,541
Cast iron	132	83.7	246
Refined copper	2,539	1,677	6,201
Crude nickel	8,059	8,641	22,728
Crude aluminum	1,520	1,298	1,619

Source: Federal State Statistics Service (www.gsk.ru)

for 87.7 per cent of Russian exports (2006) while high technology exports comprise 8 per cent of exports (2005, was 14 per cent in 2000) (World Bank Database). Booming revenues for fuel exports are related to sharply increased prices for oil and gas and the increased production of these commodities. Oil production went up from 303 million tons in 1998 to 469 million tons in 2005. The average price for a barrel of Russian oil went up from 20 dollars in 2000 to 100 dollars in 2007. The prices of other major export products also went up (see Table 3.3). By 2006, 50 per cent of government revenues came from oil and gas (finance minister Kudrin, *Itar-Tass*, 21 May 2007).

Russian merchandise exports grew from $105 billion in 2000 to $304 billion in 2006 (Federal Statistical Office). Yet, in 2006 industrial output was still 29 per cent below the 1991 level (Table 3.1). It is telling about the quality of growth in Russia that in 2006 textiles and leather production were still 25 per cent of the 1991 level while machinery production only 47 per cent of the 1991 level (Table 3.1). Russian producers can still not compete with imports on price and quality.

Foreign direct investment increased substantially from 2003 but the investments are concentrated in the extractive industries, real estate and financial sector (altogether 67.6 per cent in 2006, see Table 3.4). Also, foreign direct investment was in 2005 less than 3 per cent of GDP (in Poland it was 4.9 per cent).

The slow recovery of industry was not due to a lack of capital, capital outflow remained at a high level during the 1990s, as shown in Table 3.5. Capital outflow is understated here because much capital flight went unreported as money and other valuables were often smuggled abroad.

Table 3.4   Shares of foreign direct investment by sector of economy, % of total, 2006

Shares of foreign direct investment by sector of economy	% of total
Extraction of mineral resources	33.1
Real estate	23.5
Manufacturing	19.0
Finance	11.0
Retail and wholesale	6.1
Transport and communication	2.8
Construction	2.0
Agriculture, hunting, fishing	1.4
Electricity, gas, water production/distribution	0.4
Provision of other public utilities	0.4
Hotels, restaurants	0.2

Source: Federal State Statistics Service (www.gsk.ru)

Table 3.5   Capital and financial account balance and foreign direct investment, 1994–2006, bn US$

	Capital and financial balance account	Foreign direct investment
1994	−26.9	0.7
1995	−6.2	2.1
1996	−20.3	2.6
1997	2.8	4.9
1998	−11.8	2.8
1999	−17.3	3.3
2000	−23.2	2.7
2001	−12.7	2.7
2002	−11.1	3.4
2003	2.5	7.9
2004	−6.2	15.4
2005	−11.1	12.9
2006	6.1	30.9

Source: UNECE database

In 2006 Russians transferred $18.8 billion abroad while $7.5 billion entered the country (in 2005 $12.5 billion, $6.5 billion respectively) (*Gazeta*, 13 June 2007). The rich in Russia usually channel their money abroad. A study by consulting firm PricewaterhouseCoopers revealed that over 100,000 Russian millionaires have about $300 billion available for investment, while the whole private banking market in Russia is worth only about \$12 billion (*Reuters*, 3 November 2006).[25] This data points to continued economic imbalance and weakness, despite impressive economic growth.

For the population at large, growth seems less impressive. A representative survey showed that only 21 per cent of respondents thought that economic growth in Russia is high, 50 per cent did not agree and 29 per cent were undecided (*Interfax*, 20 July 2007). Only 32 per cent were sure that the financial condition of the average Russian had improved during the previous year. According to Dmitry Medvedev, half of the population does not feel economic growth in their private lives (*Itar-Tass*, 15 February 2008).

In 2006 respondents in a poll had to choose from a list of the most typical characteristics of authorities in the 'stagnation' Soviet period (1970–90) and in the regime of 2006. The incumbent regime was unfavourably compared to the previous period in every aspect. Only 7–9 per cent of respondents characterize the incumbent authorities as 'authoritative, respectable and competent' (*Trud*, 3 May 2006). However, these negative assessments did not apply to President Putin.[26] By the middle of 2007, 85 per cent of respondents in a representative survey approved Putin's performance as president while 14 per cent disapproved (*Vedomosti*, 24 July 2007, survey of Levada centre).

However, if asked about the achievements of Putin as president, for the vast majority of issues there were more negative than positive ratings. For example: there were 6 per cent more respondents who rated economic development as a failure than as a success (16 per cent compared to 10 per cent) and 26 per cent more people rated his attempts in combating corruption as a failure compared to those who rated it a success (28 per cent against 2 per cent) (Russlandanalysen 100, 2006). On the regional level we found a similar discrepancy between approval ratings of the political leader and ratings of concrete policies.[27] The most prominent criticism towards government was in March 2006 'cannot curb inflation and cannot stop decline in income' (51 per cent) and 'do not care about social protection of population' (39 per cent) (Russlandanalysen 100, 2006).

These negative appraisals do not correlate with official statistics that show that living standards of the Russian population have improved dramatically since 1999. Average monthly wages increased from US \$79 in 2000 to US \$395 in 2006 (Federal Statistical Office).[28] However, many struggle to make ends meet. Those who eat well but cannot afford more than basic necessities were still 43.1 per cent in the middle of 2007 (up from 40.6 per cent in 2005) while the proportion of people who, when asked about their income, say they had 'barely enough money to buy food', has gone down sharply, from 30.3 per cent in 2005 to 22.2 per cent in 2007 (*Interfax*, 28 August 2007). In a survey of the Sociology Institute and the German Friedrich Ebert Foundation (late June 2006), 40 per cent were living on or below the poverty line (5 per cent more than in 2003),[29] 77 per cent reported that they felt they were unable to 'go on living in this way' (*Novaya Gazeta*, 17–19 July 2006).[30]

During the 1990s the broad strata of educated professionals, that represented 'modernity' of Soviet society, became marginalized. Hierarchical breakdown and anomie furthered the coming to the fore of the most reckless in society. Thus, the coming to the fore of anti-modern tendencies in society is also reflected in a new social stratification. The image of the 'New Russians', lacking taste, poorly educated and rude, illustrates the problem of the new ruling elite, and, to a lesser extent, the emerging middle-class.[31]

The sociologist Maleva used three criteria to define the middle-class: professional occupation; wealth (an income of at least $200 a month); and self-assessment (Carnegie Endowment for International Peace lecture, Moscow, 9 April 2003). Only 7 per cent of respondents were middle-class in all three categories, i.e. the core middle-class, 12.2 per cent were middle-class in two categories. In Moscow and St Petersburg, 13 per cent of the population is included in the core middle-class. About 1 per cent of the Russian population belonged, according to Maleva's findings, to the upper class.[32]

According to Kostokov, the development of a powerful middle class is actually frozen: 'They are literally suffocated by the domination of state officials, local authorities and the criminal racket. There is the impression that the authorities have staked at large business and has established crony relations with the oligarchs' (*Argumenty i Fakty*, 7 June 2006).

Approximately half of the middle-class is employed by the state. Relatively few work for small and medium sized enterprises as is the case in Western countries. This, together with ingrained attitudes as discussed in Chapter 4, may explain the lack of demands of the middle-class for more rights (see Chapter 5). Also, the economic recovery (since 1999) has failed to strengthen civil society. The deep state-society divide is still one of the biggest obstacles for social and economic development.

It seems that since the introduction of market oriented reforms a familiar pattern in Russian history is repeating itself: a short-lived period of liberal reforms and attempts to emulate Western institutions alternated with a period of re-centralization while society fails to act and establish the rule of law over personalized rule. Power and property then become very much intertwined as it used to be in tsarist Russia.

More than from the intentions of subsequent governments, developments in Russia have been shaped by the correlation of forces in Russian society that unfolded on the basis of an institutional framework that included above all informal institutions. Instead of diminishing the state–society divide, it was actually sharpened. Instead of Western modernity (as Weber described), the actual functioning of Russian society is more typical of a patrimonial society. It was the neo-patrimonialism, covered under the blanket of Soviet communism, that came to the fore after the disintegration of the party-state and shaped the new institutional framework. While the market bolshevism under President Yeltsin ignored Russian path dependency, the more pragmatic policies under President Putin took this into account.

Chapter 4 shows how neo-patrimonialism is matched by social practices at the micro level, while the workings of Russian neo-patrimonialism are examined in Chapter 5.

4
National Character and Economy

In this chapter the focus is on typical social practices that can be found in Russia, especially related to political and economic life, and the relation between these social practices on the one hand and world outlook as shaped by historical experiences on the other hand. It is argued that a specific (post-) Soviet socio-psychological syndrome can be discerned that, although eroding, is able to replicate itself. Dominant social habitus inhibits the emergence of modernity in the Weberian sense. Changes in the social habitus occur more slowly than political and economic change and differences in timescales in these spheres cause major frictions. The dominant social habitus can be characterized as neo-patrimonial.

Collective attitudes and social practices are reflected in a national culture. National culture can be seen as part of the collective programming of the mind. The mental programs of members of the same nation tend to contain a common component. Other components of the collective mental programs of individuals are sub-cultural, that means shared by others of the same educational level, socio-economic status, region, ethnic group, gender etc. (Hofstede, 1984, pp. 10–15, 38). Mindsets are developed in the family in early childhood and re-enforced in schools and organizations, and contain a component of national culture (ibid.).

Although many observations have been made about the Russian national character and mental programming under Soviet communism, few systematic analyses can be found.[1] This is related to the fact that the theme was taboo under communism and that the subject-matter is difficult to grasp empirically. Generally, the systematic analysis of cultural specifics is a recent phenomenon and has been neglected so long because it transcends traditional disciplinary boundaries and it is politically sensitive. On the other hand, Russia provides an interesting case because it developed, until recently, in relative isolation from global integration.

Surveying attitudes in Russia

Often, attitudes and beliefs that people express verbally do not always match the preferences and commitments they reveal in their conduct. This problem is especially conspicuous in Russia where 'cross-thinking' and 'double-morality' has become widespread. There is also a gap between objective behaviour and subjective dispositions as Eckstein noticed (he called this an 'epistemic gap').[2] Culture is reflected in behaviour, not in lip-service. The values of a culture are revealed by the choices people actually make. It is due to these phenomena that results of surveys often proved to be contradictory.[3]

A representative survey in October 2006 found that only one-third of surveyed Russians wanted re-nationalization of privatized properties while according to another representative survey 54 pent cent of respondents want the results of privatization to be reviewed (*Interfax*, 19 April 2007; Frye, 2007).

A survey with 2000 adult respondents across Russia showed that 62 per cent are to some extent or another satisfied with their life (Interfax, 2 October 2002). But a survey of 200,000 families across Russia showed that 59.2 per cent of Russians are unhappy, while only 2 per cent are happy (Rosbalt, 22 July 2003); further questioning revealed that 25 per cent believe they live comfortably (ibid.). When respondents from several countries were asked about how they assess the situation in their country, 32 per cent of Russians are satisfied against 20 per cent in France, 29 per cent in Germany and 81 per cent in China (*Russlandanalysen 109*, 2006).

Hofstede and Hofstede (2005, p. 81) point to the phenomenon of acquiescence, that is the tendency to give positive answers to any question, regardless of its content. For questions dealing with values, this tendency was correlated with collectivism and large power distance. For questions dealing with descriptions of the actual situation, the tendency to give all positive answers was correlated with weak uncertainty avoidance. In high uncertainty avoidance countries people showed a negative tendency in describing their work and life situation (Hofstede and Hofstede, 2005, p. 177). Russia ranked very high on the uncertainty avoidance index (rank 7 out of 74 countries) and power distance index (rank 6 out of 74) but had a medium ranking (rank 39 out of 74) on the individualism index (Hofstede and Hofstede, 2005, pp. 43, 78, 168).

This suggests that both with respect to questions dealing with values and questions dealing with descriptions of actual situations there will be a rather strong bias in Russia.

It is questionable whether there is a relationship between social habitus and opinions as reflected in opinion polls. For example, most Russians (66 per cent, 1996) think that it is never justified to accept bribes.[4] However, giving and accepting small or even large bribes is an established feature of Russian society that was also widespread under communist rule.[5] Obviously, here there is a big difference between opinions related to bribery and the practice of bribery in Russia that is considered to be one of the most corrupt countries in the world.[6]

Many surveys conducted in Russia show that Russians moved to a post-modern value system and that their values do not differ very much from those to be found in most other European countries. This is, among others, the case with the World Values Surveys, conducted in Russia in 1991, 1993 and 1996. These surveys suggest that Russia's political thinking came closer to that found in Western democracies. While few objected to competitive elections, respondents did not approve of more subtle concepts of political rights. In 1989 around half of the respondents in a survey spoke out against the concentration of state power in the hands of one person, this share declined to about 20 per cent in 1996.[7] When questioned about democracy 53 per cent of respondents (1996) said that democracy led to chaos and anarchy.[8] Only 10 per cent of Russians, according to an October 2003 poll, said that the right to elect political leaders is important for them (Shlapentokh, 2004). More people have a positive view about Stalin than a negative one (February 2003, 30 per cent difference: Shlapentokh, 2004).

According to 29 per cent of the respondents, Putin's era was the most democratic era in the history of Russia while Gorbachev's era was the most democratic to only 11 per cent (Shlapentokh, 2004). In another poll, 47 per cent thought that restrictions on the media were necessary (*Izvestia*, 25 November 2002), while only 22 per cent spoke against censorship. Another poll showed that 52 per cent of respondents thought that multi-party elections do more harm than good (Pipes, 2004, p. 11). In a 2005 poll, 48 per cent of respondents believe that if the political, social and economic situation is acceptable, there is no need for opposition. Only 33 per cent of respondents saw political opposition as an essential attribute of true democracy (*Interfax*, 19 July 2005). On the other hand, in 2004 61 per cent of respondents thought that a political opposition was needed while 17 per cent thought it was not needed (Zudin, 2006, p. 142).

Since 1991 there has been a general trend in the polls that demonstrates less positive attitudes towards democracy. According to a report from the Comprehensive Social Studies department (ICSS) at the Russian Academy of Sciences, the majority of Russian citizens, as high as 64 per cent, have reservations about the values expressed by what sociologists call 'modernists'. The latter are convinced that individualism, liberalism and the western model of democracy are in most respects suitable for Russia. These views are shared by only 26 per cent of the population (*Izvestia*, 12 November 2004).[9]

Despite trends towards authoritarian rule, 52 per cent of Russian citizens consider themselves to be free while 39 per cent do not (Public Opinion Foundation, March 2005).[10] Also remarkable is the fact that 60 per cent of respondents in 2005 believed that the media enjoy absolute freedom of speech (*Izvestia*, 22 September 2005). Another survey showed that 42 per cent of Russians think Western democracy is disastrous for Russia compared with 35 per cent in 2000 (*Gazeta*, 15 February 2007). On the other hand, 57 per cent of respondents in a ROMIR poll (15–21 June 2007) were satisfied with democracy in Russia although only 26 per cent of them thought elections in Russia to be free and fair (*Jamestown Foundation Eurasia Monitor*, 16 January 2008).

Thus, results of surveys are contradictory and tend, if repeated, to change rather quickly. Of course, when interpreting results we should also take into account the political and general socio-economic context in which the surveys took place.

Alexander (1997) criticized many polls for being 'directed research', trying to apply 'objective' tests of political culture, i.e. a purposeful search for signs of a democratic and market culture. He maintains that 'the search for these two artificially constructed extremes clouds the fact that the vast majority of the population has a more complex attitudinal outlook' (Alexander, 1997, p. 117). Attitudes are varied and usually inconsistent and reflected in behaviour that lacks clear patterns and that is difficult to identify and comprehend.

The problem with the many comparative value surveys is that they claim to reveal substantial information about values and social practices rather than opinions. There is often the illusion of capturing the essence of a civilization in a few value coordinates as expressed in survey results.[11] Also, various value surveys completed in Russia, according to the Hofstede methodology, reveal very big differences although, according to Hofstede, value patterns are very inert (see Latov, 2007). Typical behavioural patterns and social practices could be explained by situational factors explored next.

The (post-) Soviet socio-psychological syndrome

One can argue that from the viewpoint of civilizing processes, Soviet power had a civilizing as well as a decivilizing impact.

The civilizing aspects were, among others, mass education, the spread of hygienic habits, the partial emancipation of women and upward social mobility. The decivilizing aspects comprised the spread and legitimacy of amoral behaviour, e.g. lying, denunciation, rudeness.

The decivilizing aspect is related, according to Zinoviev, to the fact that in Soviet civilization the usual counterbalances or safeguards of community life (law, morality, religion, etc.) were oppressed.[12] Rude manners became generalized (the communists despised 'bourgeois manners') and intellect became even more marginalized compared to tsarist times, despite the fact that so many obtained higher education. Another decivilizing impact of Soviet socialism was the fact that the opportunity to satisfy the individual's needs increasingly became dependent upon contacts with specific social groups and less so upon individual performance.

The decivilizing aspects of Soviet communism became more pronounced with the gradual disintegration of Soviet society and economy. Particularly since the collapse of the party-state it seems that all constraints on what is considered as a-social behaviour fell away. It meant that the most reckless in society came to the fore, not restrained by society at large. Society missed protective mechanisms to prevent predatory behaviour.

The pathologies of post-Soviet society should be seen in the context of deep seated social practices. Here it is suggested that Stalinist rule, and more broadly, the communist and tsarist past, has produced a system of values, norms and behavioural patterns that is quite persistent and that is able to replicate itself.[13] This coherent system of values and social practices is named the (post-) Soviet socio-psychological syndrome. This syndrome will be described below. Emphasis will be placed on the interrelationships between its component parts.

The cult of power

Although parliamentary democracy has been formally introduced in Russia, the political system and society at large is still very much authoritarian. Bureaucrats and enterprise directors reign in their domains as absolutist rulers. An enterprise director can fire an employee whenever he wants. Exercise of power in Russia has absolutist traits as power in Russia always has been, in Soviet and in tsarist times, absolutist. In general, it is difficult (if not impossible) for most Russians to think of government in terms of institutions rather than in terms of people who occupy positions within institutions (see also Barner-Barry and Hody, 1995, p. 212). 'Ponyatii' (i.e. understanding the rules of the game) is above the concept of law.

Whereas the English language differentiates between power and authority, Russians only have the concept 'vlast'. Power in Russia has a personified nature. There is no tradition of challenging power because this has been severely punished in the past. Therefore there are no obstacles for the transformation of any authority into imposed power, into the unilateral dependency of subordinates *vis-à-vis* the state and its representatives (Oleinik, 2005, p. 184). Political opponents are as a rule criminalized.

Power is exercised in a patrimonial and arbitrary way and this is reinforced by the way the ruled react. The way power relations are reproduced in Russia is partially rooted in the acceptance or tolerance by the subject people. In the words of Simon (1998, p. 131) 'The bond between the people and the ruler/state was always forged by subjugation and reward, but not by mutual rights and duties.' In Russian organizations *kommandas* can be found, a leader surrounded by his people who can be trusted. Trust underpins the cohesion of such a *kommanda*. There is also the concept of *krugovaya poruka*, a sense of common responsibility (see Sakharov, 2006, p. 11).

The all encompassing power of the communist party-state, and before that the tsarist autocracy, created a cult of power.[14] The attribute of power became so overwhelmingly important in the party-state where almost everything was subordinated to the will of the central power, that power, and therewith the lack of it, became of overriding importance in everyday life. According to Meyer (2006, p. 49):

How people relate to 'the power', intricate networking and the ability to negotiate informally become prevailing mechanisms how to achieve social status, influence and develop life perspectives, at least on the professional level and in the public realm.

Absolutist power meant that those in power wanted to control the behaviour of their subordinates as much as possible. A control mania is visible in all areas of life. At the same time, a majority of Russians do not regard the right of citizens to influence and control those in power as natural and necessary.

The availability of absolutist power generates the desire to use this power by those who exercise it. It is visible in the functionaries of public administration who are usually quite rude towards their clients. It is the powerlessness of the individuals faced with absolutist power that nurtured the rudeness of officials. It generally furthers the contempt of the feelings and the rights of individuals.[15]

There is no inclination to share power as has been shown in the recent history of both Ukraine and Russia. There is no history of seeking compromises. The prevailing idea is that the winner takes all.

Due to the nature of power as is exercised in Russia the very notion of power as such, and politics in general, becomes discredited. Power is not used to facilitate but rather to block initiatives coming from below. The usual attitude of bosses in Russia is that everything that happens in their domain should be controlled by them. Independent initiatives are incompatible with such an attitude. It means that exercise of power in Russia is usually paralyzing.

It was the above described cult of power that enabled people in power on all levels to abuse their positions during the transition to a 'market economy', when the power of the state weakened, in order to appropriate state property on a massive scale. The cult has its roots in Muscovy where the nobility had the right to do whatever they wanted on their estate (*pomestie*), as long as they paid tax and obeyed the tsar.

Power is not intended to be used in a constructive way, although in communist times there was a typical developmental ideology that helped the Soviet economy increase production. Because of the way power is exercised and the long history of absolutist power, people have generally become very compliant and accept almost everything that is imposed on them. This is also related to the atomization of society. Eventually people react by circumventing the rules. Therefore it seems that Russia can be ruled with impunity. Rulers hardly have to take the general interest into account.

Absolutist power and oppression deterred trust and the development of horizontal cooperation networks in society. Russian society, as a low-trust society, is still very much fragmented. Only the small circle of family and friends can be trusted.[16] Russian society can be considered as a conglomerate of small groups of families and clans that hardly communicate with one another. Sharing knowledge with people who do not belong to the same clan is not common.

Oleinik (2005, p. 184) observed that the lack of clear borders between the spheres of everyday life facilitates the transfer of authority from one subsystem to another.

At the workplace, relations within a worker's community retain some traces of the traditional peasant's community, the events related to private life can easily become publicly known and discussed. Supervisors feel free to control the private life of their subordinates ... the interactions with the state determine the basic parameters of domination and imposition at lower levels of the institutional structure, they structure network capitalism as a whole system.

Attitudes towards the state and the public sphere

A peculiarity for Russia is the thinking in terms of dichotomy where it concerns the state and the public sphere. This dichotomy has a moral undertone: the nation (good) versus the state (bad), 'us' (good) versus 'them' (bad), people (good) versus the rulers (bad). In this context stealing state property is not considered as a serious offence. 'Beating the system' is considered a virtue. Although 'the state' has a negative connotation, the state is held responsible for providing a large range of services.[17] Related to this peculiar attitude towards the state is the absence of solidarity that goes beyond the small circle of family and friends.

It is not typical for Russians to think in terms of universal rules applicable to everyone. There is no notion of the rule of law and the concomitant separation of powers. The law is of no relevance and can be used by the blackmail state to punish its adversaries. Related to this is the culture of legal nihilism that has always existed in Russia.[18] According to Alexander Yakovlev the law in Russia has never been associated with moral truth. 'In a situation where the law is equated only with the power of a tyrannical state, where the law is not respected but only feared, the idea of fairness is contrasted to existing laws' (quoted in Ledeneva, 2006, p. 26).

With the falling away of external social control, deviant behaviour is spreading rapidly. In this respect Elias (1987, p. lxix) draws attention to the way that:

> societies without a permanent autocratic central authority can only function and indeed can only survive for long in that form if the relative weakness and instability of the central authority, of the leading external regulating agency, is matched by the relative strength and stability of the self-regulating of their members.

In this sense there is an interdependence of the structure of society at large and the personality structure of individuals. It means that there should be a match between social habitus and political and economic structures.

In Soviet times the behaviour of individuals was framed by the rules that were imposed by the party-state. These rules were not usually internalized and in the private sphere other rules were applied. With the falling away of the party/state a moral and social vacuum appeared because the only source of external social control, apart from the family, was removed.[19] Whereas outside the post-socialist world, individuals are usually encapsulated by many institutions, formal and informal, individuals in post-socialist Russia miss such a strong institutional encapsulation. The result is, among others, widespread anomie.[20]

The culture of dependence and reluctance to assume responsibility

The cult of power, typical in all countries that belonged to the former Soviet Union, with the possible exception of the Baltic States, has led to a culture of dependence. Independent behaviour has always been punished. When Gorbachev was asked the question why Hungarian style reforms were not implemented in the Soviet Union, he answered 'unfortunately, in the course of the last 50 years the Russian peasant has had all the independence knocked out of him' (Brown, 1996, p. 143).

Within larger or traditional organizations, like (previous) state-owned enterprises, the state bureaucracy and schools, this aversion towards independent behaviour is still very much present. This attitude produced a deep-rooted lack of or fear of taking the initiative.

Passivity is also characteristic for many inhabitants of Russia. The attitude is that the world, even the immediate environment, cannot be changed. It is an attitude of 'learned helplessness', a deeply-rooted attitude that is very difficult to unlearn.

The culture of dependence not only produces a lack of initiative, but also a lack of willingness to assume responsibility. Generally, people do not feel responsible for the tasks allotted to them. Their superiors do not credit them with competence, so there is no scope to assume responsibility. Assuming responsibility for something may have negative consequences. In Soviet times, people were only expected to follow orders and not to show initiative, although people found many ways to circumvent silently the orders imposed from above.

Of course, such an attitude has very negative consequences for labour ethos in general. Industriousness, discipline and efficiency did not rank highly with most Russians. This is not to say that people in Russia do not want to do a good job – circumstances often prevent them from doing so. Usually, in order to make sure that they work, people have to be supervised constantly.

Related to a lack of accountability is the aversion to transparency.[21] Russians generally prefer informal dealings above contractual arrangements, they prefer a diffuse demarcation of competencies above a clear differentiation of competencies, they prefer mores above laws.[22] This is all related to strategies to circumvent the rigidities of 'the system', imposed from above.

The culture of dependence and the cult of power created a general inertia in society and individuals. One seldom finds an enthusiasm to undertake something, although with small industrial entrepreneurs one can find quite another attitude. But they are rare in Russia. Soviet despotism created widespread lethargy and fatalism.

Related to the culture of dependence is the inclination to blame all deficiencies in one's own environment on external factors. It is at the same time a legitimization not to change anything. The idea of shaping one's future by determined action and initiative is alien to most people. Most people are inclined to complain about the circumstances imposed upon them, without taking any action.

In Western Europe, social habitus was very much influenced by changing living conditions of families. As Rifkin (2005, p. 125) observes, 'by the eighteenth century, the public household had metamorphosed into a private domicile, and family members were often separated from one another by partitions and rooms. Privacy meant the ability to exclude others'. It meant the privatization of space. Everywhere people became less servile and more industrious, Rifkin (2005, p. 120) noted that 'possessing, not belonging dictated the terms of the human intercourse' and that 'bourgeois man learned to be self-controlled, self-sacrificing and self-possessed, to be diligent and industrious'. It is obvious that above described process has only very recently started in Russia.

Often, social practices that developed in the Soviet Union have been compared with those developed in Soviet prisons.[23] As in prison, people facing a system of suspended punishment also have a sense of vulnerability (Ledeneva, 2006, p. 114).

The marginalization of intellect

Russian society is far from being a meritocracy. Compliance with those in power is a first requirement for influential positions. All other abilities are secondary. The result is an elite that is very incompetent and incompetent people cannot tolerate competent people in their immediate environment. Thus, with the exception of some enclaves of privately owned enterprises and scientific centres of excellence, the specific recruitment mechanisms for influential positions in Russia prevent the development of competence.

Generally, and this is typical for Russian and Soviet history, the intelligentsia eschewed power.[24] In their eyes, power is corrupt and something evil. Talented people have usually sought a career in science or arts, rather than in politics. Creative intelligence in society was not only oppressed but channelled in directions that were not threatening to those in power. Not much has changed in this respect.

During Perestroika and the 1990s the intelligentsia had access to power but was discredited in this process. It was often inexperienced academicians who became government advisors and imposed their voluntarist projects upon the country.

Creative intellectual energy is often channelled towards escapist themes. Tatyana Tolstaya (Smith, 1990, p. 183) noticed that:

> Russians are prone to escapism, whether it be the 'lazy, dreamy' philosophizing of the intelligentsia, or the brutal, destructive and often self-destructive mass alcoholism of workers and peasants.

People were never asked to think independently. The educational system was geared towards the reproduction of facts rather than towards developing the ability to theorize or to analyse independently.[25] This is still a basic characteristic of the educational system. Students have an overloaded programme of classes. There are practically no seminars where texts are discussed and students have hardly any time in the curriculum for independent research or writing.

Soviet society and the Soviet educational system produced a world outlook that was very simple. The 'laws' of society and economy were laid down in the classics of Marxism-Leninism and the only question was to interpret them in the right way, which meant the interpretation of the party-state. It is also very much in line with the Muscovy legacy of a Manichean world outlook.[26]

Of course, the official world outlook and the world outlook of Russia's citizens differed but Soviet propaganda has had a profound impact on the world outlook of citizens.

Led Gudkov (2007, p. 11), the director of the Levada centre in Moscow, believes that:

> the widespread inability to understand other people, in particular their enthusiasm and deepest feelings, is of crucial significance for the anthropology of post-totalitarian and post-Soviet man. It is a constitutive element of the national identity of Russians. It is an inability for

empathy ... with the inclination to subscribe to other people, friends as well as enemies, the lowest motives.

He also points to the inclination to think in terms of black and white (Gudkov, 2007, p. 8, 9). This is related to the specific forms of exclusion that were predominant in Soviet thinking. In political life, the adage has been 'who is not with us, is against us', instead of inclusive thinking, namely 'who is not against us, is with us'. This official excluding way of looking at the world of ideas had a profound impact upon the world outlook of people. Related to the above described mechanisms of exclusion is the propensity to be intolerant towards deviant opinions.[27]

The (post-) Soviet socio-psychological syndrome as a comprehensive mechanism

As Scheme 4.1 shows, the constituent elements of the (post-) Soviet socio-psychological syndrome form an interrelated whole, reinforcing each other. This is why it is so tenacious. The system described above is a system of negative feedbacks. No features are described that can be interpreted as positive. These negative feedback mechanisms can be seen as a kind of tumour in Russian society. Understanding this phenomenon is crucial for grasping the essence of present-day Russian society.

The collective programming of the minds of individuals in Russia has been described here. It does not mean that the above description depicts adequately the average Russian. Such an average citizen does not exist. People in Russia are as diverse as they are in any other place in the world. Nevertheless, the assumption is that the majority of Russians are affected by the syndrome as described above but this does not imply that most Russians share each element of the syndrome. The cult of dependence mainly affects the subject people, while the cult of power should be mainly seen as phenomena close to the sphere of power. The (post-) Soviet socio-psychological syndrome affects differently rulers and the ruled. The idea of the (post-) Soviet socio-psychological syndrome should be seen as a hypothesis that allows a deeper understanding of the described social practices and belief systems.

Some elements need further explanation. One is the problematic relationship to truth. Under communism lying was a means of survival. In enterprises, managers had to manipulate figures and to cheat authorities. This legacy may have contributed to the widespread practice of present day cheating in economic life. Even in tsarist times, there was the widespread notion that there was nothing wrong in deceiving

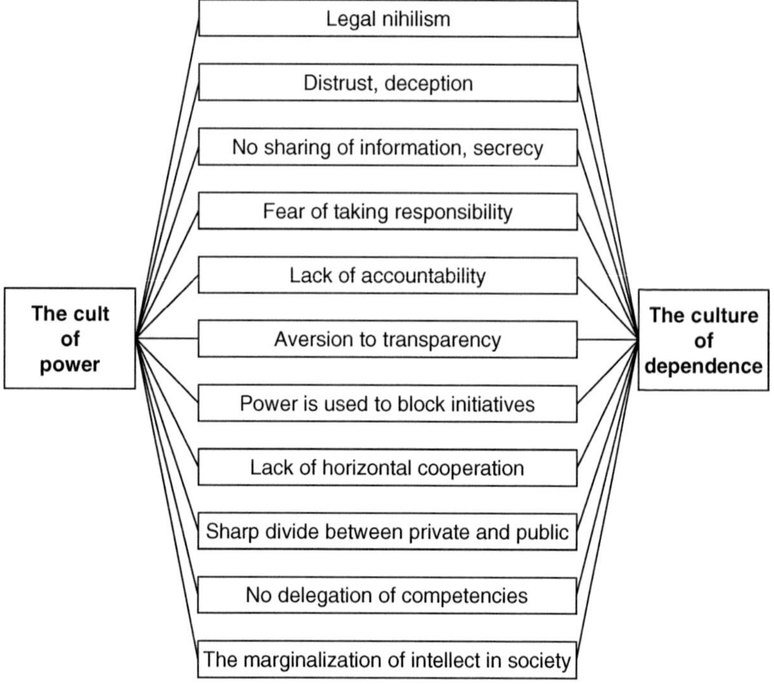

Scheme 4.1   The (post-) Soviet socio-psychological syndrome

foreigners and cheating themselves and their own country. Prince Gregory Potemkim went so far as to build an eighteenth-century stage set in Ukraine, filled with smiling peasants to show Tsarina Catherine the Great how happy he had made his serfs. Connected with this tradition of cheating is the generalized lack of trust in society.[28] A related phenomenon is the widespread opportunistic behaviour.

Conspicuous in the presentation of the (post-) Soviet socio-psychological syndrome is the centrality of the question of how power is dealt with in Russian society. The cult of power and the culture of dependence give a clue to the many social practices mentioned in Scheme 4.1.

Some attitudes that can be considered as an asset are not discussed. There is, for example, the value attached to education, resulting in many attending higher education, even under difficult economic circumstances. However, this is not activated in social practices that may further economic development. The hypothesis of the (post-) Soviet socio-psychological syndrome can be considered as an ideal type that helps to understand path dependency of Russia.

The properties attributed to the (post-) Soviet socio-psychological syndrome became most pronounced in Stalin's time, although many of these properties had already developed in tsarist times and have been described in nineteenth-century Russian literature. Almost two decades after the demise of communism it appears that this syndrome is very persistent.[29] Central is the cult of power that sustains the Russian type of neo-patrimonialism.

In Chapter 5 it will be seen to what extent the typical social practices and values discussed in this chapter influence the operating mechanisms of the political and economic systems nowadays.

5
How Russian Neo-Patrimonialism Works

In Chapters 2 and 3 the historical origins of the current political and economic system of Russia have been analysed with an emphasis on the interplay between social forces at the macro and micro level. In Chapter 4 the historically grown complex of social practices and attitudes that dominate Russian economic life has been investigated. The cult of power has been identified as being central to a series of pathologies that affect Russia.

In this chapter the operating mode of the Russian political and economic system is analysed referring to the mental models that are underpinning these systems. It is argued, among others, that the political and economic systems are so intertwined that they can not be analysed separately. Because economic success is usually ascertained through the right political connections, the nature of political power is analysed first. It is argued that although the present Russian political-economic system can be seen as a hybrid, neo-patrimonialism is dominant. The emerging capitalism is still subsumed in the neo-patrimonial system. It is also argued that there is a match between macro-structures and dominant mental models as discussed in Chapter 4. In this context the path dependence of Russia is discussed. There will be regular references to Ukraine because this country shares so many features with Russia (see also Chapter 6).

How Russia is governed

President Putin inherited a presidential system from his predecessor Yeltsin that has been enshrined in the constitution that was accepted in 1993. The President had the power to initiate and veto legislation and also the right to issue normative decrees.

Instead of focusing on formal structures that frame Russia's political institutions it is instructive to depart from the actual political process because of the huge discrepancy between form and substance in the Russian political system.[1] While there is a division of power in principle, in reality there is a merging of the executive, legislative and judiciary powers (see Belyayeva, 2006, pp. 7, 20). Real decisions are taken in the Presidential Administration, i.e. in the court of the President, while the parliament, with a majority for United Russia, has been transformed into a rubber stamping institution. The judiciary is an instrument of the executive rather than an independent force.

This does not mean that an autocratic system has been established, in contra-distinction to its democratic formal structure. The current political system is somewhere in between democracy and dictatorship. The President is far from almighty and although in all respects, the Kremlin constitutes the highest authority, the President presides over a weak state. Apart from the President, there are other important players in the political process: the various factions in the presidential court, oligarchs, the regional elites and last but not least, the government bureaucracy.

Political parties are in most cases organized around personalities, not around programmes. They are usually vehicles of clan interests. Conspicuous is that the opposition is never united. Sectarianism and radicalism are characteristic for the so-called opposition parties. Often, political parties emerge just before elections, to disappear shortly afterwards.

Even the Communist Party that functioned as the main opposition party and has the appearance of a programmatic party can be considered as a decorative opposition that tries as much as possible to accommodate with those in power (Wilson, 2005).[2]

In Russia (and Ukraine) opposition is considered to be something unnatural and 'opposition' politicians usually do their best to be incorporated in the machinery of power.

Political parties usually use black PR (public relations) to discredit opponents. It is easy to buy discrediting articles in newspapers.[3] *Kompromat*, i.e. blackmail files, are used routinely in political campaigns. The security services operate as brokers in *kompromat* markets (Ledeneva, 2006, p. 55). Manipulative patterns in politics have become known in Russia as 'political technologies'.

In the Russia of President Putin a political party emerged whose sole function was to support the President ('United Russia').[4] Through the application of political technologies and domination of state-owned or state-controlled TV channels it managed to obtain a big majority in parliament. This party is known as the Party of Power. Similar dominant parties also emerged elsewhere in the post-Soviet space and they function as an instrument of those in power. The Party of Power has access to 'administrative resources'. These state resources, and the power to influence vote counting, guarantee dominance in the legislature.

In Russia a virtual democracy emerged in which the actual function of institutions differs very much from the formal functions. Like other post-socialist countries that wanted Western assistance, Russia has felt unprecedented pressure to adopt democratic institutions although there was no strong domestic pressure. This has led to imitation democracy, which is defined by the existence of formal democratic institutions that conceal autocratic or authoritarian practices. As Ivan Krastev has noticed 'Russia is not an illiberal democracy by default; it is an illiberal democracy by design' (Shevtsova, 2006). Shevtsova highlighted the similarities of the political regime that developed under President Putin with the 'bureaucratic authoritarianism' that developed in Latin America during the 1960s and 1970s. It shares the major characteristics, with a leading role for technocrats and an active role for the secret services (in Latin America it was the military). However, Shevtsova (2006) notices that 'since previous types of legitimacy (party, monarchic and ideological) no longer work for Russians, bureaucratic authoritarianism has to be legitimized by elections'. The regime 'cannot use harsh authoritarian measures because it would discredit their democratic legitimacy and their relative popularity, but they cannot actually follow democratic rules, either, because this would threaten their position'. The central fact of imitation 'prevents it from functioning effectively as either a democratic or an authoritarian system. Thus does Russia stagnate in a twilight zone of political incoherence' (Shevtsova, 2006). According to historian Dmitry Furman, Russians 'live in a system of norms that contradicts our customs and our psychology and norms and that are not "convenient" for us and that we can not follow' (*Nezavisamaya Gazeta*, 6 April 2007).

The political system that is emerging in Russia is in many ways similar to the one-party rule democracies that evolved in many developing countries, like Mexico, and in some developed countries, like Japan. Until recently, Mexico was a one-party state in the context of a democratic multi-party system. The ruling party has, since 1917, used intimidation, electoral fraud, patronage, corruption and cronyism to maintain power. All powerful interest groups, including the media, were effectively part of the party's political machine. The dominance of the Liberal Democratic Party in Japan is another example.[5]

Real interest representing institutions for the population at large hardly exist in Russia. For example, although trade unions exist, they

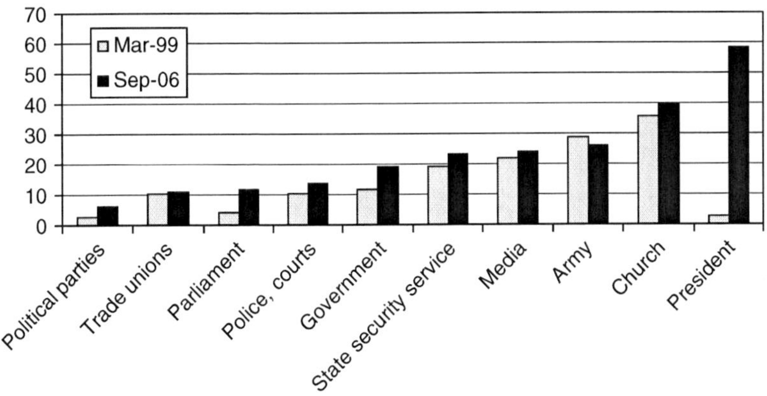

Graph 5.1   Trust in institutions (%)
Source: Russlandanalysen 122/2006/Levada Centre

hardly represent the interests of their members (for the low level of public trust in trade unions see Graph 5.1). The absence of adequate interest representing structures contributes to a deep cleavage between society and the state.

What is currently lacking is civil society, not only conceived as a system of organizations and associations that function independently of the state but also as independent organizations of citizens that will emphasize the community and collective action. Instead, a corporatist state is emerging in which government-led organizations substitute for civil society (see Peregudov, 2006).

In strong societies informal institutions operate in the same way as cement in a wall – they hold the bricks (of society) together. The Russian situation is very different – there are few rules to guide the behaviour of individuals. In Russia universal and impersonal mechanisms of social integration are very weak as are value generating institutions. Even the family, one of the few remaining 'institutions' is now faced with widespread dislocation, which has affected large numbers of youths.[6] In this context social solidarity is restricted to a limited number of primary or kin-group members.[7]

The character of elite networks

Russia remains largely a bureaucratically controlled society and economy with elite networks operating primarily in the sphere of the state and its administration. The state sets the parameters in which the elite operate.

Because the rules of the polity are not clear and because there is not a strong countervailing power, patronage-clientele networks spread.

Political patronage can be defined as an informal network of personal, political relationships, which are at the same time asymmetrical and interdependent. It encompasses the mutual exchange of political favours and is tested over time. Typically, for the Soviet Union, political patronage developed into a crucial mechanism of elite mobility, being largely unchecked by other mechanisms, such as open selection procedures on the basis of meritocratic criteria. Therefore, political loyalty to the party and the patron became a major priority. Formal decision-making procedures increasingly became a façade to mask the decision-making by a set of coteries. After the disintegration of the Soviet Union and communism, the state remained of the utmost importance for the elite because the state gave elites the opportunity to self-enrich and advance careers.

The bureaucracy did not limit itself to the role of re-distributor while levying 'administrative rent' (see Peregudov, 2006, p. 88). From the middle of the 1990s it became increasingly involved in the running of businesses. The officials turned businessmen usually kept their official posts. These businessmen-officials were in effect businessmen rentiers. In this way political-economic clans emerged in which these officials often played a crucial role. This reflects the corporate-bureaucratic symbiosis.

Elite networks in Russia are characterized by secrecy and distrust towards those not belonging to the inner circle of the clique. Important clans are grouped around specific industries and related banks and, above all, based in specific regions.

Russians believe that to join the elite, one has to have money (75 per cent) and connections with government structures (56 per cent), while vigour, enterprising qualities, talent and high qualification are of lesser importance (20 per cent). Many Russians also believe that during 1990–2005 the elite changed for the worse (42 per cent of respondents); while only 7 per cent think it changed for the better (*Vremya Novosti*, 24 August 2005).

The short-term interests of the main clans dominate the policy agenda of government. Conspicuous is the absence of strategic planning on all levels of the state machinery. State policies reflect the balance of power between various clans at a specific stage rather than a specific strategy of government. State policies are characterized by improvising. This is related to the fact that politics in Russia is overwhelmingly focused on the attainment of power and the distribution of influential positions and competition among bureaucratic agencies for competences. Politics does not turn around policy options and the strategic course of the country. Striking is the total absence, in the political class, of any clear underpinned strategic visions for the country.[8]

The state bureaucracy

In contemporary Russia there is a multi-layered policy making body in which various branches of government and bureaucracy produce a huge amount of legislative and quasi-legislative documents, which are poorly coordinated. The multitude of laws and decrees are frequently contradictory and can often be interpreted in different ways.[9] The inconsistency of the legal system gives the bureaucracy and politicians arbitrary power. It makes almost everyone punishable. Enterprises and citizens are supposed to know the law although many laws are not published. Therefore, almost anyone can be guilty of anything.

Also characteristic of legislation and decree making is a systematic use of making exemptions to general rules. In February 2001, First Deputy Prosecutor General Yuri Biryukov reported that over a period of six months, his office had uncovered 3,273 pieces of legislation adopted by the regional governments that contradicted federal law and he stated that these governments continued to draft laws as they wished (Ledeneva, 2006, p. 23). The regime of exemptions is made as a consequence of lobbying. As a result, government measures are often not implemented. Of Putin's orders 20 to 30 per cent have never been carried out (*Argumenty i Fakty*, 26 October 2005).

The main features associated with an effective system of state governance are clarity of objectives, freedom to manage by government institutions, accountability, effective assessment of performance and adequate information. In Russia there are problems with each of these issues. Diffusion of authority weakens the system of governance in Russia. The diffusion of authority delays the emergence of a stable legislative environment. The distinction between the political and the civil service aspects of government administration is blurred and the rule making authority extends to administrative sub-units.

Lack of accountability also permeates the economy, related to the lack of horizontal differentiation and a concomitant delineation of responsibilities. Few feel responsible and few can be held responsible. Related to this generalized lack of accountability there is an omnipresent control mania and a concomitant deep aversion against control.[10]

A high burden of coordination is placed on a relatively weak civil service. There is an in-built tendency for government institutions to multiply according to mechanisms akin to Soviet times. In this bureaucracy the presidential administration can be compared to the former apparatus of the Central Committee. The mode of operation of most ministries has hardly changed since Soviet times (Belyayeva, 2006, p. 21).

Both in Ukraine and Russia the administrative apparatus increased enormously in size. According to BOFIT weekly (21 April 2006) by end 2005 there were nearly 1.5 million officials in Russia. The number increased from about 1.1 million in 1998. One would expect the opposite in a transition from centrally planned to market economy (in China, another bureaucratic country, with more than 1.3 billion people, there are 5 million officials and their number is declining).[11] Including army personnel and other armed forces, the state sector totalled 5 million people, i.e., more than 15 per cent of the adult work force.[12]

The army of bureaucrats is occupied regulating: During the 1990s more than 80 per cent of commodities were subject to state certification before they were put up for sale, as was the case in Soviet times (Ledeneva, 2006, p. 24). The certification procedures are difficult to follow, are often contradictory and the published standards are difficult to obtain. For example, the State Committee of Standardization sells its published volume of norms and procedures for more than $7000 (Ledeneva, 2006, p. 24), well beyond the reach of most citizens. Regulations are enforced by decrees and resolutions rather than by law because the former are more easily passed and prepared.[13] This follows the stereotypic Soviet thought that good government responds to small changes in the economy, rather than creating a stable legal environment.

Given the enormous significance and influence of the bureaucratic apparatus in post-Soviet Russia, one cannot treat this machinery as a 'dead weight' in the political process. The bureaucracy pursues its own interests and has powerful instruments to defend its interests. The Russian bureaucracy can be considered as a sovereign bureaucracy. President Putin has said that: 'to a significant degree, our bureaucracy is now an exclusive and arrogant caste that views state interests as a form of private enterprise' (*Gazeta*, 2 November 2005). A study by the Sociological Institute of the Russian Academy of Sciences, in cooperation with the German Friedrich Ebert Foundation, also found that the bureaucracy has transformed into a separate caste, living according to its own laws. According to Institute director Mikhail Gorshkov, 'They (the bureaucracy) strive to retain their power, shaping a class consciousness in which their own interests are placed ahead of the public interest' (*Gazeta*, 2 November 2005). In the study 1500 'average' citizens and 300 low- and mid-ranking officials were studied. The survey found that bureaucrats have more opportunities to secure better food, clothing, housing, a higher social status and obtain financial security. Most respondents found that the growing army of bureaucrats have become less efficient and more corrupt, with 71 per cent of the 1500 respondents agreeing that officials were hampering Russia's development (*Gazeta*, 2 November 2005). All agreed that the primary goal of officials was to keep and increase personal wealth and power, even at the expense of the people (*Moscow Times*, 11 November 2005).

A public service ethos is almost absent in Russia. Dmitry Badovsky, a researcher with the Institute of Social Systems at Moscow State University, said that Russia has undergone a 'true bureaucratic revolution' since the Soviet collapse (*Moscow Times*, 11 November 2005). 'Today, bureaucrats strive to own their official functions, sell them at the market price, and then pass the newly acquired property to their heirs. This was different from Soviet times, when a bureaucrat almost always enjoyed relatively large perks, but only while he was employed in the job' (ibid.). Now selling a function is financially enhancing, e.g. a senior job at any Russian ministry costs from $150 000 to $1 million and a job as a traffic policeman costs from $3000 upwards (*RIA Novosti*, 6 March 2006).

Relationships within the bureaucracy are personalized and the system of 'mutual favours' is entrenched. The state bureaucracy is not considered an impartial implementer of government policies while functioning within the framework of the law. Instead it is used by those in power as an instrument to maintain and expand their power base. Therefore the militia, the tax office, the fire brigade and all other state services can, in principle, be used by politicians in extending and employing their power. If an enterprise or citizen is not complying with political authorities, however illegal demands of the latter might be, the tax office or another public service will impose penalties. The middle and lower tiers of the bureaucracy, in particular, are out of control and not at all constrained by higher authorities.

The judiciary is *de facto* treated as a part of the state bureaucracy and subordinate to the Kremlin (or regional and local bosses). In the whole of Russia, 99 per cent of criminal cases result in a guilty verdict (*Financial Times*, 22 October 2005). Nevertheless, there has been some progress and increasingly citizens and enterprises turn to the court for dispute solutions (see also Chapter 3). However, often court decisions are not implemented and judges are often bribed.[14] Recently Dmitry Medvedev has identified one of his key tasks is to make the judiciary independent: 'What is the use of talking about equal opportunities if everyone knows that those with sharper teeth are always right, not those abiding by the law? We need to deal with the practice of unlawful decision by request' (*Itar-Tass*, 15 February 2008).

The weight of the bureaucracy in Russia is so overwhelming and dominated by patron-client relations that post-Soviet Russia can be characterized as a bureaucratic form of semi-feudalism or as a bureaucratic regime.[15] The centre of power is the Kremlin, i.e. the President and his entourage, but the government is always to be blamed for policy mistakes. Like the tsar, the President is above the parties and does not assume responsibility. The President tries to be a balancer of interests of various factions in his court.

The majority of respondents in a survey of 1500 Russians found that 'the bureaucracy and financial capital have merged and have become utterly corrupt' (*Interfax*, 1 November 2005). We can also say that Russia has developed into what Max Weber long ago called pseudo-constitutionalism and pseudo-democracy (see Wells and Baehr, 1995).

No polity has been created that is a reflection of society and that could adapt political structures to changing social needs, creating preconditions for evolutionary institutional change. The continuing deep divide between the state and society can be considered as one of the major causes of failed modernization attempts. The Russian state is a typical Hobbesian state, i.e. 'an impersonal entity, separate from society, which does not allow any residual authority other than its own' (van der Pijl, 2006, p. 6).

Many advocates of the liberal market economy argue that the middle-class is the major social force that is supporting liberalism. Developed civil society and liberalism is associated with a developed middle class. When the Orange Revolution occurred in Ukraine, many saw this as an expression of modernization of society, the force of civil society and an emerging middle class. However, the Russian middle class is relatively small with half dependent on state funded jobs (see Chapter 3). They do not pose a challenge to the new authoritarianism nor do they demand a regime of rights. This is very much in the Russian tradition as Chapter 2 has shown.

A survey in Russia showed no evidence of liberal attitudes among the middle class (*Russlandanalysen 127*, 2007). The survey (January 2007, Levada centre) showed that 31 per cent of respondents intended voting for the Party of Power, i.e. 'United Russia' (27 per cent 'no answer' and 27 per cent 'will not vote'). Among the highest income category (more than 4000 rubles a month) 29 per cent would vote for the Party of Power; 33 per cent of those aged 18–35 would vote for that party as would 34 per cent of those with tertiary education and 31 per cent of those living in a megalopolis. Another survey revealed a drop from 5 per cent in 2004, of the Russian population who were active in non-governmental organizations, to 3 per cent in 2005 (*Russlandanalysen 138*, June 2007).

How the economic system works

First of all, in the case of Russia one cannot speak about an economic system that can be analysed separately from the political and social system. In developed capitalist countries the markets operate as the dominant coordination mechanism due to the fact that they function in the context of a law governed economy. Economic subjects have a high degree of freedom to operate due to a strong state that is able to guarantee the implementation of the law. In the case of Russia the market fulfils a very limited role as a result of which there are few economic 'laws' that operate irrespective of the will of economic subjects.

For instance, when Gorbachev launched his market reforms and asked enterprises to seek partners in the market for themselves, it was not the market that delivered, in free competition, the required supplies and customers, but the *tolkachi*, i.e. the 'pushers' who accommodated for the inconsistencies of central planning and organized in an informal way inputs for enterprises. They then broadened their scope of activities. Whole departments within enterprises took over their role, but also new intermediating institutions, like independent agencies and banks (Ledeneva, 2006, p. 177).

A second example: in a market economy one would expect mass unemployment in a situation in which enterprises are faced with a collapse of production such as occurred during the 1990s. However, employment hardly fell in industrial enterprises during the 1990s. Registered unemployment in 1995 was approximately 2.7 per cent, only 8 per cent of which was attributable to mass lay-offs. However, many employees did not receive salaries. The break from the centrally planned economy was less abrupt than appeared on the surface. During the 1990s, state controlled holding companies emerged, which replaced the ministries but were hidden from foreigners. Eleksbank (electrical industry) increased its staff from 55 (1990) to 1800 immediately after independence. Essentially, it became an industry-like institution. The process of financing the subsidies to the enterprises was a complicated administrative task (Hough, 2001, p. 38). The economy ministry retained a staff of approximately 2000 (Hough, 2001, p. 40). According to Hough (2001, p. 31), it

> can be confidently asserted that the Russian economy was centrally regulated and directed from January 1992 through to the end of 2000.

> The central government had overwhelming power vis-à-vis the enter-
> prises, oligarchs, banks and regions ... no one should continue to
> assert that the Russian government was not strong or that institutions
> did not exist.

Through his leverage President Yeltsin could use enterprises as a social service instrument by allowing enterprises to be overstaffed. Under President Yeltsin a shift in redistributive capacity occurred from the holdings in Moscow towards the regions, in order to secure the region's leader's loyalty. In the regions numerous new federal bodies emerged.

A third example was the liberalization of prices that would have created an equilibrium that could have been beneficial for consumers and that could, in principle, have pushed to bankruptcy inefficient enterprises. However, monopolies dictated prices to such an extent that it led to hyper-inflation (together with inflationary financing by government). Also, many prices remained regulated at the central level. Even in 2005, the prices of 221 out of 445 goods and services surveyed (among which 73 were food products) were regulated (*RIA Novosti*, 17 May 2005).

The problem was that, instead of a smoothly functioning market economy, a hybrid economy appeared in which the market was not the dominant mechanism, at least not in most sectors.

The reforms that started under Gorbachev removed the core institutions of the centrally planned economy, especially the economic role of the party, on the assumption that in this way preconditions for the development of market relations would unfold. Instead, a formal institutional vacuum emerged in which the less visible informal institutional arrangements of the centrally planned economy, especially the shadow economy, imposed itself as the main operating mode. It was an extension of the economy of favours, with a bigger role for organized crime and clan networks, while the pursuit of self-interest of enterprise management was not at all restrained. Once the 'glue' of the party-state, i.e., the coercive role of the party, was removed, the hidden world of semi-feudal economic relations that served as oil for the centrally planned economy, but at the same time undermining it, was released. This resulted in robbers rather than entrepreneurs coming to the fore. It was a far cry from the proclamations of government officials who professed that their actions were inspired by the aim of introducing a well-functioning market economy. Too often observers, especially in the West, were misled by government declarations. In hindsight, we can see that many decision makers profited enormously from the predatory system that they helped to create.

Despite a qualitative break with the falling away of the party-state in 1988–91, the new socio-economic formation developed organically out of the previous one. In 1991 Russia was not a *tabula rasa*. A reconfiguration of elements from the former economy and society led to a new social and economic system. The 1990s also meant an extreme inconsistency of formal rules that allowed informal practices to develop further.

The disintegration and abolishment of the communist system has usually been analysed in terms of economic incentive structure, changing international economic environment and corrosive political structures. Attention has been on macro-economic and political structures while the changing sociology of communism has been neglected.

Some scholars say that in the case of Russia it was mainly situational factors that determined economic behaviour. For example, Shiller *et al.* (1992, p. 179) claimed that 'the biggest obstacles to a successful transition do not seem to lie in the basic attitudes or psychological traits held by people in the ex-communist countries'. They interviewed people in Russia, Ukraine, East Germany, West Germany and the USA, asking how they would behave in hypothetical situations. Surprisingly, the survey found that the East Germans were more optimistic, more committed to produce in the current system and more likely to adopt long-term thinking then the West Germans. Generally, Shiller *et al.* claim that their evidence suggested that attitudes in ex-communist countries do not consistently differ from attitudes in advanced capitalist countries. However, the basic assumption is that there is a high correlation between what people say they would do in hypothetical situations and their actual behaviour if these situations were to materialize. As has been argued earlier in Chapter 4, this is a dubious assumption.[16]

The misconception that economic rationality and modernity will be accepted by society if appropriate macro-economic policies are pursued and the right (formal) institutions are put in place, led to the revolutionary voluntarism of the champions of the free market in Russia.

Economic behaviour cannot be fully understood by referring to formal economic institutions only. According to Meyer (2006, p. 17):

> Institutions are stable patterns of interaction in social relations. They can be just factual social practices or regular behaviour. But in most cases they are based on some kind of rules, norms or conventions, which are more or less accepted and habitualized, maybe even taught. Formal institutions are based on explicitly defined rules and norms, on rights and duties to enable and to limit social interactions, to achieve certain goals and to structure the distribution of power.

Formal and informal institutions together form a framework of both constraints and structures of opportunity. They constitute the 'rules of the game' in society. Economic development and economic institutions can be seen in the context of the nature of social interaction in a given society. Generally, economists have displayed a lack of interest in psychological or cultural issues.[17] They assumed that the behaviour of individuals is basically the effect of broader forces at the macro-level, related to formal institutional arrangements of a society. However, institutional economists now generally accept the idea that well-functioning markets can only be conceived in the context of specific generally accepted and enforced norms. In his writing, Douglass North (1990, p. 36) drew attention to this idea:

> In the modern Western world, we think of life and the economy as being ordered by formal laws and property rights. Yet formal rules in even the most developed country make up a small (although very important) part of the sum of constraints that shape choices. In our daily interactions with others, whether within the family, in external social relations or in business activities, the governing structure is overwhelmingly defined by codes of conduct, norms of behaviour, and conventions.

For example, trust underpins the efficient functioning of markets in developed market economies. North pointed out that 'how effectively agreements are enforced is the single most important determinant of economic performance' (North, 1990, p. 36). It is obvious that in Russia, where cheating in business is common practice, trust is largely lacking in economic life.[18] Here it is argued that a general lack of trust in society is not only a legal problem and related to the weakness of the state, but also a sociological problem.

A minimum of trust is needed to allow all kind of transactions to take place. Once relations of trust have been established, behavioural patterns conducive for economic development may be stabilized and expanded. According to Winiecki (2004) the presence or absence of 'civilizational fundamentals' of liberty, law and order and trust, that predate the socialist past, determine to a large extent the transition's failure or success.

Table 5.1 shows how extremely low the level of general trust in Russia is compared to developed market economies.

In Russia, the level of institutional trust was 9 per cent in 1998 while in 1999, after the financial crisis of 1998, 3.4 per cent (Oleinik,

Table 5.1   The level of general trust in a comparative perspective %

Country	General trust				
	1976	1986	1991	1996	1999
Denmark	86	94			
Germany	93	90			
France	92	89			
Great Britain	84	83			
Greece	79	74			
Italy (North)	70	72			
Italy (Sicily)	50	53			
Russia (USSR)		54	36	31.5	32.1

Source: Oleinik, 2005, p. 181

2005, p. 181).[19] Also, trust in most institutions that are important for a democracy is extraordinarily low as shown in Graph 5.1.

Corruption

> Power tends to corrupt, and absolute power corrupts absolutely. (Lord Acton, letter to Bishop Mandell Creighton, 1887)

Russia and other states of the former Soviet Union are perceived to be among the most corrupt in the world (see the corruption perception index, Table 1.2). Corruption in Russia should be seen in the context of the age old institution of 'legal nihilism' and the absence of a universal legal order. In Russia there is, typical for patrimonial societies, contempt for law, an inclination towards personalized relations and an ethical dualism. In these circumstances corruption can flourish (see Suhara, 2004).

The phenomenon of corruption is seen as a way to smooth transactions in all spheres in an environment in which the state cannot or is not willing to enforce contracts. This also applies to the relationships between enterprises.

When studying corruption in South Asia, Myrdal (2005, p. 51) associated it with a fragmentation of loyalties and, in particular, minimal loyalty to the community as a whole, whether on the local or the national level. In modern societies, according to Myrdal (2005), these wider loyalties are backed by firm rules and punitive measures, by which certain behavioural reactions are kept apart from considerations of personal benefit. A stronger loyalty to less inclusive groups would encourage moral laxity and implies a low level of social discipline.

In the West, the phenomenon of corruption arose as a contradiction between the requirements of modern bureaucracy and patrimonialism. In tsarist times corruption was not seen as morally wrong. Exchanging presents was an essential means of nourishing client-patron relationships and created some stability in the social system. The ambivalent attitude towards corruption was highlighted by Vladimir Rushaylo, Minister of Interior (2001), who insisted that it is 'wrong to mistake bribe taking for corruption' (*RIA Novosti*, 13 March 2001).

Corruption is in Russia not an aberration but a crucial component of a neo-patrimonial society. Corruption and clientelism can be described as an ultimately institutionalized reaction to insecurity inherent in the neo-patrimonial system (Engel/Erdman, 2002 quoted in Zimmer, 2006, p. 288). In Russia corruption serves different state institutions as an instrument of control and power. It is a system of rewards for those who comply and blackmail for those who might resist.

The extensive surveillance apparatus does not serve the fight against corruption but rather uses corruption to gain control over individual actors and whole groups (Zimmer, 2006, p. 289). This practice goes beyond the state. 'The selective application of laws enhances the degree of insecurity, so that one can dare speak of a "purposeful creation of insecurity" which extends to the upper echelons of the power apparatus' (Prizel 2002, quoted in Zimmer, 2006, p. 289).

At the same time corruption undermines central power and makes governance less efficient, because officials can be bribed by the public to circumvent official rules. At this point it becomes important to distinguish between the many forms of corruptions. Karklins (2005, p. 25) developed a typology of corrupted acts in which she lists 15 different kinds of corruption. For our purpose it suffices to distinguish between the petty corruption of the public aimed at circumventing cumbersome rules and ensuring proper public services (*blat* and gift giving) that lubricates an otherwise rigid system and, on the other hand, the big corruption that results in state capture and allows the seizure of the nation's assets.

Corruption does not necessarily undermine economic development. According to David Kang (2002, p. 3) there are certain conditions in which it can be beneficial:

> Developing countries typically have weak institutional structures. In that case, if there is a balance of power among a small and stable set of

government and business elites, money politics can actually reduce transaction costs and make long-term agreements and investments more efficient, even while enriching those fortunate few who collude together.

However, it seems that in Russia these conditions are not fulfilled. Even in Moscow and St Petersburg, the most Westernized environments in Russia, repossession of assets through changing the rules and laws by corrupt bureaucrats and judges is so widespread that it raises the question whether the government is willing to control this trend. Legal nihilism means that property in Russia is conditional.[20]

The omnipresence of corruption is reflected in the following: after questioning 1600 respondents of 128 populated areas in October 2005, the Levada Centre reported that only 1 per cent of those surveyed felt protected against the arbitrary actions of the police, courts and prosecutors (Interfax, 2 November 2005). According to Radaev (2002), over 80 per cent of Russian entrepreneurs have suffered broken contracts. According to another Levada survey, 88 per cent of businessmen thought that their property and assets could be confiscated at any moment (*RBC Daily*, 27 December 2007).

According to UNESCO data, in 2007 Russians paid a total of $520 million to bribe university officials (*Novye Izvestia*, 18 March 2008). The average rate to buy justice in court was $275 (often lawyers function as a kind of broker between judge and defendant). The average amount of a bribe on the business market in Russia in 2004 was $135,800. The total business corruption market is, according to the prosecutor general, worth $240 billion, i.e. close to the total annual state spending (*Ekho Moskvy* radio, 23 May 2007).

The argument goes that corruption spread during the 1990s because the salaries of officials were so devalued during the period of hyperinflation that they were forced to take bribes. This is certainly not the only reason, as the recent increase in corruption, in circumstances of high economic growth and rising living standards shows. Business bribes are usually taken by high ranking officials who have good salaries and under President Putin these salaries increased substantially.

Business corruption, in particular, boomed. Uniformed extortionists have squeezed out organized bandits. The Indem Foundation in Moscow found a five-fold increase in corruption income between 2001 and 2005. Bribery costs amount to an average of 7 per cent of turnover per month for Russian companies (both legal and shadow). Researchers relate this rapid increase to the lessening oversight of the bureaucracy: less political competition, less freedom of press, less transparency of government and more restrictions for non-governmental organizations (*Vedomosti*, 12 July 2006). Accusing an official of corruption may lead to suing under the new law on extremism.

Surveys of the World Bank showed that the quality of state governance turned from bad to worse. The number of firms that complained they had to frequently give bribes rose from 13 per cent in 2002 to 21 per cent in 2005.[21] The World Bank sees the root cause of corruption in vague legislation (*Itar-Tass*, 16 October 2006). However, vague legislation is created on purpose to give bureaucrats and politicians arbitrary power and to permit the asking for and payment of bribes.

It seems that the fight against corruption is not taken seriously at the highest levels.[22] Dmitry Medvedev admitted in a speech in Krasnoyarsk that the struggle against corruption had so far failed (15 February 2008).

Corruption is increasingly focused on those who are gatekeepers, i.e. usually bureaucrats, either in the state administration, or in the health and education sectors.

Economist Alexander Buzgalin described the problem in the following way:

> There are four paradoxes about the Russian bureaucracy: the more liberal reforms are implemented, the greater the bureaucracy's power grows; the stronger the power of the bureaucrats, the more widespread are illegal methods among them. This calls for tough action, but the stronger this demand becomes, the faster the number of bureaucrats grows.
> (*Gazeta*, 2 November 2005)

Dmitri Oreshkin, head of the Mercator Group, says:

> Corruption is a significant mechanism in maintenance of the balance inside the elite. This means that everyone understands that authorities buy the loyalty of the bureaucratic class. Authorities buy state officials with a possibility to live on an income that is not quite legal. Definitely, there are a huge number of absolutely honest and decent officials but there is an informal rule of the game: you can receive additional income within certain limits in exchange for loyalty. This is even encouraged.
> (*Novye Izvestia*, 2 June 2006)

In Russia corruption is not an aberration, but the system.

It is important to note that it is the small- and medium-sized enterprises that suffer greatest difficulties from corrupt officials. Large enterprises have the leverage to minimize the burden of taxes and bribes. Apart from higher bribe payments, small- and medium-sized enterprises also face a higher tax burden and bureaucratic harassment. As a result, many of these enterprises move into the grey or black sphere.

All enterprises are faced with the problem of how to enforce contracts and agreements. The judiciary is not of much help as it is usually not independent. The variety of sanctions employed by enterprises as part of informal practices is described in Scheme 5.1.

Type	Action	Institution manipulated
1. Provoking administrative actions	Arranging for raids, inspections, and citations for administrative violations; arranging clashes between local/regional/federal levels of administrative control	Administrative institutions
2. Interfering with legal procedures	Opening, suspending, and closing cases and official investigations and sanctions	Legal institutions, tax police, state security organs
3. Interfering in personnel issues	Forced resignations and fixed appointments; staff reorganization	Employer institutions Use of blackmail files (*kompromat*) collected by private security firms
4. Applying financial pressure	Freezing assets, demanding repayment of debts, raising the level of kickbacks, and purchasing debts	Financial institutions
5. Organizing informal pressure	Using *kompromat*	Media institutions, PR agencies, private security firms
6. Using violence/threat of violence	Informal negotiations (*razborki*) and physical attacks	State and private security services and agencies

Scheme 5.1   Types of sanctions as part of informal practices
Source: Ledeneva, 2006, p. 173

The overview shows how the range of sanctions enterprises can use is much broader than in developed capitalist countries. The influence and performance of enterprises is less related to its market performance than it is to its ability to mobilize administrative support. Enterprises often function in the context of clans that have access to state institutions. Therefore enterprises can often use resources (like administrative and law enforcement resources) that in liberal market economies are not accessible for enterprises. Therefore, in a clan state there is no clear separation between the sphere of the state and the private economy. Clan structures convert resources that in liberal market economies are inconvertible.

Because of the uncertainty inherent in a clan economy, business groups try to conduct, as far as possible, business within their own group. Business groups constitute a closed system of associated companies organized in a non-transparent way. Non-transparency is furthered to allow tax evasion, to avoid raiding and to facilitate rent-seeking. With help of transfer pricing and shell firms, members of the network that control the business group, including officials, can obtain rents. Business groups can be seen as dispersed companies where management is decentralized but in which decision making is coordinated (see Avdasheva, 2005, p. 291). According to Avdasheva (2005, p. 299) 'a 'dispersed company' can only operate through the use of very strong extralegal mechanisms'.

Between, and above all within, business groups, network coordination is more important than hierarchy and market coordination. The loose organizational structure of business groups implies high transaction costs.

Network, hierarchy and market coordination

Networks are often localized and closed. They provide a context in which business transactions attain some degree of predictability. It is extremely difficult for an outsider to be accepted by these networks and a precondition is the acceptance of the in-group morals. Transactions between networks are very difficult. The aim of the network is, among others, the closure of social and economic opportunities to outsiders. Russia can be seen as a complex amalgam of local economic networks (business groups) with localized and personalised relationships. Often, a bureaucrat plays a crucial role in these business groups. This bureaucrat opens the way to the cooperation of the state.[23] Russian enterprises rely on a network of contacts in order to minimize uncertainties stemming from the unstable context. It is the same type of network contacts, centred around *tolkachi*, that were extensively used to coordinate economic activities in Soviet times. They involved long-term personal relationships with other enterprises.

Rather than visualizing the network of contacts around institutions, like enterprises, networks should be seen as clan structures, centred on chieftains. Clans usually consist of business people, officials and, in many cases, criminals. Usually the chieftain of a clan is charismatic, enjoys full control over the clan and expects complete loyalty from the core members of the clan. There is a disincentive to invest. Betrayal is considered the gravest crime in the clan's ethics. If a core member of the clan deserts, he risks expropriation. It was the clan networks, rather than individuals or formal institutions that became the main actors in the withdrawal from communism.

Karl Polanyi (1957) distinguished three types of coordination in the economy: networking, hierarchy and the market (see Scheme 5.2). In the capitalist world it can be said that no general optimal mixture exists, rather there is a wide variety of mixtures of various elements. The optimum blend may vary from country to country.

Since the beginning of the transition, Russia moved closer to (clan) 'networking' than to the market. The state transformed into a clan state. In the clan state the convertibility of different types of resources is guaranteed. Rather than competition, clan wars appeared in the transition process. Kosals (2007) argues that the conversion of resources, in which corruption is involved, is part of the normal activities of clans. Because the state agencies are linked to clans, the state cannot act as an arbiter that stands above the parties and cannot implement the law in an impartial manner.

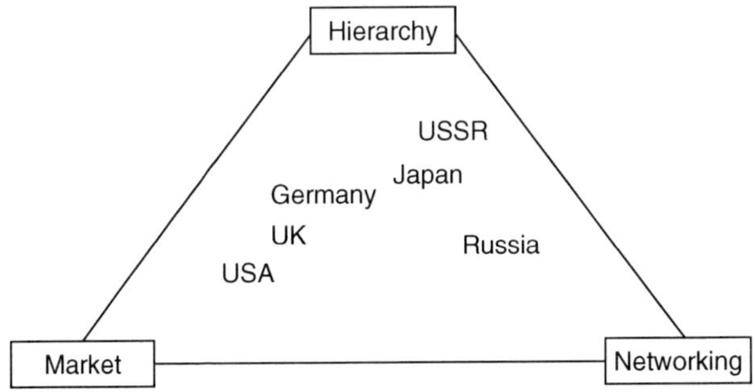

Scheme 5.2   Co-ordination mechanisms in various countries

An important characteristic of the clan state is the institutionalization of the shadow economy, which in Russia (and also in Ukraine) has attained a size of 40–50 per cent of real GDP.

Path dependence

Path dependence prevented a quick and easy transformation towards a modern capitalism. Path dependence is conceived by North (1990, p. 6) as the persistence of established informal rules:

> Although formal rules may change overnight as the result of political or judicial decisions, informal constraints embodied in customs, traditions and codes of conduct are much more impervious to deliberate policies. These cultural constraints not only connect the past with the present and future, but provide us with a key to explain the path of historical change.

According to North (1990, p. 112), path dependence is a way to conceptually narrow the choice set and link decision-making through time. Path dependence points to the nature of constraints from the past imposing limits on current choices and therefore making the current choice set intelligible. Path dependence is the key to an analytical understanding of long-term economic change (North, 1990, p. 112). It is not 'a story of inevitability in which the past neatly predicts the future' (North, 1990, pp. 98, 99).

According to Hedlund (2005, p. 17) 'we are faced with strong path dependence where failures to seize opportunities for positive change reflect obstacles to change that are deeply embedded in the institutional matrix of the society at hand'. We can speak in this case of an institutional lock-in. This exists in the case of Russia because the change-over to a more efficient incentive system that would create more wealth for the whole of society was prevented by a predatory state and a kleptocratic elite that emerged in the context of a neo-patrimonial polity. This polity was matched by corresponding mental models in the elite and the population as a whole.

Pleines (2005, p. 149) uses the concept of cultural dependence, pointing to the fact that the specific thought, perception and behavioural patterns of a social group hamper or further specific developments. The concept of cultural dependence goes beyond that of path dependence in two respects. First it captures not only the rules but also the thought and perception patterns that underpin these rules and that may be compatible with the expression of concrete rules. Secondly, the concept of cultural dependence is not only about established rules as retarding moments for change but sees these also as the innovative potential of cultural factors (ibid.).

The perception of economic interests, that informs economic behaviour, is mediated by specific belief systems. Scheme 5.3 sets out the dominant belief systems in Russia and the West with respect to the functioning of state, society and economy.

The description of Western and Russian models is ideal-typical and abstracts from the variety of capitalism in the West. For example, with regard to the function of enterprises it can be said that the goal of profit maximization is much more prominent for a typical company in the US than for a typical Japanese or German company. The juxtaposition of Russian and Western models can be equated with the Weberian dichotomy of traditional/modern. Traditional societies are often patrimonial. Weber's definition of the patrimonial state is:

> Where the prince organizes his political power – that is his non-domainial, physical power of compulsion *vis-à-vis* his subjects outside his patrimonial territories and people, his political subjects – in the same essential manner as he does his authority over his household, there we speak of a patrimonial state structure ... In such cases, the political structure becomes essentially identical with that of a gigantic landed estate of the prince. (Quoted in Hedlund, 2005, p. 125)

Under a patrimonial system there can be no clear distinction between state and society in so far as such a distinction postulates the right of persons other than the sovereign to exercise control over things and (where there is slavery) over persons. In a patrimonial state no formal limitations on political authority, no rule of law, nor individual liberties exist (ibid.).

Dominant Russian belief systems can be characterized as close to patrimonial. Nevertheless, the structure of Russian society nowadays differs in many respects from the patrimonial societies as described by Max Weber: Russia is industrialized, urbanized, the educational level is high and the state is over-powerful.

However, Weber's characterization of social practices and the nature of power in patrimonial societies fit Russian contemporary society well. Therefore we propose here the term neo-patrimonialism for current dominant belief systems and behavioural patterns in Russia. New, compared to tsarist patrimonial culture, is the general lack of trust in society and anomie. New, also, is that the social structure is not sanctioned by religious beliefs and that traditional value-generating institutions have disappeared or weakened.

	Western model	Russian model
Economy and politics	Clear distinction between spheres of economy and politics Sphere of economy has relative autonomy	Blurred distinction between spheres of economy and politics
Rule of law	Rule of law	Mores are more important than laws
Demarcation of competencies	Horizontal differentiation within and between organizations, clear demarcation of competencies Contractual obligations are important Hiatus between rules and decisions (procedural rationality)	Opaque borders between and within organizations Wheeling and dealing Economic transactions based on personal trust No accountability No hiatus between rules and decisions
Enterprises	Enterprise headed by manager/entrepreneur Networking in and between enterprises important, social engineering through sophisticated management methods	Enterprise headed by *khozian* (lord) Top-down hierarchical management methods
Role of state	State as facilitator, provider of basic public goods such as education Soft governance mechanisms are important State rules over citizens, with mutual rights and obligations State bureaucracy is rule follower	State as a predator. Neglect of public services Rule by decree Blackmail state State rules over subject-people State bureaucracy is rule maker
Approach towards economic problems	Economic rationality, analytical approach, transparency. Economic calculation possible Methodical rational acquisition	Political rationality. Lack of transparency. Economic problems ignored. Economic calculation very difficult. Often, external factors blamed for economic problems Aversion against 'book-keepers' mentality'

Scheme 5.3   State, economy and society: Russian and Western models

The neo-patrimonial state is characterized by the mutual penetration of patrimonial and legal-rational bureaucratic elements in a structure that is dominated by a patrimonial logic. It is often described as virtual because the appearance, i.e. the formal structures, is legal-rational, although the substance is predominantly patrimonial.

Neo-patrimonial rule is exercised within the structure of and with the claim to rational-procedural bureaucracy and 'modern' statehood. Political participation and interest articulation are dominated by patronage structures. The access to rent-seeking is organized in a neo-patrimonial way.

Officials hold positions in bureaucratic organizations and exercise power as far as they can, not as a public service but as private property. Loyalty is based on the common interest of a *khozian* and his personal *kommanda* (Zimmer, 2006, p. 284).

In Chapter 4 we discussed the primordial importance of the way Russians deal with authority and how this influenced a range of Russian social practices. Here, on another level, it is shown to what extent the cult of power is related to almost all features identified in Scheme 5.4.

Stanislaw Menshikov (2005, p. 69) compared the Russian economy to an inertial system moving along a trajectory that in the long run is self-destructive but extremely difficult to change. He mentioned the following features:

- a prevalence of oligopoly/monopoly over competition;[24]
- the dominance of oligarchic financial/industrial groups together with a relatively weakly developed banking system;
- a close fusion of business oligarchy with the state;
- a shadow economy that is inordinately big;
- an excessively high share of gross profits in GDP;
- high inequality; and
- a strong reluctance to invest capital on a long-term basis.

Menshikov points to the fact that gross profit exceeds 40 per cent of GDP, while labour accounts for 43 per cent and gross capital investment only 16 per cent. It is exemplified in the large number of Russian billionaires.[25] Low investment ratios and a high level of capital exports point to the extractive character of the Russian business elite.

Oleinik (2005) prefers the term 'network capitalism' to describe the system that emerged in post-Soviet Russia. By preferring a closed network to an open market, the economic subjects in Russia try to protect themselves against the negative impact of the government and the laws affecting their business. Market transactions and the informal norms that

The state	State	– State dominated economy/society; over-powerful state, from point of view of citizens and enterprises – Inefficient and weak state, not able to implement decisions – Dispersal of power within the state – No rule of law, rule of exceptions, no transparency in laws, legal nihilism, much regulated by decrees. No separation of powers – Parasitic state, predatory state – High degree of state capture by business oligarchy. This prevents the emergence of a developmental and facilitative state – Secret service is crucial in maintaining cohesion of the polity (among others through the mechanism of blackmail state)
	Role of bureaucracy	– The public serves the civil servant (system of *kormleniye*) – An independent political force, rule maker – Bureaucratic semi-feudalism. Clientelistic networks dominate state bureaucracy – Overlapping competencies within bureaucracy – Control mania – Merging of bureaucratic and criminal networks – Corrupt officials erect barriers to entry for new businesses
	Role of government	– Government acting as fire brigade. Tendency to improvise – Command and control reflexes to crisis situations – Rule by uncertainty
	Polity	– Deep society–state divide. Polity is not adequately reflecting societal interests – No culture of compromise. No developed sense of complexity of social-political processes – Marginal role for parliament, though it is important for oligarchs – Emergence of a strong 'party of power' – Emergence of corporatist institutions
The economy		– Property rights not well protected – Prevalence of oligopoly/monopoly over competition – Small SME sector – Low level of organizational capital – Centre–periphery dynamics – Large black economy
Society		– Atomized society – High levels of inequality – Weakness of conflict regulating and value generating institutions

Scheme 5.4   Features of Russian neo-patrimonialism

govern network relations are very localized. Radaev (2002) describes the substitution of laws for informal norms in terms of 'deformalization' (see Oleinik, 2005, p. 153). The close interpenetration of power and property leads to power-property. Political leadership grants a right to own property, whereas the property rights naturally assume that their holder is invested with some political authority (Oleinik, 2005, p. xxiii). Results of sociological surveys in Russia show that the relative significance of 'network barriers' did not decline during post-Soviet reforms (Oleinik, 2005, p. 166). Networks are often localized and frequently lead to regional clans.

In our view the term 'network capitalism' does not capture the essence of the hybrid system that emerged in Russia with its contradictory logics but in which the neo-patrimonial logic is dominant. This is not just an academic dispute about labelling, it has important consequences for diagnosing the actual working of the system. If departing from the idea that the dominant system in Russia is a form of capitalism, one might assume that the logic of private capital accumulation dominates and the economic system has a high degree of autonomy. In this view corruption and legal nihilism can be considered as aberrations that can be dealt with relatively easily. If defining Russia as a predominantly neo-patrimonial system, corruption, illegality and rent-seeking are central and crucial to the system.

Rent-seeking is furthered in Russia because the absence of a law governed economy and therewith the high degree of uncertainty in economic life, imposes a short time perspective upon businessmen. Getting richer by cultivating good relations with corrupt bureaucrats and politicians who can open venues for expanding business empires and securing markets is easier than investing in productive outlays and innovation. Rent-seeking is institutionalized in the organizational form of business groups with shell firms created for creaming off rents for members of the network, including officials that control the group. The state actually furthers rent-seeking through the failure to create a stable economic and social environment. Property rights are not well-protected and this therefore creates a disincentive to invest. The state also allows and even encourages businessmen to put their money in foreign bank accounts rather than investing in Russia.

Rent-seeking is also stimulated by allowing monopolies in many sectors and regions. Instead of improving the quality of products, monopoly rents can be achieved simply by raising prices.

North (1990, p. 99) explains a rent-seeking equilibrium as follows: 'the increasing returns characteristic of an initial set of institutions that provide disincentives to productive activity will create organizations and interest groups with a stake in the existing constraints'. The history of Russia provides ample examples of such an inferior equilibrium. It means that 'stationary bandits' are not necessarily interested in introducing the rule of law.

According to Hellman (1998) transition towards liberal market economy can be frozen by a coalition of vested interests centred on oligarchs who want to trade off the benefits of fully secure property rights against those of rent-seeking profits. This is facilitated by state capture. But why is rent-seeking so much more prominent in the CIS countries than in Central European countries? Havrylyshyn (2006, p. 91) discards the idea that the notion of 'time under communism' is an explanation. 'That one additional generation may add somewhat to entrenchment of communist rent-seeking is plausible, but that it would make a dramatic difference is harder to accept.' Havryslyshyn, like many other transitologists, overlooks the fact that socialist and above all pre-socialist legacies produced a variety of societies that dealt with power, wealth and wealth creation in very different ways.

6
Ukraine and the Russian Type of Neo-Patrimonialism

Like in a laboratory, the properties of a system in change or turmoil are more easily discernable than one in a stable condition. Therefore, Ukraine, with its recurrent political crises, is an interesting case. Ukraine shares many social, political and economic features with Russia. The histories of both countries are closely intertwined and as such the contents of Chapters 2, 4 and 5 also apply to Ukraine. The recent history of Ukraine, above all its Orange Revolution (2004), provides much of the material that sheds a light on the character of the Russian type of neo-patrimonialism that is dominant in the eastern and southern parts of Ukraine. Therefore, in this chapter we analyse the driving forces of socio-economic change in Ukraine and its regions in order to learn more about Russian-type neo-patrimonialism.

Although Ukraine shares a long common history with Russia many differences came to the fore in its post-socialist transition. Ukraine's economic performance was among the worst in the post-Soviet environment. The difference between Russia and Ukraine is particularly notable (see Table 1.1). Admittedly Russia has the benefit of natural resources and did not face the same challenge of nation building. In Soviet Ukraine the communists were generally more conservative than in Russia. During President Gorbachev's tenure, Ukraine was largely shielded from processes of democratization and *glasnost*. The larger part of the communist elite transformed into nationalists and capitalists overnight. The reforms in Ukraine were much slower; the focus of the first 5 years of independence was on nation building with a relative neglect of economic reform. Global economic governance agencies such as the IMF had less influence in Ukraine because Ukraine was less in debt.

The early 1990s were characterized by hyperinflation that gave huge opportunities for speculators to enrich themselves. Between 1991 and

1999, gross national product (purchasing power) fell by approximately 60 per cent.

From the beginning there was much more elite competition in Ukraine compared to Russia. This was related to: the absence of stable formal institutions at the national level; and to regional divisions in the country. During the first half of the 1990s the parliament and the president had about equal influence but there was continuous haggling and confusion about the division of powers. During President Kuchma's first term (1994–9), after the constitution of independent Ukraine was adopted (1996), the power was gradually concentrated around the President. He skilfully applied a divide and rule policy with respect to the regionally based clans, mainly between the clans of Dnipropetrovsk, Donetsk (both Eastern Ukraine) and Kyiv. He also tried to find a balance between Western and Eastern Ukraine. Nevertheless, his powerbase remained weak, when compared to Russian presidents, and prime ministers regularly distanced themselves from the President. During his second term (1999–2004) President Kuchma increasingly relied on the Donetsk clan, appointing one of the leaders of the Donetsk clan, Viktor Yanukovych, as Prime Minister (2003). He also failed to create a stable Party of Power. Instead he relied on *ad hoc* coalitions supporting him in parliament. For example, during the parliamentary elections of 2002, the bloc 'Our Ukraine' of Viktor Yushchenko (a former Prime Minister) won the elections while the electoral bloc of the President (For a United Ukraine) came in third place. However, the latter party prevailed in the single mandate constituencies. In addition, after the elections, independent candidates joined the presidential bloc (often after having received big sums of money or after having been threatened) so that this bloc appeared as the strongest. However, soon this bloc fell apart into rival factions while still seemingly supporting the President. It showed the weak institutional support base for the President. However, the opposition was also continuously weak and divided. Their leader, Yushchenko, refused to organize an open opposition to the President.

Under President Kuchma regional fiefdoms and regional bosses consolidated their power, and the political system increasingly began to resemble feudalism. The regional clans always maintained a limited autonomy with regard to the centre. They supported President Kuchma – conditionally. Here the situation compared with Russia was and still is very different. Although regional clans are powerful, the primacy of the centre under President Putin, unlike under President Yeltsin, was not disputed. Local and regional clans often act as they please in contemporary Russia, but they will not challenge the authority of the Kremlin.

We can distinguish different types of neo-patrimonial rule in the post-Soviet environment. There is the one of 'dominant power politics', with a restricted but real political domain with little possibility of a change of power. The boundary between the state and the ruling group is indistinct, and the resources of the state are used by the ruling group for its own purposes. The Russia of Putin and Medvedev belongs to this group. On the other hand there is the type 'feckless pluralism' (Carothers, 2002), characterized by a significant degree of political freedom, regular elections and changes of power between distinct political groupings. Nevertheless, democracy remains superficial. This is the case with Ukraine.

During the second term of President Kuchma it looked as if Ukraine was moving in the same direction as Russia, namely in that of a non-competitive authoritarian regime. During the campaign for the presidential elections of November/December 2004 many Ukrainians, businessmen and regional clans were frightened by the prospect of official candidate Viktor Yanukovych winning the election. He is a representative of the clan from Donetsk (Eastern Ukraine) where a neo-Soviet polity was already firmly established and where local oligarchs exercised monopoly power. Many feared that a victory for Yanukovych, who was at the time Prime Minister, would mean a definitive turn to Russia, authoritarianism and one clan rule. Few expected a victory for opposition candidate Viktor Yushchenko during the presidential election because the instruments the official candidate had at his disposal, above all the 'administrative resources', seemed overwhelming. So far Ukraine had remained relatively quiet, civil society underdeveloped and most Ukrainians were passive with a view to the authoritarian tendencies in the country. Added to this most opposition politicians, including Yushchenko, did not pose a real challenge to the President. Only socialist party leader Oleksandr Moroz, and Yulia Tymoshenko, a former gas tycoon and former vice-prime minister, were actively engaged in challenging the President.

Differences between Western and Eastern Ukraine became most voiced during the Orange Revolution, when Prime Minister Yanukovych was declared winner after the second round of elections with the help of massive fraud. Hundreds of thousands of demonstrators came onto the streets and forced a re-run of the elections, supported by part of the security apparatus, while many civil servants and city councils, in Western and Central Ukraine, defected to the opposition. With this support and the significant support of the West[1] the election was won by Yushchenko.

Notable was that Orange supporters were generally very eager to demonstrate on the streets. Surveys show that approximately 29 per cent of Ukrainians were in some way or another active during the Orange Revolution. However, of these 29.2 per cent 21.2 per cent constituted Orange supporters while 6.7 per cent were Yanukovych supporters (*Zerkalo Nedeli*, 3–9 September 2005). Many of the Yanukovych supporters were paid. It shows the deep cultural divide between the masses that brought about the Orange Revolution and the bastions of neo-Soviet culture.

The Orange Revolution can be seen as an attempt to break with the trend to impose authoritarian neo-patrimonial rule in Ukraine. It can also be seen as the culmination of a conflict between different clans in which elite pluralism was enforced with the help of the mobilization of the population and support from the West. Often the Orange Revolution has been depicted as the victory of the millionaires over the billionaires.

The Orange Revolution was based primarily in Central and Western Ukraine. In Eastern and Southern Ukraine demonstrations were limited and the public authorities stayed on the side of Yanukovych while continuing to harass Yushchenko supporters. Also, a clear majority of the electorate in Southern and Eastern Ukraine supported Yanukovych. The election results of the relatively fair re-run on 26 December 2004 showed Ukraine geographically even more polarized than on 21 November 2004 (see Map 6.1).

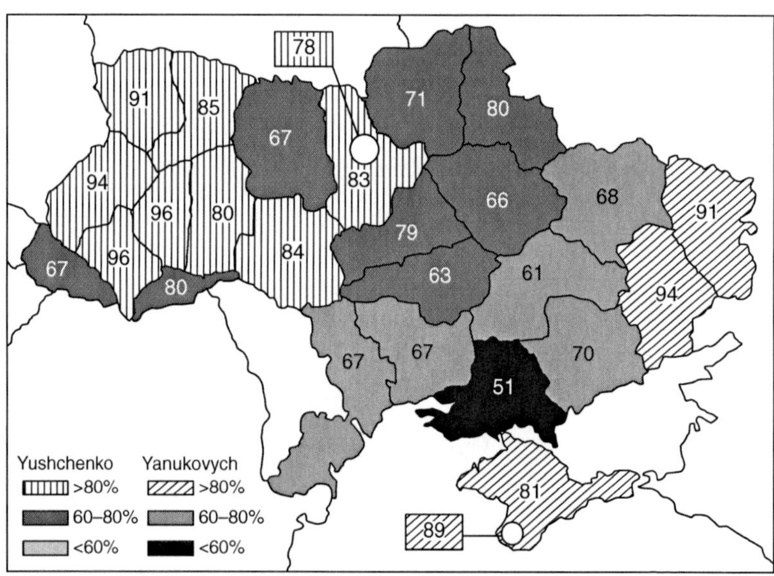

Map 6.1 Results of the re-run of the Ukrainian presidential elections, 26 December 2004

The vote not only reflected a political preference but also a political culture. Some observers even speak about a cultural–civilizational divide between Eastern and Western Ukraine. In the Eastern and Southern Ukrainian provinces most voters always voted for candidates proposed by local and regional authorities. A Soviet style political culture dominates in which dissidence is criminalized and punished, independent media have little or no chance and political and economic power is merged. The semi-feudal enterprise paternalism in which bosses interfere in all aspects of life of their employees is much stronger in Eastern and Southern Ukraine than in Western and Central Ukraine due to the concentration of big industrial enterprises in the east of the country.

One should not equate the difference between Western and Eastern Ukraine as a difference between modern and traditional. Western Ukraine is largely agrarian and less urbanized than the east and the south of the country. In many respects traditional value systems dominate. There are no indications that Western Ukraine is less corrupt than Eastern Ukraine. Dominant political forces in Western Ukraine are looking to the West and are very nationalistic. Discernable is a correlation between the degree of civic activism and the experience of having been ruled, for some time, by non-Russian, more democratic powers. Galicia, for example, which was incorporated in to the Soviet Union during World War II has some experience with representative democracy. In early tsarist times, Kyiv had been a Latinized city and functioned as a gateway to the West.

During the Orange Revolution the allies of Yanukovych promoted intolerance towards the opposition that was not mirrored in the Orange camp. In Donetsk and other eastern provinces conspiracy theories found fertile ground. Many in the east could not believe that the Orange supporters were not paid.

In the account of the Orange Revolution the inadequate behaviour of the politicians from the Yanukovych camp was remarkable. The siding of Yanukovych with separatist elements just before the re-run of the presidential elections pushed many Ukrainians away from him as did the open way he falsified election results. His reliance on the support of Russian advisors and President Putin himself showed an utmost ignorance of the public mood in Ukraine. Apparently Yanukovych and his supporters thought that 'administrative resources' would ultimately crush the opposition.

The clumsy actions of the Yanukovych camp are related to the environment in which they socialized. The cult of power in post-Soviet patrimonialism leads to command and control management of political processes and a contempt for democratic procedures. Political leaders are insensitive to the complexities of social engineering and coalition building. They are usually helpless in situations of managing dissent and pluralist interest structures.[2]

The failure of the Kuchma and Donetsk clans to retain power was related to the fact that the political opposition was not fully neutralized, that there was disunity in the political elite and business class due to a lack of balancing of interests of various regional clans and that there was no strong party of power that could control the political process. In the Russian tradition, the country's leader should balance the various factions of the court. Authoritarian tendencies during Kuchma's second term were masking a gradual weakening of his power base. But, at the regional level, especially in Eastern and Southern Ukraine, the political process was under the control of regional clans and neo-patrimonial rule consolidated.

The Orange Revolution also showed how unreliable oligarchs are as a support base for those in power. Many oligarchs shifted support to the opposition. Oligarchs usually have accounts and assets abroad and have a certain degree of autonomy *vis-à-vis* political power. This explains the opportunistic behaviour of most oligarchs. If they think their interests are better served by the opposition, they shift support. President Putin had learnt this lesson and did not tolerate political dissent from the side of oligarchs any more. Only those oligarchs who support the President can do business.

After the Orange Revolution the political forces that represent Central and Western Ukraine came to power. It was reflected in the new government, under Tymoshenko, in which there was no representation from political forces based in Eastern and Southern Ukraine, the economic powerhouse of Ukraine.

Although the government of Prime Minister Yulia Tymoshenko (January–September 2005) introduced some measures against corruption and more press freedom emerged, at the local and regional level most officials stayed in power and business went on as usual. Additionally, the parties in power were open to former Kuchma cronies. For example, the party of Yulia Tymoshenko offered party positions in exchange for money while pushing aside democratically elected party functionaries (*Ukrayinska Pravda*, 9 August 2005). 'Our Ukraine', the party of Yushchenko, proved to be a business party centred around Yushchenko himself. Political parties remained clan organizations rather than organizations of citizens around a political programme. Also lacking was a strategic governmental and presidential vision.

Initially, this all happened in a context of divisions about the future course of the country. The government under Tymoshenko wanted a national capitalism with certain safeguards with regard to foreign economic relations, while the presidential administration wanted an opening up to the world market with full privatization and liberalization. Tymoshenko generously increased the minimum wage, pensions and salaries of public service workers. It appeared that a programmatic Our Ukraine stood closer to the Party of the Regions than Tymoshenko's party.

Later, political infighting became increasingly related to the division of property (re-privatization of illegally acquired enterprises under former President Kuchma), and the distribution of power and influential positions, than about policy directions. All parties exhibited contempt for law. As a result, the authority of the judiciary was undermined.

The President maintained an opaque system of government in which the Security Council obtained competencies that are usually the privilege of government. These competencies were moreover not clearly delineated. This led to a daily interference of the Security Council in government affairs. The Security Council became a shadow government. Government ministers received orders from the Presidential Administration *and* the Security Council. The Presidential Administration decided to control major financial flows, such as those from the gas trade, while forbidding the government to deal with it. Allegations of corruption against people in the President's environment followed.

In the 9 months following the Orange Revolution a situation emerged in which there were various power centres that openly competed for influence. With the sacking of Tymoshenko and the appointment of low profile technocrat Yekhanurov (September 2005), a close associate of Yushchenko, the President sought to redress the situation. However, he needed the support of his former foe Yanukovych and in exchange for the support of the Donetsk Party of the Regions, Yushchenko promised to stop the reviewing of privatizations and to stop suing his former opponents, even if they had been involved in election fraud and corruption.

Old methods for informal decision making (rule by telephone) were not abolished. In fact, the way most Orange politicians tried to rule was very much entrenched in Soviet practices. Yushchenko even put someone with a criminal record (for smuggling among other charges) in charge of the customs office (*Ukrayinska Pravda*, 15 September 2005). Nevertheless, the situation was very different from the late Kuchma era; the press was free to report and there was open debate about government politics.

However, crucial features of neo-patrimonial rule remained in place and with the sacking of the government of Tymoshenko these features were even strengthened. According to former Ukrainian Minister of Finance, Viktor Pynzenyk, the machinery of power had not changed with the Orange Revolution (*Zerkalo Nedeli*, 13 May 2006).[3] The functions of government bodies often overlap, while many agencies wield insufficient power to fulfil their tasks. The government often does not and cannot govern while parliament often fulfils functions that the government should fulfil. For example, more than 90 per cent of draft laws are proposed by MPs, which means that legislative activity is not well coordinated, often badly prepared and going in many different directions. Subsequently, the Constitutional Court takes the right to block laws, not only those that contravene the constitution, but any law. For example, a law that put an upper limit to pensions, preventing the disbursement of extremely high pensions to former state bureaucrats was blocked. Parliament not only approves the government budget but also takes the right to unilaterally change items in the budget. State officials or employees of state owned companies often sign agreements that affect crucial aspects of the future of the country.[4] On the other hand, the government sometimes assumes legislative qualities, for example when deciding about tax privileges. Sometimes parts of the executive apparatus refuse to support ministries. For example, the statistics office can refuse, by law, to give specific information to ministers.

After the Orange Revolution a widespread disregard and abuse of rules and procedures continued to exist in the political process. Regional and local assemblies pass bills on matters which do not fall under their authority (*Zerkalo Nedeli*, 7–13 April 2007). Legislators continue to enjoy immunity from prosecution. This is the reason that three quarters of MPs are owners of big business (ibid.). The parliament tolerates voting by delegates who are not present. The parliamentary speaker allows balloting to be repeated as often as necessary to get the desired result. The Verkhovna Rada abused its formal obligation to conduct the swearing in of the constitutional judges in order to paralyze the activity of the Constitutional Court. The independence of the Constitutional Court is openly questioned. A survey by US judge Futey found that 'what credibility the courts gained as a result of Yushchenko versus the Central Election Commission in 2004, has disappeared and there has been a steady erosion of the judiciary's authority'.[5] Experts interviewed for the report on 'Corruption, Democracy and Investment in Ukraine' (Neutze and Karatnycky, 2007) alleged that corruption is widespread in legislative circles, particularly in cases where parliamentary deputies pursue their own business interests (Neutze and Karatnycky, 2007, p. 17).

According to a survey in May 2007, 77 per cent of the population believe that 'corruption levels have remained the same or have increased since 2004' (ibid.).

Since the Orange Revolution 'raiding', which involves the seizing of property with the help of bribing and flouting the law in commercial disputes[6] has become increasingly common. During 2005–7 around 2500 Ukrainian enterprises were allegedly raided (Neutze and Karatnycky, 2007, p. 13).

With respect to the dissipation of power, overlapping competencies and the inability of government to govern, little progress has been made since independence. The chaotic situation profits those people who are feeding from the state coffers. It gives advantage to the many in the state machinery that are in a position to influence decision making. But importantly, the political system grinds to a halt without a strong man at the top.

The parliamentary elections of March 2006, that confirmed the deep regional divisions revealed during the presidential elections, gave the Orange parties the opportunity to form a coalition government. However, the contradictions within the Orange camp, above all between the Tymoshenko bloc and the businessmen in Our Ukraine, were so big that Our Ukraine decided in an early phase to open secret parallel negotiations with the Party of the Regions. After three months of haggling, an Orange government under Tymoshenko was announced; it was immediately made redundant by the defection of the Socialist Party, a defection provoked by Our Ukraine.[7] This enabled Our Ukraine to finish negotiations with the Party of the Regions and in August 2006, five months after the parliamentary elections, Victor Yanukovych became Prime Minister again but in a much more powerful position because the new constitution gave him more powers than the President.

It meant that 18 months after the Orange Revolution, the Kuchmists were in government again. It also appeared that neither Yanukovych nor Yushchenko were interested in power sharing. Both tried to impose their will on each other. But Yanukovych gradually prevailed. After Yanukovych lured (i.e. bought or blackmailed) 24 MPs from the Orange camp while attaining almost 300 seats in the 450 seats in parliament, enough to impeach and overrule the President, Yushchenko decided to announce early elections. This decision was contested and declared illegal by government and parliament and a stalemate emerged that almost led to clashes between armed forces. The stalemate was not only caused by the unwillingness of all sides to compromise but also by the fact that a legal chaos emerged after the acceptance of vague and contradictory changes in the constitution. Moreover, during the political conflict all major political institutions, including the Constitutional Court, were de-legitimized. Politicians were not and hardly could be guided by the institutions that were created for conflict resolution. As has happened before in Ukraine, politicians played with the rules but not according to the rules. It exhibited a deeply rooted legal nihilism. Ukrainian politicians do not value institutions as institutions. Also, there was the attitude that the winner takes all: political players from all sides were not willing to compromise. In the contest for power and money, all means were allowed, including blackmail, bribery and intimidation. Yushchenko prevailed, above all through his leverage over the armed forces.

The parliamentary elections held in September 2007 did not change the situation substantially (the Party of the Regions and the Tymoshenko bloc won while the Orange parties achieved a slight parliamentary majority as in 2006).

The major development was the strengthening of the influence of the Presidency. The second Tymoshenko government that obtained, almost three months after the elections, a razor-thin majority of 2 in parliament, was characterized by the preponderance of Our Ukraine ministers, 13 out of 24, although Our Ukraine achieved only 14 per cent in the parliamentary elections. Yushchenko also managed to clip the wings of government by subordinating the government to the Security Council, presiding over half of the Cabinet of Ministers sessions, having an ally appointed as the Chairman of parliament and forcing the government majority in parliament to adopt a new law on the cabinet of ministers that would transform Ukraine into a presidential system, contrary to the constitution. The President also re-created a broad coalition outside the government by appointing high ranking politicians from the Party of the Regions to influential positions such as the chair of Security Council, the post of general prosecutor and positions in the presidential administration.

It does not mean that all the gains of the Orange Revolution had been lost. There was, especially in Kyiv, a more pluralistic power structure, and there was more media freedom than just before the Orange revolution. However, no culture of democracy developed and the institutions underpinning a democracy did not strengthen. Modes of governance, in the economy and the polity, hardly changed.

Ukrainian neo-patrimonialism was still very much in place, while the Party of the Regions, with its power base in Donetsk, was in a position to further the socio-economic model that had emerged in their home region. The Party of the Regions also managed to unite, behind its banner, the major business interests from the eastern and southern part of Ukraine. Paradoxically, it appeared that Russian-style neo-patrimonialism became strengthened as a result of the Orange Revolution, at least in Eastern and Southern Ukraine.

Many observers in the West saw the Orange Revolution primarily as a victory of civil society, reflecting changes in the younger generation and the strengthening of the middle-class. Many argued that democratic Ukraine should be given the prospect of EU membership. The fact, that the Orange Revolution was also a reflection of inter-elite rivalry and that also the foreign factor plaid an important role, was downplayed.

In Ukraine the core middle-class constitutes around 9 per cent of the population. According to a survey conducted by the Kyiv based Horshenin institute in May 2007, 36 per cent of the middle-class would vote for the Party of the Regions (from Eastern Ukraine) and 22 per cent for the Tymoshenko bloc. It demonstrates a voting behaviour similar to the population as a whole (other polls at the same time show 32 per cent of the general population for the party of the regions and 20 per cent support for the Tymoshenko bloc (*Zerkalo Nedeli*, 19 May 2007). The survey, comprising 2000 people, found that the more people earn the more they withdraw into a private circle, curtailing all other contacts (*Den*, 22 May 2007). Despite the political turmoil that commenced in late 2004, economic growth was robust (7.2 per cent annual growth in 2000–7, 8.9 per cent annual decline during 1990–9). Like the situation in Russia, it was facilitated by the use of under-utilized capacities, a resurgence of the domestic market and prudent macro-economic policies. Although to a lesser extent than in Russia, booming exports, mainly of steel and chemicals, helped the recovery. But as in Russia, robust economic growth has not led, so far, to much development. Telling is the fact that according to a survey by the statistical office, 84.5 per cent of Ukrainians see themselves as poor (*Zerkalo Nedeli*, 6–12 October 2007).

The case of Donetsk: the winner takes all

Donetsk, in Eastern Ukraine, is the home base of Viktor Yanukovych. Although Donetsk represents 10 per cent of the population of Ukraine, it produces 20 per cent of Ukraine's industrial output and 23 per cent of exports (2006). Heavy industry and coal mining emerged in the nineteenth century and workers flocked to Donetsk from all corners of the Russian Empire. Nowadays Donetsk is perceived as the prime neo-Soviet civilization in Ukraine and is seen by many within the Ukrainian elite as an example to follow because of its relatively stable economic and political development. Therefore it is instructive to examine how the Donetsk model emerged and has been consolidated. First, the process of re-distribution of state assets will be analysed.

In Donetsk the myriad of trading firms that emerged around big state enterprises during the early phase of transition were linked to the enterprises through close personal links. The trading firms who provided services to these state-owned companies, or purchased their products, were often headed by close relatives of the directors of the companies or sometimes by the directors. This squeezing of state-owned enterprises was overseen by the local and provincial public authorities, especially the secret services and the judiciary. They were complicit in this state-managed economy and profited directly from the plunder of state-owned companies. Often, state functionaries were involved in the commercial firms. Without the approval of state functionaries, the squeezing of state-owned enterprises would not have been possible.

During the period of hyperinflation (1992–5), that followed independence, the commercial firms boomed as prices were freed and opportunities for speculation widened. Especially in energy trade and steel exports huge fortunes have been made. In Donetsk the origins of many fortunes lay in coal mining. A very popular business arrangement was to supply steel, equipment and other materials to coal mines in exchange for coal (especially coke coal) and then supply it to coke-chemical plants, metallurgical enterprises and power plants. Through their influence upon public authorities in Donetsk such firms arranged themselves as sole suppliers.

Part of the profits of these trading firms disappeared to off-shore accounts. Another part was used for the purchase of other firms. In the waves of privatization trading firms acquired a broad range of enterprises. Initially it was not manufacturing enterprises but, for example, the local football club, hotels, shops, cafés and restaurants. Privatization in Ukraine proceeded very slowly, and the big strategic enterprises that dominate the economy of Donetsk, were privatized from the late 1990s onwards.

In 1993 and 1994 the power of the Donetsk clan was at its highest, shortly after the miners' strike of 1993 that brought Efim Zviagilsky, a leader of the Donetsk clan, to the head of the government in Kyiv. Miners' strikes were used by local politicians to their advantage in their negotiations with Kyiv.

After the commencement of the transition, former communist leaders stayed in power. They were gradually supplemented by representatives of the new commercial groups and criminal elements. Elections were manipulated and the popular voice was hardly represented in the polity of Donetsk.

During the period 1995 to 1997 the unification of fragmented elite groups started under the banner of regional autonomy. Politicians from Donetsk wanted regional autonomy in order to get a hold on local energy resources and to maintain the freedom to develop economic relations with Russia. Also, groups that were previously involved in the shadow economy became active in legal business. This period was also marked by the criminalization of the political sphere.

In May 1997 the appointment of Viktor Yanukovych was a compromise between Donetsk and the authorities in Kyiv. He had business interests in Donetsk and was close to oligarch Akhmetov but was at the same time supporting President Kuchma.

After the violent clashes of 1997, in which several leading members of the Donetsk clans had been killed, the Donetsk clan built up their empires in silence, without openly challenging state power in Kyiv. A silent compromise emerged between Kyiv and Donetsk: Donetsk organized support for the President, guaranteeing a majority for him in Donbass, while Kyiv would let the Donetsk clan manage its own affairs. The arrangement was, in effect, 'politics is done in Kyiv and business in the Donbass'. It meant that the Donetsk clan could constitute its own fiefdom, with its own rules that were different from those in Kyiv, under the condition of loyalty to President Kuchma.

After gaining control of the coal mines and coke factories, the major commercial groups turned their attention to the steel enterprises, most of which were privatized from 1998 onwards. The major commercial groups transformed themselves into financial-industrial groups. The financial-industrial groups were so powerful, financially and politically, and so well-organized, having eliminated thousands of small commercial competitors, while forging unity among the few remaining holding companies, that the takeover of the big state-owned enterprises in Donetsk was an easy task.

The Donetsk clan controls the three most important production chains in Donetsk: coking coal–coke–metal; energy coal–electricity–steel; and gas–steel–gas pipes. Privatization was meant to create more efficient economic structures and competition. Instead, privatization in Donetsk created a quasi monopoly that controlled the whole regional economy. It led to obstacles for new enterprises and the monopolization is reflected in the very low number, even by Ukrainian standards, of small and medium sized enterprises.

Local tycoons are not despised and in some cases are even quite popular. Rinat Akhmetov, the richest man of Donetsk and Ukraine, is popular, partly related to his financing of the local football club and charity work. Although there is widespread dissatisfaction with living conditions in Donetsk, it is not the local politicians and oligarchs that are usually blamed, but the government in Kyiv that does provide enough in subsidies. Rent-seeking behaviour of local oligarchs is not denied but belittled.

Since 1999, after a prolonged economic decline, output began to increase in Donetsk and Ukraine as a whole. Despite the stabilization of the economic and political situation in Donetsk, investment levels hardly increased and local clans preferred to use their financial power to expand their empires by buying up enterprises everywhere in Ukraine. Although investment levels went up, in 2006, the province of Donetsk accounted for 10.8 per cent of the total capital assets put into operation in Ukraine, although Donetsk accounts for about 20 per cent of industrial production. The low level of investment is reflected in the extremely high proportion of archaic Martin ovens in steel production.[8]

There is the argument that with the gradual demise of coal mining and related state subsidies, lessening opportunities to gain with gas trading and limitations of the international steel market, rent-seeking opportunities will be severely reduced. However, this does not necessarily push the oligarchs of Donetsk into abandoning rent-seeking activities. It seems that over the past few years they have shifted their activities from channelling money abroad or using it for conspicuous consumption towards expanding their empire of enterprises in new sectors and regions. Since 2000 part of the flight capital has been used for this purpose that is reflected in the increasing investments from Cyprus, the Bahamas and other tax paradises.

There has been since the late 1990s a high degree of trust and cooperation within the upper echelons of the regional elite and there is a highly integrated regional economic complex, although since around 2002 two distinct conglomerates have begun to dominate Donetsk: SCM Holding owned by Rinat Akhmetov; and Industrial Union of Donbass in which Sergey Taruta is the main stakeholder.

As argued before, the main bottleneck is the monopolization of the major part of the regional economy by a coherent group of clans that is mainly interested in rent-seeking and has a short term outlook. Their rule is facilitated by a belief system and related social practices that help to perpetuate dominant social and economic relations in Donetsk. The paternalism is also rooted in the big enterprises that take care of many aspects of their workers' lives while telling them how to vote. It also should be recalled that 96.3 per cent of the Donetsk electorate voted for candidate Yanukovych in the relatively fair re-run of the presidential elections. Have they not heard about the massive electoral fraud, about the mismanagement of enterprises and state assets in Donetsk under Yanukovych's tenure as governor?[9]

After Yushchenko appointed Yanukovych as Prime Minister (2006) he sought to counterbalance the influence of the Akhmetov clan from Donetsk by appointing in key positions people from rival clans in Donetsk. Therefore, after the parliamentary elections of 2006, representatives of both Donetsk conglomerates arrived at the top of the power pyramid. This may help to reverse the problems of the Donetsk economy which, since early 2005, has started to lag behind the rest of Ukraine.[10] This lag may be related to the fact that many earning opportunities, such as VAT fraud, and tax concessions for the special economic zones in Donetsk, were withdrawn shortly after the Orange Revolution. For example, industrial production declined in Donetsk by 8.7 per cent in 2005 (cf. growth in Ukraine of 2.9 per cent) and in 2006 grew by 5.6 per cent (cf. 5.6 per cent in Ukraine). After Viktor Yanukovych became Prime Minister again and again appointed Azarov (from Donetsk) as minister for taxation, immediately VAT arrears started to accumulate in Donetsk.[11] Plans were also announced to reinstate special economic zones (*Associated Press*, 7 August 2006).

The situation in Donetsk is very similar to the situation in Russia where, as a rule, local rulers are playing the political-economic game among themselves and consciously employ strategies that prevent newcomers from entering. They keep much of the information about local affairs to themselves and establish an exclusionary system of elite politics (see Mendras, 1999, pp. 304–6). A kind of state corporatist alternative for civil society emerges. About 150 organizations in Donetsk formed an umbrella committee that supported the plan for regional revival and supported the Party of the Regions. It is a kind of hegemonic bloc policy. There also seems to be a correspondence between the values prevailing in society and the behaviour of the power elite.

It has been shown why Western and Central Ukraine have reacted differently to government policies under President Kuchma who during his second term tried to impose the Eastern Ukrainian variant of neo-patrimonialism, which is very similar to Russian neo-patrimonialism, upon the whole of Ukraine. The Orange Revolution revealed the regional split in Ukraine and the existence of very different political cultures. The Orange Revolution and its aftermath showed both the strengths and the weaknesses of East Ukrainian neo-patriminonialism. In Donetsk a form of state corporatism has emerged that is based on a rather broad popular support and has shown economic and political stability. Many in Eastern Ukraine see this as the model to follow.

Events in Ukraine after the Orange Revolution showed that neo-patrimonialism is very resilient and that once in power most Orange politicians did not behave very differently to their opponents. The Orange Revolution was as much a clan war as it was a democratic revolution. After this revolution, legal nihilism remained dominant and power sharing appeared not to be possible. In Eastern and Southern Ukraine very little changed after the Orange Revolution while the Party of the Regions consolidated its position. It shows that the Ukrainian variant of neo-patrimonialism, that is very similar to that to be found in Russia, is very resistant to democratic challenges.

7
Path Creation: A Comparative Perspective

In preceding chapters a number of structural obstacles for social and economic development in Russia have been identified. The most important are all related to the peculiarities of governance mechanisms in Russia: corruption, rent-seeking, legal nihilism, etc.

In order for Russia to fully exploit its development potential, knowledge about how to 'unlock' Russia and to move it out of its pathological path-dependence is fundamental. Opportunities, as well of constraints, of Russia's institutional legacy should be taken into account.

First, a comparison between Russia's development potential and the factors that made Western economies successful will be made. Second, lessons for Russia will be drawn from the experience of successful neo-patrimonial countries such as those in Eastern Asia. Finally, from the perspective of the most dynamic sectors of the world economy Russia's position will be identified.

Some elements of a policy aimed at path dependent path creation are suggested. Ways of accommodating the new organizational-technological paradigm with Russian path dependence are explored.

Russia from the perspective of the experience of Western economies

Economic transformation of Western developed capitalist economies can be analysed in terms of problem-solving capacities. Developed capitalism entails a search for the most efficient solutions at the micro-level involving a social engineering that is largely absent in Russia. Russians have learned, during ages of despotic rule, to live with rather than solve problems. In Russian society conflict and problem-solving mechanisms are weakly developed. The most dynamic societies are learning societies. However, collective learning, by trial and error, has been made very difficult in Russia because of the lack of feedback mechanisms.[1] When comparing Russia's predicament from the perspective of the process that led to economically successful capitalist economies, the nature of authority patterns comes to the fore as a crucial factor.

Generally, if looking at developed capitalism, one can say that each of these economies, apart from having an important market sector (autonomous economic system) has a strong state that is able to impose the rule of law (hierarchy) as well as a strong society, where norms of reciprocity are prevalent (networking).

The problem with Russia is that in each of these three spheres there are major and deeply rooted deficiencies. Russia is not only faced with market failure, but also with hierarchy failure and network failure. The roots lie in a blocked society. At the core of this blockade is the inability to limit the power of the boss, on all levels, through the development of transparent procedures for conflict management.

Gradually, in developed capitalism, network coordination became more important together with the coordination mechanisms of the market and hierarchies. Network structures exist within and between firms and organizations and are linked to public authorities. According to Messner (1997, p. 180), networks are social innovations, institutional inventions for solving complex problems in view of which both market-like allocation (due to the production of negative externalities, a lack of long-term orientation, insufficient redundancy relations) and hierarchical forms of decision making (due to rigidity, a lack of flexibility, imperfect information, a lack of variety) prove dysfunctional. In Russia, these innovative networks are largely absent.

In developed capitalism, a new socio-technological-organizational paradigm is gaining ground, characterized by a complex organizational and governance pluralism. In Russia, the emergence of such a paradigm is hindered by the general lack of trust in society, the lack of co-operative attitudes among enterprises and organizations and the obstructive attitude of the state towards non-state organizations. It seems that Russia is actually moving away from the above-mentioned paradigm.

In the 1990s anomie, a lack of trust and deviant behaviour spread in society. This all reflected the lack of a social texture and social capital that contribute to the imposition and internalization of the norms for civilized behaviour. Social capital is defined by Putnam (1993, p. 35) as, 'features of social life, networks, norms and trust – that facilitate cooperation for mutual benefit'. As Rose (1997) has pointed out, pre-modern societies also have social capital, and social capital can also be mobilized against another social group, as in the case of Northern Ireland, or against society as such, as in the case of the Mafia in southern Italy. In the case of Russia, social capital exists but often assumes pre-modern forms and anti-modern tendencies.[2]

The peculiarity of Russian society is that anti-modern network capital predominates while organizational capital, which is characteristic of modern societies, is very weak. Organizational capital is a society's stock of organizations that are formal, i.e., legally recognized by the state, rule-bound, bureaucratic, and hierarchically coordinated (Rose, 1997, p. 112). Organizational capital is weakened by anti-modern networks.

The lack of rules governing social relations and relations between institutions, resulting in high barriers to cooperation, in all spheres, can be considered as one of the major obstacles to social and economic development in present-day Russia.

Russian-style clan networking contrasts sharply with the 'network society' emerging in the developed capitalist world. It is extremely difficult for an outsider to be accepted by these clan networks and a precondition is the acceptance of the in-group morals. In all successful economies, both markets and competition are embedded into cooperative networks that act as uncertainty reduction devices and as buffers to both instability and to predatory practices. The lack of horizontal cooperation and the closed character of clientele networks in Russia inhibit the diffusion of innovations. It is related to a lack of trust in Russian society (see Chapter 5). Russia always has been a low-trust society. According to Winiecki (2004) trust is a consequence of a long tradition of civil society, the ability and willingness of citizens or inhabitants to organize themselves for the joint pursuit of various common activities.

In modern capitalist economies, there is a complicated horizontal differentiation within society and economy in which various actors have clearly demarcated competencies and tasks. The differentiation occurs within enterprises, between enterprises, and between all institutions that are part of society. There is a high degree of insulation of institutional spheres from each other and a limited convertibility of status attributed from one sphere to the other (Elster *et al.*, 1998, p. 31). Agency in industrialized societies is institutionally encapsulated (Elster *et al.*, 1998, p. 27). In the words of Elster *et al.* (1998, p. 27),

> modern industrialized societies have a well institutionalized social order in which the (contingent, 'non natural') rules according to which political and distributional conflicts are carried out are

relatively immune from becoming themselves the object of such conflict there is, in other words a solid hiatus between rules and decisions.

Typical for Russia is the lack of organizational differentiation and clear demarcation of competencies and borders between and within organizations. This lack of horizontal differentiation is related to the aversion towards transparency and clear procedures in the guidance of economic life.

In the West complex regulations that guide the behaviour of individuals and enterprises emerged in a long process of trial and error in which conflicts were made productive in the context of conflict resolving mechanisms. In this way contradictions in society could be managed and bring coordination and governance mechanisms to a higher level with beneficial effects for social and economic development. In Russia these conflict resolving mechanisms are largely absent.

Given the characterization of Western economies above, transformation from a centrally planned to a market economy can also be conceived as the splitting up of encompassing and multi-functional institutional compounds into smaller and functionally more specific units (Elster *et al.*, 1998, p. 28).

While in the developed capitalist countries a complex social fabric emerged to sustain economic development, in the Soviet Union it was the vertically structured party-state that organized industrialization in an authoritarian way. While in developed capitalist economies a horizontal organizational differentiation occurred in which new institutions had a large degree of autonomy that enabled collective learning, in the Soviet Union, technological progress and innovation was conceived in a linear, top-down way. Contemporary Russia is still faced with this legacy.

The economic success of most developed economies does not lie in an unrestrained free market but in institutions combining competition with cooperation. Within the firm sustained social bonding and common organizational culture sustains cooperation. In a learning economy modalities of cooperation within firms also affect relations between firms. Forms of cooperation are often rooted in cultures that often pre-date capitalism and are often alien to capitalism. According to Hodgson (1999, p. 68):

> capitalism has survived because it has combined, in different ways and with different degrees of success the fluidity and incentives of property exchange with different social cohesion and moral obligation to keep the contract system going in a complex environment.

Looking from this perspective at the Russian economy it can be seen that there is a problem with the lack of cooperative traditions and trust. This complicates the build-up of organizational capital which is not just a question of transferring codified knowledge. It also involves the transfer of tacit knowledge.

Russia from the perspective of patrimonial societies

Instead of looking at the experience of Western developed capitalist economies it is in many respects more fruitful to look at the examples of successful neo-patrimonial societies.

The Soviet state could be considered as a developmental state in which the state propelled the nation forward in its peculiar way. Comparative analysis of the conditions under which newly industrialized countries create innovative conditions for private enterprises shows that the role of the state is crucial in economic development. In post-socialist Russia it is necessary to determine what kind of state intervention is required. According to Evans (1995) social and economic development occurs if state structures fit into the social environment. The state should be able to resist capture by rent-seeking actors. Developmental states show that state institutions should be embedded in a dense network of ties that bind them to societal allies with transformational goals. However, in order to further development, the state and its bureaucracy should have a certain level of autonomy. 'Autonomy complements embeddedness, protecting the state from piece meal capture, which could destroy the cohesiveness of the state itself and eventually undermine the coherence of its social interlocutors' (Evans, 1995, p. 248). According to Evans, it is the delicate blend of autonomy and embeddedness that makes the difference. He also argues that political elites should share a common sense of purpose and direction, an *esprit de corps*.

Looking at Russia from this perspective, it seems that some crucial ingredients for a developmental state are missing. Politicians and top executives do not seem to share a sense of common purpose and direction. Usually, their first loyalty is towards their clan and the private interests of this clan. The bureaucratic domain they are occupying is considered as their private lot and connected enterprises can freely feed from state resources. A sense of public accountability is missing. Patron-client networks dominate the state apparatus that has become predatory with respect to society at large. Thus, the state hardly enjoys autonomy with respect to private business networks, although at the national level, there is the primacy of politics. Also, professionalism within the bureaucracy is very low because meritocratic recruitment principles are minimally applied. In many respects, the Russian bureaucracy is reminiscent of the bureaucracies of the Ottoman and Byzantine empires.

The state should also be crucial in bringing about stability, trust and creating a physical and regulatory infrastructure for development. What actually happened in Russia was that the state, at least in the 1990s, contributed to de-development. Instead of minimal state intervention Russia needed a state-led development while introducing markets. The state actually furthered rent-seeking by not creating a stable economic and social environment. Rent-seeking was also stimulated as a result of the absence of a functioning capital market that could further the efficient allocation of resources.[3] The absence of a law governed economy creates a high degree of uncertainty in economic life and imposes a short-term perspective. Getting richer is easier by cultivating good relations with corrupt bureaucrats and politicians who can open venues for expanding business empires rather than investing in productive outlays and innovation. The state also allows and even encourages businessmen to put their money in foreign bank accounts rather than investing in Russia. Instead of using government budget surpluses for improving the country's crippling infrastructure it was, until recently, potting up money. Government should also have participated in investment projects. However, an industrial policy was, until recently, totally absent.

In Russia power is located in places other than it should be according to constitutional rules. This situation happens frequently across the world. In many East and South Asian parliamentary democracies there is a separation between form and substance of authority. More often than not, the formal structure of authority is completely fictitious. Therefore, the virtual democracy of most post-Soviet countries is far from unique. One would assume that in (neo-) patrimonial societies authority patterns should be clear and concentrated if the polity is to function smoothly. However, this is not always so. Japan, although having undergone a fast modernization process, retained many elements of traditional society and it is far from what is generally seen as liberal capitalism. There is, for example, the weak rule of contract law, the powerful industry-finance alliances, the sectoral cross-share holdings, lifetime employment, state planning institutions and mercantilist foreign trade policies. Japan has a similar party of power to Russia and this party has also used 'administrative resources' to stay in power. Japan also knows 'decorative opposition parties'. But, Japan has known political stability for a long time. However, peculiar for Japan is the fact that there is no clear centre of power. Power is shared by big enterprises, bureaucracy and government. There is no focal point in the polity. Unlike Russia there is a strong consensus among the political and business elite about what policies to pursue. Whereas it seems that in Ukraine and Russia strong leadership is only possible if power is concentrated in the hand of a strong leader while power sharing is problematic, in Japan strong leadership is guaranteed by the institutionalized consensus building mechanism (see Van Wolferen, 1989). A shame culture supports behaviour that conforms to societal expectations.[4]

It seems that in any positive scenario, given current dominant social practices and belief systems, Russia requires a strong political leadership as a prerequisite for a gradual transition to a rule-based society and economy. The developments in Ukraine after the Orange Revolution bear testimony to that. In the absence of trust in society, the state has an important role to play in bringing about trust and predictability to social and economic life. This is of course only feasible if the state apparatus is thoroughly reformed and the state bureaucracy purged. This can, in principle, be accomplished with the help of a vibrant civil society that functions as a countervailing power for the state. At the same time the state has to fulfil an important role in furthering the cohesion of society.

In the current situation of rampant rent-seeking in the private sector, it seems very important that the state develops a physical infrastructure while ensuring the reproduction of basic services like education and health care and protecting the country from predatory behaviour, which implies certain forms of import protection and control on international financial exchanges. A corporatist, state-led model of development that takes into account the deeply rooted social practices, attitudes and belief systems, while at the same time acknowledging the need to transform these, can lead Russia out of the deadlock situation of underdevelopment.

According to a World Bank study, China has developed an impressive set of informal institutions that support the same kind of dynamic activity (entrepreneurship, market entry and exit) and competitive markets that underlie the innovation economy of the United States (World Bank, 2006b, p. 15). However, in Russia it is still typical for markets to be captured by a few incumbent firms who are likely to be in cooperation with regional and local officials. The latter receive quasi-fiscal services from larger firms on their territories. This creates a natural bias against outside competition (World Bank, 2006b, p. 16).

In China, the decentralization of considerable autonomy to the provincial level of government has been critical in 'allowing China to develop the market dynamism needed for an innovation economy even in the absence of strong formal market institutions' (World Bank, 2006b, p. 17). However, in Russia decentralization initiatives have been stifled.

Whereas in Russia the bureaucratic apparatus expanded enormously during transition, in China it shrank.[5] Whereas the share of private consumption in GDP in China is rather low (44 per cent, 2003), compared to Russia (49.1 per cent during 1998–2005), the share of private consumption plus capital investment together in China is much higher than in Russia (86 per cent, 2003, versus 66.1 per cent) (Menshikov, 2005).

A comparative analysis with China showed that China liberalized markets first and privatization occurred later, at a slower pace and was moreover much more limited, compared to Russia (Bhaumik and Estrin, 2005). In China, enterprises, including state owned, were much more responsive to market signals than enterprises in Russia. In China new enterprises were encouraged whereas in Russia they were discouraged.[6] During the period of investigation (1995–9) a severe de-capitalization occurred in Russia while in China the real capital stock of companies grew substantially. Unlike in China, markets in Russia remain geographically and institutionally fragmented. The Chinese case confirms that market incentives are sufficient to ensure some degree of efficiency in enterprise activity without immediate full privatization. Bhaumik and Estrin (2005) conclude that neither 'big bang' reform policies nor early privatization, such as occurred in Russia, is the *sine qua non* of successful transition. In China, since the late 1970s, government has been pragmatic, following the dictum that it does not matter what colour the cat is. What matters is whether it can catch mice.

In China the state–society divide is less deep than in Russia. According to a survey (2003–5) only 37 per cent of polled Russian entrepreneurs trust government against 82 per cent of polled Chinese entrepreneurs (Chen *et al.*, 2007). According to other survey results, the sum of positive answers on the survey question 'Can the majority of people be trusted?' was in Russia 37.9 per cent, while in China it was 64.3 per cent (Yasin, 2007, p. 39). The fact that the state–society divide in China is less pronounced than in Russia is related to the Chinese policy of corporatism. The Chinese state initiated the establishment of numerous interest representing organizations that were initially state controlled but that, gradually, got more scope for manoeuvre (see Unger and Chan, 1995). It allowed a shift from a party command system that dominates directly, to a system which dominates partly through surrogates. Research showed, for instance, that in the tripartite negotiations between trade unions, employers' organizations and the state, the first two had very distinct voices reflecting the different interests of their constituencies (ibid.).

In China there has been a shift from an authoritarian state corporatism in the direction of societal corporatism in which the leadership is beholden to their membership.[7] A similar process also occurred in other East Asian countries. Thus, corporatism created a mechanism through which the grip of the state could be loosened. However, a precondition for this is a 'hard' state that is relatively immune to the pressure of lobbies.

Social preconditions for social and economic progress

Often, societies in communist countries were depicted as progressive while the regime was seen as regressive. Or, pluralist civil society was contrasted with mono-organizational official society. Implicitly, it was often assumed that communist societies in Central and Eastern Europe were converging towards modern Western societies. There were rising standards of living, higher educational levels, urbanization, the emergence of a youth culture, the coming to the fore of a social strata of professionals and the impact of globalization, etc. After the demise of communism and the coming to the fore of the pervasive impact of globalization, ideas about homogenization were reinforced because society was freed from the chains of the oppressive party-state.

However, once the party-state fell away in Russia, distrust and cheating became rampant in society, at all levels. Nowadays, neo-patrimonial social practices constitute an obstacle for introducing an efficient economic system. Paternalism remains strong and transparency would undermine an economic system in which economic relations are personalized. Also, economic relations are embedded in a polity where politicians and bureaucrats have a strong leverage over entrepreneurs. Compromising material (*kompromat*) gives political leaders arbitrary power. *Kompromat* is generated through the Byzantine legal system in which no one can fully comply with the law and in which almost everyone violates the law.

In Russia a neo-patrimonial polity and society emerged in which there is a close match between generally accepted social practices and the *modus operandi* of the political, economic and social systems. Political power is primordial and political power can easily be converted into wealth, but not vice versa as the recent political history of Russia shows. Russian politicians have an interest in keeping the neo-patrimonial polity as it is. Oligarchs are allowed to accumulate wealth under the precondition of loyalty to the political leader. In the neo-patrimonial polity the bureaucracy emerged as an independent political force and it strengthened its position in the post-Soviet transition.

The bureaucracy has become a maker of the rules of the game and not a 'rule-follower'. A neo-patrimonial kleptocracy emerged in which interests of new businessmen and bureaucracy merged.

It is the personalized, patrimonial character of the state that creates personalized and patrimonial rules in the economy. Government leaders often have an interest in resisting an institutionalization of rules that will restrict their political power and advantages in gaining wealth. In the patrimonial state, law does not exist to enforce justice but to maintain order. The state is not subject to legal constraints.

Towards a knowledge-based and innovative economy

Compared to Western economies, Russian economic growth since 1999 looks impressive. However, compared with other emerging economies, the record looks less impressive. Whereas during 1999–2007 average GDP growth in Russia was 6.7 per cent, in Nigeria and Iran, other major oil exporters, it was 6.2 and 5.0 per cent. But average growth in India was during that period 6.9 per cent, in China 9.3 per cent and Pakistan 5.1 per cent. During 1992–2007 Russian GDP grew by 73 per cent, that of Pakistan by 158 per cent, Nigeria by 145 per cent, India by 281 per cent and China by 632 per cent (IMF database: www.imf.org/external/data.htm). Despite robust economic growth since 1999, the record of Russia on a range of key economic indicators, especially innovation indicators, is not impressive.

Expenditures on information and communication technology are very meagre. High tech exports as a percentage of manufacturing exports was 9 per cent in 2006, whereas the average for low- and middle-income countries was 20 per cent (for China it was 30 per cent) (see Table 7.1).[8] The proportion of new or improved technological products in total exports was just 2.8 per cent over the period 1999 to 2005, compared to 38 per cent of total exports in EU-15 countries (World Bank, 2007b, p. 20). Only 0.7 per cent of Russian exports towards the European Union (25 countries) consisted of machinery and 0.1 per cent transport equipment, whereas 64.4 per cent related to energy (Eurostat, 2005). Cooper (2006) showed that the export performance of Russia compared to Brazil, India, Turkey and China is extremely weak especially in high technology fields,[9] for example, in civil aviation, Russia lags behind Brazil.[10] In car manufacturing Turkey, Brazil and even India are now outperforming Russia. Furthermore, Russia's integration into global production chains remains limited and only a small share of exports is part of producer driven networks (see World Bank, 2007b, p. 19).

Table 7.1 High tech exports, foreign direct investment, small- and medium-sized enterprises, domestic credit to private sector and gross capital formation

	Gross national income, Atlas method, per capita, current $, 2006	High tech exports as % of manufactured exports, 2006	Foreign direct investment 2005, $ million	Net inflow of foreign direct investment 2004 as % of GDP	Micro, small and medium sized enterprises, 2000–2004 % of total employment	Domestic credit to private sector (% of GDP), 2004	Gross capital formation (% of GDP) 1990	Gross capital formation (% of GDP) 2006
Russia	5,780	9	15,151	2.1	49.0	24.5	30	20
Ukraine	1,950	3	7,808	2.6	20.2	25.0	28	24
Belarus	3,380	3	305	0.7	9.7	14.0	27	30
Hungary	10,950	24	6,435	4.6	55.8	46.5	25	25
Poland	8,190	4	9,601	5.2	68.0	27.7	26	19
China	2,010	30	79,126	2.8	78	120.1	35	45
Low and middle income countries	2,000	20		2.6				27

Whereas in successful economies small- and medium-sized enterprises are a driving force, in Russia the role of this sector is modest. According to Dmitry Medvedev, only 1.2 per cent of small businesses are connected to science and innovation and only 18–20 per cent of all employees work in small businesses (Rosbusiness Consulting, 19 February 2008). According to minister Elvira Nabiullina the contribution of small business to GDP is in Russia two to three times less than in many developed and developing countries (*Vremya Novosti*, 29 February 2008). Most small businesses are in traditional consumer trades and some in traditional handicraft. There are scarce examples of vertical integration with large firms, and barely any horizontal networks (see Dallago, 2003). According to minister Nabiullina the treatment of small businesses is like a developed kind of feudalism: 'The municipalities have issued a huge number of different enactments in the sphere of trade regulation, creating a system with major administrative barriers.' And 'there is only one way for the small businesses to 'claw back' its expenditure on oiling the administrative mechanisms: by increasing prices. The prices of a number of products in regions that are close neighbours sometimes differ by tens of percent' (*Vremya Novosti*, 29 February 2008).

Peculiar for Russia is the extremely high share of people working in very big plants (larger than 2,500 people, 29.3 per cent of the working population in 2001). More important is the monopolistic market control in many sectors that could stifle innovation. In a sample (2003) representative of the Russian economy 22 large financial industrial groups, controlled by oligarchs, were controlling 47 per cent of employment and 45 per cent of sales in a sample (World Bank, 2005a, p. 136). Above all strategic sub-sectors, with a large average firm-size, suffer from monopolistic control: gas; oil; automobiles; and chemicals. According to minister Nabiullina, in the production of cement, one of the most important components of the costs of infrastructure projects, one firm accounts for 40 per cent of the market and more than 50 per cent in the European part of Russia, 'The result is that we are constantly financing monopoly prices out of the budget' (*Vremya Novosti*, 29 February 2008). According to the Finance Minister, Alexei Kudrin, the absence of competition represents the greatest challenge for Russia's economy (Interfax, 23 March 2007).

Gross capital formation was only 20 per cent of GDP in 2006 whereas in China it was 45 per cent. Domestic credit to the private sector as a percentage of GDP was 24.5 per cent in Russia against 120 per cent in China (2004). During the 1990s, the average age of Russian capital stock increased from 10.8 to 17.9 years and the share of capital stock of less than 5 years old (i.e., modern) was a mere 3.9 per cent (Hedlund, 2005,

p. 290). Under President Putin the investment ratio was far too low to have had a substantial impact on the capital stock. According to Yasin, the restructuring and modernization of Russia's infrastructure would cost about $3.5 trillion over the coming 20–25 years (Hedlund, 2005, p. 291).

According to Dmitry Luchshy, owner of a distribution company, the cost of transportation adds as much as 50 per cent to the cost of final products in Russia. He said: 'That's three times more than in developed countries... A few kilometres from Moscow and the roads are not lit up at all, you go into complete darkness. The transport system here is dangerous. We still have lots of bandits on the roads. In some regions some racketeers just approach the driver and ask for a hundred dollars because he passes their territory. There is not any control, any unified system and the drivers themselves lie about their expenses on the way, cheating on the businesses they work for (www.russiatoday.ru, 20 February 2008). After almost a decade of high economic growth, the Russian government did not manage to build new highways.

Although since 2006 large sums out of the stabilization fund have been used to prop up public services and infrastructure, very little has been done to tackle ingrained inefficiencies.

The priorities of Russian government are different from most countries at a comparable level of development (see Table 7.2). In 2007 total spending on national defence and security plus law enforcement amounted to 4.7 per cent of GNP, whereas government expenditures for education amounted to 3.6 per cent of GNP (World Bank, 2007b, p. 12).[11] Russia's educational system has deteriorated since 1991. Russia is faced with a corrupt and broken health care system that prevents an effective battle against rapidly spreading AIDS, tuberculosis and diphtheria. Only 14 per cent of Russians are satisfied with the health care system while only 24 per cent had access to proper medical care (Radio Free Europe/RL, 1 March 2008). This contributes to high mortality and declining life expectancy (see Table 7.3).

While China attracts a lot of foreign direct investment (FDI), Russia attracts FDI mainly in the energy and services sector (see Table 7.4).[12] FDI accounted in 2007 for about 2.2 per cent of GDP, half that received by Ukraine. More important is capital flight. Russia records the highest level of capital outflow among developing nations.[13] Russian citizens are holding $219.6 billion in foreign bank accounts according to the Bank for International Settlements (*Izvestia*, 15 December 2006).

By 1 October 2007, Russia had accumulated $450 billion of foreign currency reserves and another $150 billion in the federal stabilization fund (World Bank, 2007b, p. 12). In addition, private Russian capital

Table 7.2 Armed forces as percentage of total labour force, defence expenditures as percentage of GDP, expenditures on education

	Armed forces as % of labour force 1995	Armed forces as % of labour force 2004	Defence expenditures as % of GDP, 2005	Expenditures on education, 2005
Russia	2.5	2.0	4	3.6
Ukraine	2.0	1.2	2	6.4
Belarus	2.1	3.8	1	6.0 (2002)
Hungary	1.8	1.1	1	5.5 (2002)
Poland	1.7	0.9	2	5.4
China	0.6	0.5	2	1.9*
Middle income countries	1.8	1.2	2	

Notes: *The Chinese Education and Research Network gives for 2000 a percentage of 3.41 while the aim of Chinese government is to quickly raise the percentage of GDP spent on education to 4 per cent (www.edu.cn)
Source: *World Development Indicators* 2006

Table 7.3 Life expectancy at birth 1990, 2005

	1990	2005
China	69	72
Russia	69	65
Ukraine	70	68
Belarus	71	68
Poland	71	75
Hungary	69	73

Source: World Bank

invested abroad is estimated at about $200 billion (Menshikov, 2005). It brings the total of domestic under-investment to $800 billion. Menshikov (2005) concludes that 'the surplus profit received in the export sectors due to natural and export rent continued to go abroad, rather than being used in capital-deficit sectors'.

A worrisome trend is the short-term foreign borrowing of state corporations and the banking sector that attained $55 billion during the first nine months of 2007 (World Bank, 2007b, p. 8). This contributed to the growth of the corporate debt that attained $400 billion in early 2008 (*The Economist*, 1–7 March 2008). As *The Economist* observed, cheap foreign credits have oiled the emergence of Russian state capitalism and its foreign expansion (ibid.).

Table 7.4 Knowledge economy indicators

	Information and technology expenditures as % of GDP, 2005	Information and technology expenditures $ per capita, 2005	Internet penetration, as percentage of population, December 2007	Telephones per 100 people fixed main line, 2006	Telephones per 100 people mobile subscribers, 2006	Expenditures for R&D % of GDP, 1996–2003	Computers per 1000 inhabitants, 2007*
Russia	3.6	191	20.8	30.8	105.7	1.28	122
Ukraine	8.0	141	12.0	26.8	106.5	1.16	38
Belarus			56.3	34.7	61.4	0.62	
Hungary	5.8	632	35.2	33.4	98.9	0.95	146
Poland	4.2	331	36.6	29.8	95.4	0.56	193
China	5.3	90	15.9	27.8	34.8	1.31	41
Low and middle income countries	4.6	82		125	187	0.85	

Notes: *For comparison: Brazil had 16.09 computers per 100 inhabitants, Mexico 13.08 and Malaysia 19.16 (ITU)
Sources: *World Development Indicators* 2007, for Internet penetration Internet World Stats, for telephone penetration International Telecommunications Union

Table 7.5   Profit margins in various branches of industry (profit/sales %)

	2000	2003	2005
Industry average	24.7	13.5	15.3
Oil	66.7	20.7	34.7
Natural gas	30.0	20.5	
Steel	25.6	21.8	26.7
Non-ferrous metals	51.6	33.8	
Electric power	13.5	10.1	18.0
Machine-building and metal working	14.1	8.7	8.2
Chemical and petro-chemical	17.0	7.0	19.3
Wood and paper	16.5	7.0	11.2
Construction materials	9.0	9.5	3.9
Light industry	7.2	1.7	2.7
Food industry	10.1	8.5	7.9

Sources: For the years 2000 and 2003: Menshikov, 2005; for the year 2005: *Rossiiskii statistisheshkii ezhegodnik*, 2006, p. 657

The lion's share of investment in Russia is still going to energy, transportation, real estate and services and most of it is by state corporations (World Bank, 2006b, p. 4). Even in these sectors there have been insufficient investments.[14] In the oil and gas sector the infrastructure is obsolete and levels of waste are enormous. Production at three of Gazprom's four major fields is already declining and since 1991 no new gas fields have been opened up. The ministry of Industry and Energy warned that soon Russia will be faced with a shortage of gas if the decline in gas production continues (*Newsweek*, 7 January 2008). To keep production at current levels an annual investment of $11 billion is needed. But Gazprom is acquiring companies abroad and investing in the non-gas sector instead of securing future gas production. Gazprom can export gas to Europe thanks to cheap imports from Central Asian producers but the latter are finding new customers and alternative pipeline routes are developed in order to circumvent Gazprom's pipeline monopoly.

Other than metals, manufacturing received only 13 per cent of fixed capital investment during January to October 2006. Lack of investment is not related to a lack of money given the high level of capital flight. It seems that in Russia, economic restructuring hardly takes place and no adequate response to new technological challenges has been formulated. The state of physical infrastructure is very bad, especially public utilities services that are debt ridden and not able to modernize these services. As a result many are faced with power and heating supply interruptions.[15]

Often the growth of the service sector is seen as a positive development. However, the increase in Russia's services is largely based on a variety of real estate dealings and other trade activities. Between 1990 and 2004 construction and agriculture contracted to less than a third of their value. Profit margins in many industrial branches are relatively low and in some even declining (see Table 7.5).

In 2006, production output exceeded the 1991 levels only in two sectors of the national economy, namely oil and gas production and the paper and pulp industry (see Table 3.1). Only 32 aircraft and 95 helicopters were built in Russia in 2004, compared to 500 and 300 respectively in 1984.

There is a big problem with domestic demand as 15 per cent of the population appropriates 57 per cent of all income (*Newsweek*, 7 January 2008). Much of the spending power of the rich is used for purchasing imported luxury goods.

Between 2000 and 2008 macro-economic stability has been achieved but the economy has hardly been restructured and institutions that should underpin a modern economy have deteriorated rather than improved. As a result innovation has stalled. Reform in public services did not occur. Therefore political leaders admitted during the campaign for the presidential elections that the policy followed so far has led to a deadlock. Dmitry Medvedev emphasized that the key priority is innovation based development. Rather than being interested in economic growth rates he pointed to the quality of economic growth. According to Medvedev, 'this boom is characterized by investment being concentrated in the big companies, above all the state-owned companies. We have to admit that we have been running the economy in manual over these last years' (speech in Krasnoyarsk, 15 February 2008, www.medvedev2008.ru).

Employment in agriculture counts for 11 per cent of the Russian population in 2004 and the sector accounted for 5.1 per cent of GDP in 2005 (Federal Statistical Office). It means that the agricultural sector is important for Russia. However, state support for agriculture was withdrawn suddenly in January 1992 and agriculture has been left to its own devices. Only in 1999 was some state support reintroduced, in the form of import quotas (among others). In 2005 agriculture received 3.2 per cent of the total investment in the economy while it was 28 per cent in the period 1965 to 1985 (Ioffe, 2005, p. 180 and World Bank, 2006a, p. 7). As a result output in agriculture diminished drastically. In 2005 the output of grain was 75 per cent of the 1986–90 level, that of eggs 77 per cent, milk 57 per cent, pork 45 per cent, wool 21 per cent and sugar beet

64 per cent (*Rossiiskii statistisheshkii ezhegodnik*, 2006, pp. 445, 456). The number of cows in 2005 was 46 per cent of the 1990 count and that of pigs 35 per cent (*Rossiiskii statistisheshkii ezhegodnik*, 2006, p. 456). Restructuring hardly took place. The dominant type of agricultural enterprise is still the collective farm. Family farms cultivate just 7 per cent of the arable land and private plots comprise 11 per cent of the land. Half the farms are bankrupt *de jure* (this means their bank accounts are frozen) and another 25 per cent are *de facto* bankrupt. Between 14 and 20 per cent of all arable land has been abandoned, mainly in fertile regions (see Ioffe, 2005, p. 181). According to the federal statistical office sown land areas have decreased by 44.4 per cent between 1992 and 2005.

Recently the production of private farmers increased considerably in some segments: from 8.4 to 18.3 per cent of all grain production between 2000 and 2005 and from 14.2 to 26.6 per cent of all sunflower oil during the same period (Federal State Statistics Service: www.gks.ru/). In 2005, 80.3 per cent of all vegetables and 91.6 per cent of all potatoes were provided by private plots.

Between a third and half of all adults in the countryside are chronic alcoholics (Ioffe, 2005, p. 191). This leads to, among other things, rampant theft in the countryside. Many doctors and teachers have left because of low (or no) pay. This means that a supportive infrastructure has collapsed. Agronomists and other specialists have left, because after the reorganization of the collective and state farms they were no longer needed. Due to the breakdown of the supply system of pharmaceutical products, 38 million people in the countryside are without medicine (*Nezavisimaya Gazeta*, 25 December 2007).

Instead of innovating, the rural economy has deteriorated enormously since the start of the transition to a market economy. As a result, imports of food products soared.[16] Food import dependence became a particular problem after the prices of a number of staple goods started to rise sharply on the world market, fuelling inflation in Russia.

According to Voigt,

> current growth rates of Russia's economy in aggregate numbers can be attributed neither to the general success of transition nor to Putin's reforms. Moreover, they seem to camouflage a rather heterogeneous picture (divergence among regions and sectors). (Voigt, 2006, p. 138)

High growth rates in Russia since 1999 are mainly related to the rise in oil and gas export receipts, the usage of spare capacities in the manufacturing sector, the import substitution taking place after the devaluation of the ruble (see also Chapter 3), the new tax regime that stimulated production and the recent consumer credit boom.

The question emerges as to what extent is resource abundance good for Russia. According to a World Bank report:

> Resource abundance itself is not necessarily a disadvantage for economic growth but resource dependence does indeed appear to correlate with low long-run growth. On the other hand, a growing literature in development economics demonstrates that success in achieving comparative advantage on international markets in manufacturing and tradable services, particularly in knowledge-intensive and technologically sophisticated products, can be associated with rapid economic growth. (World Bank, 2006b, p. 12)

Resource abundance has contributed to an extremely high level of energy consumption. Energy use per capita in Russia is 3.6 times higher than in China (World Bank, 2005). The energy intensity in the iron and steel industry is about 0.31 toe/t in Russia compared to 0.17 toe/t in the USA, 0.12 toe/t in Germany and 0.1 toe/t in Japan (*Russian Analytical Digest*, 23 July 2007, p. 6).

To what extent is Russia's educational base a positive factor in building up a knowledge economy? Russia has, in principle, a good educational base but it is eroding fast due to long-term neglect causing the quality of education to deteriorate. Nowadays the wealthy send their children to study abroad. Or they buy Russian diplomas, even from prestigious institutions. Between 1991 and 2002 more than half a million scientists and computer programmers emigrated.[17]

Only two Russian universities are placed in the global top 500 in a recent rating of the world's universities. Just 1 per cent of GDP is dedicated to higher education while the European average is about 2 per cent (Sergei Guriyev, *Moscow Times*, 30 January 2007).

The share of trained skilled and unskilled workers is very low in Russia (7.7 and 1.4 per cent respectively). About 44 per cent of Chinese skilled workers are trained and 28 per cent of Chinese unskilled workers (World Bank, 2006b, p. 22). Many Russian enterprises are already experiencing shortages of skilled labour. Among investment climate constraints, larger Russian manufacturing companies rank the importance of 'lack of skilled and qualified workers' only behind taxation. In the survey, twice as many enterprises (27 per cent) complained about being understaffed, as opposed to overstaffed (13 per cent) (World Bank, 2006b, p. 22).

Russia has an impressive number of researchers per 1 million of population (around 3400, slightly higher than South Korea and Germany

(World Bank, 2006b, p. 20).[18] This contrasts sharply with the manufacturing value added per worker (less than \$10,000 in Russia against about \$40,000 in South Korea and almost \$70,000 in Germany).

Nevertheless, Russia is doing well in terms of patents. The Russian patent office ranks ninth according to the total number of patent filings in 2004 (Japan was first, the USA second, Korea third and China fourth). If counting resident patent filings per million inhabitants Russia is doing less well, i.e., ranked sixteenth with 160 patents, 2004, while Japan is ranked first with 2,884 patents and Korea second with 2,189 patents per million inhabitants.[19]

If looking at the patents filed in the US patent and trademark office, an alternative indicator, given the importance attached internationally to patents filed in the USA, the picture looks less impressive for Russian research. The number of patents filed in the USA was for Russia during the years 2004 and 2005 160 and 148 (and continuously declining from 234 in 2001) whereas the figures for China are 597 and 565, for South Korea 4,671 and 4,591, for Hungary 52 and 48, for Norway 243 and 220 and for The Netherlands 1,273 and 933 (patent counts by country/state, all patents, all types, 1 January 1977–31 December 2005).

The number of patent filings is just one output indicator for research and development. Unfortunately, the Russian good record in domestic patent filing does not translate into international competitiveness of Russian industry or a willingness to spend on innovation. R&D as a share of sales in Russia amounts to 2.6 per cent, as compared to 3.1 per cent in Brazil, 3.9 per cent in India and 5.9 per cent in China (World Bank, 2006b, p. 20).

The problem with Russian research is that it has been squeezed since transition began, as a result the majority of the very best sought employment in the West. There was also an internal brain drain: researchers moved to other occupations in order to survive. Many researchers kept their jobs but had second or even third jobs in order to survive.

Despite high enrolment in higher education, the high share of researchers in the population, and aggregate outlays for R&D in GDP, that place Russia on the level of Germany and South Korea, Russia still lags well behind OECD and other large middle-income countries in R&D outputs. Also the number of scientific publications per capita is low. Researchers in Poland, India, Brazil and South Korea generate two to three times as many scientific publications per person. German and Spanish researchers generate six times as many (World Bank 2006b, p. 19).

About 60 per cent of all R&D is financed by the government in Russia, against less than 20 per cent in Korea, about 25 per cent in Germany and about 50 per cent in Hungary. The public science sector is large, fragmented and largely cut off from the enterprise sector. The public science sector is also cut off from education. In the Russian tradition, research is not done in universities but in separate research institutions.

Russia has an advanced IT solutions industry and Russian computer engineers and software developers are very well trained. They are in demand in the West. However, they are generally bad in implementation. According to 2005 data from the World Economic Forum, Russia occupies 62nd place out of 104 in implementing new information and communications technology (*RIA Novosti*, 18 December 2006). Government departments are also unwilling to introduce modern computer based management methods or to use IT in order to interact with the public. According to a World Bank report (2007b, p. 19), ICT only plays a small role in productivity growth.

Other newly emerging industrializing countries, like India, China, Brazil and Mexico are rapidly catching up with Russia on key knowledge economy indicators which are shown in Table 7.4. It will be difficult for Russia to compete with these countries given lower wage levels and given the fact that these countries are moving successfully up market, being able to compete in markets where Russia assumed it might develop a competitive advantage.

Despite strong economic growth Russia continues to face a big development problem: spatial imbalances; deteriorating infrastructure; low investment rates; a demographic crisis; and lack of competitiveness in industry. The 2007 United Nations Development Report found that over the past 15–20 years all indicators show a worsening of human potential in Russia. Furthermore there is the lack of competition in many regions and sectors, low skill-levels of employees, a deteriorating R&D sector, mass poverty and big inequalities, bureaucratic interference and massive corruption.

Why are these problems in Russia so much more pronounced than in Central European countries? The comparison with China is also compelling. The argument in this book has been that there is a major problem in economic governance structures that goes beyond the question of private and state, or plan and market. Russia is faced with a bureaucratic regime that stifles economic development. Still, in most cases, the way to economic prosperity is the right connections in the bureaucracy and politics. There is hardly a notion within the economic and political elite of the public good. As Ledeneva (2006, p. 139) has noted, entrepreneurship 'is used up in circumventing difficulties and scheming to go around formal rules and procedures rather than focusing on improvement and innovation'.

The new capitalism in Russia is embedded in a semi-feudal political order that furthers rent-seeking rather than productive activity. This has been clearly shown in the case of extracting industries. Russia can be compared, in this respect, with a range of other petro-states. Russia is different compared to most other petro-states with respect to the research base and the educational level of the population. However, here there is a huge discrepancy between the high level of human capital and the low level of social and organizational capital. Therefore President Putin identified as the main problem of the Russian economy 'its extreme ineffectiveness' (*Itar-Tass*, 11 March 2008).

The problem with most studies dealing with the Russian economy is that they ignore the socio-political causes of economic underdevelopment. They fail to see that the economic system is socially embedded. The challenge is to show how insight into inter-linkages between society, the polity and the economy may contribute to recommendations for economic policies.

Any path towards sustainable development goes through the abolishment of crucial features of Russian neo-patrimonialism. On the other hand, path creation should take into account the legacy of the past that is constraining policy options.

Path dependent path creation will not lead to an Anglo-Saxon styled liberal capitalism. A successful Russian path shows state-led economic development with an important role for the market but a crucial role for the state in strategic sectors. It also implies protection against foreign hostile takeovers and capital flight.

As Schienstock (2006, pp. 23–4) observed:

> Path creation is a collective and even inter-organizational undertaking, in which an organization's capabilities and relational aspects are more important than individual competencies and personal characteristics... Path creation can not be conceptualized as a rational decision making process; it involves vested interests and power games. The path creation period is a period of trial-and-error experimentation and confrontation between the forces of change and those of persistence, but also between different groups of modernizers.

A new path is a contested terrain. Russia needs what North (1990, p. 81) characterized as social flexibility,

> an adaptively efficient path . . . allows for a maximum of choices under uncertainty, for the pursuit of various trial methods of undertaking activities, and for an efficient feedback mechanism to identify choices that are relatively inefficient and to eliminate them.

The state should be a coercive force able to monitor property rights and enforce contracts effectively (Hedlund, 2005, p. 312). It should be recalled that there is no private property without government. One of the greatest mistakes of the 1990s was to see the state as standing in opposition to markets.

In a positive scenario, in all likelihood, the emphasis will be on administrative regulation rather than the rule of law as rooted in the separation of powers. The state will have Hobbesian traits rather than Lockean. But crucial is that property rights are respected although there may be a less exclusive concept of property rights compared to the Anglo-Saxon tradition. Russia will resist the unrestricted opening up of its economy. In a positive scenario a national capitalism will be developed with a strong protectionist bias and an effective industrial policy.

Fostering modernization of society and economy

According to Weber *et al.* (1979, p. 1095), production oriented capitalism is not compatible with patrimonialism: 'The patrimonial state lacks the political and procedural predictability, indispensable for capitalist development, which is provided by the rational rules of modern bureaucratic administration.'

This does not imply that capitalism cannot develop in Russia. First all, Russia has been identified as having a state and society that has strong patrimonial features but also has been characterized as a hybrid. It has been described as neo-patrimonial. Moreover, recent history shows many examples of patrimonial societies transforming into modern industrialized societies, sometimes retaining features of a patrimonial and/or traditional society. Japan, Taiwan, Singapore and South Korea are examples. However, these societies had a strong state. It seems that in any positive scenario, the state should start enhancing trust in society by establishing and maintaining clear rules and therewith predictability.

Reform of the state administration and state governance should get top priority. Legal change is itself not sufficient as reform should have a social base. The state can not act as a *deus ex machina* and needs to find support from within society.

148

	Polity/state	Economy
Authoritarian liberalism	– Authoritarian state – No attempt at building national consensus – Army/secret service fulfil crucial role – Comprador bourgeoisie – High degree of state capture	– Export driven growth – Opening to world market – Aiming at FDI – Increasing import competition – Washington Consensus/ Free market – Some strategic industries disappear
Predatory clan state	– Bureaucratic and repressive regime – Comprador bourgeoisie – Nationalist – Symbiosis big business and bureaucracy	– Rent seeking dominates – Petro state – Corruption – Involution – Further privatization
Fragmentation	– Bureaucratic regime – Fragmented elite/weak government – Lumpenbourgeoisie – Growing power and autonomy for regional elites – High degree of state capture – Continuous elite infighting about all aspects of policies	– Spatial fragmentation – Secession wars – No clear-cut economic policy – Rent-seeking dominates – Involution
Developmental state	– Elite and societal consensus – Democratically elected Party of Power – Corporatism – National bourgeoisie with a clear notion of 'national interest' – Low degree of state capture – Big business encapsulated – Lesser role for bureaucracy	– Managed trade regime – Developmental state – Protection of infant industries – Limits to capital flight and currency convertibility – National capitalism – Less corruption
State corporatist/ nationalist	– Bureaucratic regime – Authoritarian state corporatism – Coalition of siloviki/ nationalist forces/business elites/bureaucracy – Consensus building – Big business submitted	– Managed trade regime – National capitalism – State led development – Stop capital export – Corruption – Managed trade regime

Scheme 7.1   Possible alternative scenarios for Russia (timescale 15 to 20 years)

Society	International	Driving force
– Growing inequality – Fragmentation – Coercion more important than consensus – Mass poverty	– Pro-Western – Free trade	– Big internationally oriented business
– Growing inequality – Coercion over consensus	– Pro-Western	– Bureaucracy and business
– Growing inequalities – Drastic deterioration of social situation	– Conflicts with neighbouring states – Foreign capital controls strategic sectors – Major concern for international community (smuggle of weapons of mass destruction) – internationalization of conflicts	– Centrifugal forces (especially regional elites that strive after autonomy)
– From state to societal corporatism – Less inequality – Cohesion policies – Investment in human capital	– Distance to Western led institutions of global economic governance – Alliance with China/India	– Broad coalition of forces (business, power structures, bureaucracy, societal organizations) around 'national interest' and harmony
– State corporatism – Less inequality – Organic conception of people and nation	– Anti-Western – Protectionism – Conflicts with neighbouring countries – International isolation	– Siloviki and domestically oriented business – Reactionary harmony-of-interest ideology

The restoration of the Kremlin's authority, especially over the regions, seems important because it restrains the opportunities of local lords to plunder their regions. However, at the same time regional actors should have a certain degree of autonomy because they are better able to exploit the regional development potential than actors in the centre. The regain of control over natural resources also seems a strategically positive move to prevent the drain of resources through the oligarchs that are controlling the nation's natural wealth. In this context the government should strictly regulate international capital transfers.

So far the government has neglected the development of the physical infrastructure of the country. Here the state can and should play a central role. Also, the government could do much more to combat corruption and discipline bureaucrats.

Because civil society is so weak, government should play a leading role in combating abuse of power at all levels. But how can the government be made accountable? It is public knowledge as to what extent (former) officials of the secret service are dominating the upper echelons of the bureaucracy. At the same time many among them are involved in business. How can these men play a leading role in cleaning up the state bureaucracy?

The same question emerges in the case of China that has experienced dynamic economic development for almost 30 years. Although corruption in China is widespread, as is abuse of public power, the Chinese authorities seem committed to combat the worst abuses, given the periodic anti-corruption campaigns. Corruption is not so widespread as to paralyze economic development. Dmitry Medvedev noticed that corruption 'weakens when the public becomes strong, when this phenomenon is being opposed by the public themselves along with a strong government' (*Interfax*, 19 March 2008).

In elaborating alternative scenarios for Russia for the coming 15/20 years, we have first to define the major problems then the major actors and factors. Subsequently, driving forces have to be identified for each of the scenarios. These are detailed in Scheme 7.1.

Major difficulties include governance problems, centrifugal tendencies, widespread poverty and international competitiveness. Major actors include the state bureaucracy, the secret services, the oligarchs and their clans and regional elites, major factors comprise, among others, the West and its institutions, ethnic minorities and energy prices.

The first scenario is authoritarian-liberal. With coercion economic liberalism is imposed that translates into the unchecked rule of internationally oriented big business. Economic policy is aimed at attracting foreign direct investment and opening up to the world market. There are no restrictions for rent-seeking and capital export. The armed forces assure stability. State corporations are privatized.[20]

A second scenario is that of a predatory clan state in which rent-seeking is dominant and a bureaucracy suffocates economic life. It is the scenario of a clan state in which the 'national interest' is subordinate to the private interests of the ruling clans. Instead of economic development there is involution, i.e. a system that eats it own economic base.

A third scenario comprises a gradual falling apart – a fragmentation. The scenario can be compared with the dissolution of the Soviet Union. A weak state cannot prevent a secession of several autonomous republics, especially in Southern Russia, while many regions are governed like feudal fiefdoms, imposing their own order irrespective of the policies of the centre. There is state capture by big financial-industrial groupings on the federal and regional levels.

A fourth scenario is a societal-corporatist scenario (developmental state) in which the sharp edges of a national capitalism are softened by social policies and in which corporatist organizations try, to a certain extent, to channel interest articulation. There will be a gradual transformation from state- to societal-corporatism as is visible in China. As a result corporatist organizations take over tasks of the state bureaucracy with the net result of less bureaucratic interference and corruption. Elements of the welfare state remain. The development model is soft-authoritarian. Half of industry remains state controlled with a very limited opening up to the world market. The regions would receive more autonomy and there would be a gradual extraction from neo-patrimonialism.

The fifth scenario (state corporatist/nationalist) is an authoritarian-nationalist scenario in which the secret service plays the major role and controls a significant part of the economy. The power structures fulfil a crucial role in politics and the economy. In this scenario there is a resurgence and revitalization of the Russian army. The ideology is nationalistic and xenophobic and ethnic minorities are oppressed. Oligarchs play an important role in the economy but they are submitted to the political authority and their power is curtailed. There is a partial opening up towards the world market but there are strained relations with neighbours. There is very limited autonomy for the regions and little attention for consensus building. That is in line with the inertia scenario identified by minister for economic development Nabiullina which implies 'that we continue the current policy, changing neither the institutions nor the economy and exploiting the competitive advantages that we currently have.'

Conclusion

After the abolishment of the centrally planned economy and the introduction of a formal institutional framework for market economy a pre-modern form of networking rather than the market became the main coordination mechanism in the economy. Behind the façade of a market economy a clan economy emerged. The transformation from plan to clan built on the Russian legacy. In 1991 Russia was not a *tabula rasa*. A reconfiguration of elements from the past combined with some aspects of a liberal market economy, resulting in a hybrid that is more like patrimonialism than a liberal market economy. The new rules are very different from those in liberal market economies but show consistency and resistance to change.

Many will argue that the market is emerging and that institutions of market economy have been strengthened and that these will increasingly discipline the participants in the market. Also, a middle-class is growing that, it is argued, will support a market economy and democracy. Above all, the economy has, since 1999, experienced robust growth with foreign investors flocking towards Russia.

However, here it is argued that despite growth there is not much development. It is reflected in: deteriorating education and health provision; the deteriorating physical infrastructure; a brain drain; poor performance in high technology sectors; low productivity in research; capital flight; widespread poverty; and increasing spatial imbalances. Russia has a major development problem.

It has been shown that this is related to major deficiencies in governance structures, on all levels, that produce deficient incentive structures. The problem lies with the rules of the game in society and economy.

Business groups dominate the economy. They are organized like clan networks with shell companies created with the aim of siphoning off profits. They often constitute monopolies that prevent competition emerging. They are often helped by officials that participate in these groups. The new Russian businessman is more often a squeezer than a builder.

The bureaucracy is a major player in the economy. It has expanded enormously in size and acts not as a facilitator but as a gate keeper to economic opportunities. Officials take bureaucratic rents. They, rather than a free market, are the way towards economic success. They are only in a limited way rule-followers. Bureaucrats often make the rules. Together with politicians, they are purposeful creators of an uncertainty that they are using as a means to discipline the actors they ought to serve. The state and its bureaucracy are not only privatized by wealthy businessmen who buy influence but also by bureaucrats who consider their position as their property, and by politicians who are using the state to further their private interests. Political power and property are increasingly merged. A casualty is the rule of law.

However, this privatization of the state has limits as has been shown in disciplining dissident oligarchs. On the national level there is the priority of politics in the sense that the Kremlin defines the framework in which economic actors can act. Oligarchs who were in opposition to the Kremlin were neutralized. Private property, in Russia, is conditional.

President Putin strengthened the state after the anarcho-liberalism of President Yeltsin in which the Russian state was threatened by centrifugal forces. However, despite authoritarian tendencies the Russian state is not almighty while government is often not able to implement its policies. Authoritarianism masks a weak state.

State governance is undermined by a bureaucracy that is well-equipped to circumvent the rules in order to further its own interests. The role of the bureaucracy has become so overwhelming that we can characterize Russia as a bureaucratic regime.

Corruption and rent-seeking are not aberrations but central to Russian neo-patrimonialism. It is part of the mechanism of power and economic governance. Moreover, criminal networks are linked to the world of business and politics. It goes together with short-termism and holds a large share of the shadow economy. Russia has an in-built inferior equilibrium that furthers rent-seeking over productive activity.

In many ways economic life in contemporary Russia is reminiscent of Soviet and even tsarist times, especially when comparing the informal institutional framework that governs the behaviour of organizations, enterprises and individuals. When considering Russia's history and its economic backwardness it is easy to see that this state has persisted over the ages. When compared to the most advanced economies it can be seen that Russia's attempts to catch up contain many similar features (see Chapter 1).

There is a match between dominant social practices and attitudes on the one hand and the functioning of the polity, bureaucracy and the economy on the other hand. The rules of the game in society and economy are not so much mirrored in the formal institutions but internalized by the people in the form of deeply rooted attitudes and social practices. Crucial within the set of persistent social practices that are significant in political and economic life is the cult of power that underpins the legal nihilism, the aversion to transparency, the preference of mores over laws and the aversion to accountability. A cult of power prevents conflict resolving mechanisms from developing that might adapt formal institutions to social and economic change. The cult of power prevents the development of feedback mechanisms that might induce appropriate evolutionary change. The cult of power determines the mode of operation of Russia's institutions.

Although Russia has been faced with major social change, specific attitudes proved to be quite inert. Persistent, throughout Russian history, was the preference of personalized rule over a regime of rules. Even when a window of opportunity opened, Russians typically failed to demand a regime of rules. Powerful constituencies could be easily silenced once their vital interests were threatened. This was shown, for example, by the lack of resistance on the part of the oligarchs when the Kremlin, under President Putin, turned on them. This is in line with a long history of submission to authoritarian rule. The middle class, also affected by the long history, did not resist authoritarian tendencies.

The result is, among others, a deep divide between the state and society and the elite and society. The weakness of interest representing institutions is correlated with weak feedback mechanisms in society that prevent evolutionary institutional change taking place that might correct ill-conceived policies. Also, weak conflict regulating mechanisms prevent complex governance mechanisms from emerging that are characteristic of the most advanced economies.

In this book, the functioning of the state bureaucracy has been pictured as a major obstacle for social and economic development. At the same time, it is argued that the state should transform into a developmental state, in a similar way to the transformation experienced by the states in eastern Asia. However, important preconditions for a developmental state are now lacking. There is no major constituency discernable within the ruling elite that is willing to tackle the problem of corruption and abuse of economic power. However, if the emerging corporatism transforms into a societal corporatism it can eventually contribute to a transformation of the role of the state as the examples of various East Asian states have shown. In this way a necessary dispersal of power away from the state and big business can be accomplished. The road ahead is full of obstacles. The example of Ukraine, with its Orange

Revolution, has shown the opportunities and constraints encountered in the transformation of Russian type neo-patrimonialism.

This book underlines the enormity of Russia's development challenges, especially when compared to the newly industrialized countries in South-East and East Asia. Highlighting cultural factors does not imply a cultural determinism. The eventual changeover from authoritarianism to democracy has to be carefully managed and is the result of a changing correlation of forces in society. Societal constraints, i.e., path dependence, have to be taken into account. The shift to a new economic development trajectory and a knowledge-based economy implies a fundamental change in economic governance mechanisms and authority patterns in society. It also implies a change in the functioning of the ruling and business elites and a redefining of the role of the state.

Russia is not doomed to under-development and authoritarian rule. It has major assets: human capital; natural resources; and a large internal market. Russia has a huge development potential that only can be exploited once governance mechanisms are developed that allow the human and natural potential to be converted to wealth. Markets have to be developed in conjunction with an efficient and strong state that allows a plurality of interest representing institutions to develop and respects property rights.

Notes

1 Divergence in Post-Socialism: The Role of Culture

1. For example; the studies 'Monitoring European Integration – The Impact of Eastern Europe (1990, CEPR Annual Report, London) and the study 'Reforms in Eastern Europe and the role of the ECU' – a report by the macro-financial study group of the ECU Banking Association (1990, Paris) expected that the transition to a smoothly functioning market economy could be completed in Central Europe within a time frame of five years, given the assumption that no major social and political instability would occur. Both studies envisaged growth rates amounting to 6–7 per cent during the 1990s.

2. We are not taking into account the 'progress in transition indicators' of the European Bank for Reconstruction and Development because instead of transition they measure the degree to which recommendations of the global institutions of economic governance are followed up. In other words, they measure the degree to which institutions of a liberal market economy are introduced, i.e. the degree of privatization and the degree of liberalization. This resulted in Slovenia achieving, in 2006, a lower rank in the composite transition progress indicator (2.85) than Bulgaria (2.96) although Slovenia shows better performance on all economic performance indicators. There are alternative methods to assess corruption, for example: the percentage of respondents who had been victimized by administrative bribery (1996–2000, the UN International Crime Victim Surveys, see Shleifer, 2005, p. 179). This gives a slightly different picture to the corruption perception index. Then countries like Belarus, Lithuania and Romania appear to be more corrupt than Russia.

3. Many transitologists analysed correlations between extra-economic factors and economic performance. With respect to differences in initial conditions Havrylyshyn mentions (2006, p. 126): natural resources; landlocked status; distance from Brussels; years under communism; levels of per capita income; share of industry; concentration of heavy/military industry; type of first government (communist/other); ethnic homogeneity; major religion; educational attainment; war/civil conflict; membership of international organizations; and continuity of old elites. Among the non-economic aspects of transition policies Havrylyshyn mentions: effectiveness of rule of law; type of government (left/right); frequency of government change; degree of democracy; and amount of foreign aid.

4. According to Hedlund (2005, p. 17) culture is a wide range of informal, mainly norm related factors that underpin the formal rules. Hofstede and Hofstede (2005, p. 3) used the analogy of culture as 'software for the mind', seeing culture as acting mental programmes. 'It is the collective programming of the mind that distinguishes the members of one group or category of people from others' (p. 4). For literature about the relationship between economy and culture, see Hedlund, 2005, p. 9.

5. The Baltic provinces also knew special arrangements. A special charter spelling out individual rights and privileges for the nobility was in force (Hedlund, 2005, p. 207).
6. Value patterns grouped according to the variables 'power distance', 'individualism', 'uncertainty avoidance' and 'masculinity' show a clear regional grouping that comprises Russia, Romania, Bulgaria, Serbia, Croatia and Slovenia that correlate among each other to a high degree (calculated on the basis of data in Hofstede and Hofstede, 2005). Remarkable is that the Catholic nations of Slovenia and Croatia are grouped here with Orthodox nations. Other pronounced groups are Poland and the Czech Republic on the one hand and Finland and Estonia on the other hand. However, correlations point to similarity of patterns. If also taking into account the cumulative differences in the scores on four variables it appears that the distance between Russia on the one hand and Serbia and Romania on the other hand is much smaller (31 and 23 points) compared to the distance between Russia on the one hand and Bulgaria, Croatia and Slovenia on the other hand (46, 45 and 58 points respectively). Bulgaria is very close to both Croatia (11 points) and Slovenia (28 points). The distance between Poland and Croatia (89 points) and Poland and Slovakia (132 points), all Catholic nations, is notable. The distance between Poland and the Czech Republic is 69 points.
7. Also in terms of subjective well-being (the satisfaction with life, on a 1–10 scale, happiness index, 2006) the regionalization given above is very pronounced: Bulgaria (4.2) and Romania (5.0); Ukraine (3.6), Russia (4.4) and Belarus (4.0); Hungary (5.6), Czech Republic (6.4), Slovakia (5.5) and Poland (5.9); Estonia (5.1), Lithuania (4.6) and Latvia (4.7). The Baltic States are very similar to the Balkan States. Here we should take into account the large proportion of Russians in the Latvian and Estonian populations (29.2 per cent in Latvia and 25.6 per cent in Estonia) and the fact that the transitional recession there was very severe (see http://www.eur.nl/fsw/happiness/).
8. Belarusian human rights defender Ales Byalatshn said on 31 January 2007 that there are seven political prisoners in the country (Radio Free Europe, 1 February 2007).
9. Several independent polls (among others Gallup) showed support for President Lukashenko of over 50 per cent. According to a letter, allegedly from Belarusian KGB officers who were involved in the counting of the vote, Lukashenko got not the official 83 per cent in the vote for the presidential elections of 19 March 2006, but only 49 per cent (*Gazeta Wyborcza*, 27 April 2006).
10. While in Belarus real wages were, in 2005, 95 per cent higher than in 1990, in Russia they were 19 per cent lower (*Rossiiskii Statistisheshkii Ezhegodnik*, 2006, p. 757).
11. Industrial production in 2005 was 53 per cent higher that in 1990 while in Russia 32.7 per cent lower (*Rossiisii Statistisheshkii Ezhegodnik*, 2006, p. 773).
12. According to Ioffe (2004) 63.6 per cent of Byelorussians work in the public sector.
13. The interdependence of cultural and economic change is not widely researched by economists mainly because of the difficulties involved in

establishing a clear and unambiguous link between cultural and economic change. It is mainly non-economists who focus attention on this issue.

14. According to Bourdieu (1990, p. 56), habitus is the acquired mode of acting and thinking, which is executed in a semi-automatic, unconscious manner in everyday conduct. Habitus is 'embodied history, internalized as a second nature and so forgotten as history'. It is 'the active presence of the whole past of which it is a product'.

2   Soviet Russia: Revolution and Continuity

1. There are numerous accounts of the darkness of the Russian countryside, especially in nineteenth century novels. Maltreatment of women and children was common. As peasants were completely unprotected against the arbitrary violence of the police and the nobility, violence was reproduced in the smaller circle of the family. Figes described the history of Russia, including the Bolshevik revolution, as a 'people's tragedy', implying that the people at large were not merely witnesses or victims of events, but active participants in the historical drama. According to Figes, 'It was the weakness of Russia's democratic culture which enabled Bolshevism to take root. This was the legacy of Russian history, of centuries of serfdom and autocratic rule, that had kept the common people powerless and passive' (Figes, 1996, p. 809).

2. Private ownership of land was not created until 1785 (Pipes, 1974, p. 157).

3. Until the nineteenth century townspeople did not own their houses or the land on which they stood (Pipes, 1974, p. 11).

4. Per capita output of industry remained far below those achieved in the West (Spulber, 2003, p. 144). While electricity output in Russia was 16 kWh per capita, it was 320 in Germany, 2029 in Britain and 875 in France (1913, Spulber, 2003, p. 144). Iron and copper mining was dominated by Dutch and German engineers and the oil industry by the British. In 1899, at least 60 per cent of coal was produced by foreign companies. Although most industrial enterprises were created by foreigners, in 1900 just under half the capital in industry was of foreign origin (Sowell, 1998, p. 212). In 1914, 47 per cent of all Russian Government bonds, 74 per cent of all Russian municipal bonds, and 40 per cent of all other kinds of bonds were in foreign hands. Of the capital exported to Europe by the leading industrial nations, 25 to 30 per cent had found its way to Russia (Berend and Ranki, 1982, p. 85).

5. For example, only 3 per cent of Russian international shipping was in Russian vessels (Sowell, 1998, p. 211).

6. The rural population in 1914 accounted for 84.7 per cent of the population of Russia (excluding Finland and Poland). Most of the cultivated land belonged to the traditional subsistence sector (Spulber, 2003, pp. 139, 140).

7. In the nineteenth century, the initiative to establish a new factory almost always came from the government. New enterprises had to be personally approved by the tsar. By the onset of World War 1, foreign corporations accounted for one third of Russia's corporate capital (Goldman, 2003, pp. 36, 40).

8. The merchant cities of Novgorod and Pskov, which had emerged beyond the Mongol reach, were regarded by the Hanseatic cities as creditworthy. This trait disappeared on their annexation to Muscovy. The Hanse forbade all credit to Russians. It was observed that cheating became endemic. This was commonplace in report after report over the centuries. A British ambassador to St Petersburg in Catherine the Great's time remarked more broadly 'The form of government certainly is and will always be the principal cause of want of virtue and genius in the country, as making the motive of one and the reward of the other both depend upon accident and caprice' (*The Times Literary Supplement*, 17 May 2006, review of Hosking, 2006).
9. Friedrich Engels wrote about a possible revolution in Russia: 'Once it starts, it will drag along its peasants and then you will see scenes by which those of '93 [the French Thermidor-HvZ] will fade' (quoted in Visnevskii, 2005, p. 12).
10. Voslensky, 1980, p. 91.
11. See also Hoffmann, 1994, and Hosking, 2006, pp. 112–113, 119.
12. The concept *Homo Sovieticus* has first been used in a Soviet collective work published in 1974. Later, the concept was taken up by critics of the Soviet regime to describe the character promoted by the Soviet system. According to Maximov (Hirszowicz, 1980, p. 172), *Homo Sovieticus* is a man who is docile, amoral, anti-social, anti-democratic, an opportunist mainly concerned with organizing his own life without much regard to his fellow citizens. Sheila Fitzpatrick (1999) describes *Homo Sovieticus* as 'a string puller, an operator, a time-server, a freeloader, a mouther of slogans, and much more. But above all, he was a survivor' (p. 227).
13. Vasily Grossman let in 'Life and Fate' (1985, p. 283) one of the personages say that 'our Russian humanism has always been cruel, intolerant, sectarian. From Avvakum to Lenin our conception of humanity and freedom has always been partisan and fanatical. It has always sacrificed the individual to some abstract idea of humanity'.
14. Gershenkron wrote about the pre-revolutionary intelligentsia: 'There are almost no normal people among us – everybody is acerbic, withdrawn, restless, faces contorted in a grimace, because one was either crossed or saddened ... we infect each other with bitterness and have so saturated the atmosphere with our neurasthenic attitudes towards life that a fresh person, say, one who lived abroad for a while, could not help feeling suffocated in our midst' (quoted in Shalin,1996, p. 89).
15. This is reminiscent of the practice of Ivan the Terrible. If an individual incurred Ivan's distrust, not only the victim died, but in some cases his wife and children, servants and friends. Sometimes even his livestock perished with him (Hedlund, 2005, p. 155).
16. The Russian Orthodox faith consists mainly in the belief in the magic effect of ritual and the Church failed to impose demands with respect to the social responsibility of believers and the importance of learning. By sticking to Church Slavonic and discouraging the study of Latin and Greek, the link with Greek and Roman thought was cut off. In Russia, the authority of the tsar, who got his authority directly from God, stood above individual morality. The subordination of the Church to the tsar was shown by Joachim when he addressed the tsar on becoming patriarch in the seventeenth century: 'Sovereign, I know neither the old nor the new faith, but whatever the

Sovereign orders I am prepared to follow and obey in all respects' (Billington, 1970, p. 145). Russian spirituality glorified non-resistance to evil and voluntary suffering. Russian Orthodoxy helped to provide the religious foundations for Russian autocracy and helped to insulate Russia from the influence of Catholic and Protestant Europe.

17. This predisposition was accompanied by a lack of action and numbness. Nadezhda Mandelstam (1970, p. 44) describes how in the 1930s a kind of numbness, the first symptoms of lethargy appeared, 'a plague that infected our minds'.

18. Nadezhda Mandelstam writes that among the people of her generation, 'only a very few have kept clear minds and memories. In M's generations everybody was stricken with a kind of sclerosis at an early stage.' (1970, p. 298).

19. The ratio of salary difference between an engineer and a worker went from 2.15 in 1940, to 1.15 in 1980. In the building industry this ratio changed from 2.42 down to 0.98, and in agriculture (state farms) from 2.43 to 1.43 (Shlapentokh, 1989, p. 81).

20. As quoted in Shlapentokh, 1989, p. 47.

21. According to Nadezhda Mandelstam (1970, p. 266), 'not everyone wants to be a Napoleon, but people cling desperately to what little power they have and will do their best to get all they can out of it. There has never been such a proliferation of petty tyrants, and our country is still swarming with them'.

22. Sociological research shows that up to the middle of the 1980s the majority of Russians were satisfied with their life. The one-third that was dissatisfied constituted the least educated and least active part of the Russian population. A national survey conducted in 1976 found that on a 5-point scale, most Russians evaluated their lives with a grade of 4. The American way of life did not deserve more than a 2 or 3, with the best life being in Czechoslovakia, which scored almost 5. Of Russian immigrants in the USA, interviewed in the middle of the 1980s, 59 per cent claim to have been satisfied with their standard of living, while 14 per cent were very dissatisfied (Shlapentokh, 1998, pp. 34, 35). The question is, of course, how we should interpret these survey findings. See Chapter 4.

23. Although most people have victims of repression in their families, it remained, usually, a sublimated part of their histories. Usually, parents kept silent about Stalinist repression with regard to their children. People stayed far from discussions about politics although everybody was joking about it. In a certain way, the Russian people can be considered as a people without a past. One can speak in the case of Russia about structural social amnesia, brought about by the party-state. Nadezhda Mandelstam (1970, p. 58) noticed in this context that 'Soviet citizens have achieved a high degree of mental blindness, with devastating consequences for their whole psychological make-up'. The sublimation of history has been stimulated by the communist authorities who reduced history to a sequence of decisions of party congresses and successes of Soviet economy and science.

24. Only with the coming to power of Andropov did the party initiate a honest analysis of the situation in the country (see G. Zoteev, in Ellman and Kontorovich, 1998, p. 95). Some of the leaders were very critical. Nikolas Ryzhkov, the future Prime Minister under Secretary General Gorbachev, wrote

in 1982 'the atmosphere in the country is suffocating, beyond that is death...
In 1982, for the first time since the war, real incomes of the population
stopped increasing. Everything was blocked: living standards; house construction; shops; kindergarten, schools, etc. The worst was the moral climate'
(Ryzhkov in his memories '*Perestroika: istorii predatelsv*', quoted in *Le Monde
Diplomatique*, June 2005, p. 18). The future minister of foreign affairs Eduard
Shevardnadze said to Gorbachev, during the winter of 1984: 'Everything is
rotten. Everything should be changed' (*Le Monde Diplomatique*, June 2005,
p. 18). Alexander Yakovlev, the chief ideologue of the CPSU, had on 3 December 1985 recommended, in a report addressed to Mikhail Gorbachev, the
restoration of market economy and the 'private property owner as a subject
of liberties', a capital market and an end to the monopoly of the communist
party (Alexander Yakovlev, 1994, Gorkaya Tsjasja, in *Le Monde Diplomatique*,
June 2005, p. 19). However, in 1986 Gorbachev still believed that fine tuning
the centrally planned economic system would be enough (Goldman, 2003,
p. 52). At that time the majority of the Politburo and Central Committee
believed this.
25. Between 1985 and 1988 the anti-alcohol campaign cost the Soviet Treasury
67 billion rubles. In 1985, the state's annual income from the sale of alcoholic
beverages constituted between 12 and 14 per cent of total budget revenues
(Aron, 2006). By the middle of the 1980s spending on alcohol accounted
for about 15 per cent of household disposable income (Hanson, 2003,
p. 179).
26. V. Mozhin, in Ellman and Kontorovitch, 1998, p. 121.
27. In this context it is striking how little resistance there was in the provinces
and republics against the coup attempt of August 1991. Almost the whole
elite kept silent and/or followed the orders from the Kremlin.
28. For the spread of organized crime see Volkov, 2005a.
29. In October 1988 a team from the West headed by George Soros went to
Moscow in order to advise the Soviet leadership about an eventual transition
to a market economy (Ellman and Kontorovich, 1998, p. 238).
30. This is not to suggest that a majority or a large part of the population engaged
in this kind of activity. However, the situation invited the worst elements in
society to come to the fore.
31. About 15 million people participated in various political actions. But the wave
of civic activism had faded by 1991. On February 4, 1990, 250,000 people
demonstrated in Moscow for the abolition of article 6 of the constitution that
mandated the leading role of the Communist Party. On 20 January 1991,
200,000 people demonstrated in Moscow against the military intervention
in the Baltic republics, which had declared their independence.

3 Post-Soviet Russia: Captured by the Past?

1. Vladimir Putin succeeded President Yeltsin on 31 December 1999 and was
elected as President on 26 March 2000.
2. Padma Desai in the Council on Foreign Relations Meeting, New York, 15 May
2006, quotation from her book *Conversations on Russia*, 2006.

3. By 2000 university professors received about $100 a month, forcing them to moonlight. Even in 2008, average wages in education are only two-thirds of the national average wage. Spending for education fell to 3.7 per cent of GDP in 2003 (Belarus 5.9 per cent; Ukraine 5.3 per cent; Germany 4.6 per cent (2002); and France 5.7 per cent (2001)) (UN ECE database: http://w3.unece.org/pxweb/Dialog/Default.asp). Nowadays more than half of students in higher education pay student fees and/or bribes. According to the Ministry of Education itself, only 10 to 20 per cent of Russian institutions of higher learning have preserved Soviet standards of quality. The state now provides less than a third of their funding. Bribes to pass examinations are commonplace (Anderson, 2007).

4. In 1998, 16.6 per cent of all Russian factories had a workforce of 1000 or more compared to 2.4 per cent of all West German factories (Goldman, 2003, p. 95).

5. According to the 'Who Owns Russia' study by Moscow based Troika Dialog, state ownership does not negatively affect corporate governance. It is not so much the type of ownership that influences the standard of corporate governance as the sector in which the company operates (*Business New Europe*, 5 February 2008).

6. In a February 1995 poll, only 3 per cent of people said they intended to vote for Yeltsin. However, he managed to obtain 35 per cent in the first round of the elections and subsequently won the second round against the communist Zyuganov. According to Aleksei Sitnikov, later president of the largest PR group Image Kontakt: in the 1996 presidential elections 'the communist won, but did not want to win. In the second round we miscounted ten million votes' (quoted in Wilson, 2005, p. 76). In the second round Zyuganov trailed by 32.5 to 35.8 per cent, but in the third round he lost with 40.7 per cent (Yeltsin 54.4 per cent) (ibid. p. 77). In Chechnya Yeltsin got 64.1 per cent of the vote. It seemed the more remote and inaccessible the region, the greater the support for the President; The people of Chujotka peninsula in the far North-East gave him 75 per cent of the vote, in Daghestan Zyuganov won 66 per cent of the vote during the first round, against 26 per cent for Yeltsin. During the second round Yeltsin won with 51 per cent. The Italian paper *La Stampa* analysed the results of the presidential elections during the first round in Tatarstan (6 July 1996). The correspondent had access to the voting figures at different levels. At the lowest level Yeltsin got in one area of Tatarstan 171,000 votes. However, the official vote count at the highest level came to 207,000 votes. Votes were systematically subtracted from all other candidates, and transferred to Yeltsin's list. Other areas of Tatarstan showed similar discrepancies.

   However, the OSCE election observers believed that the 'declared result of the election accurately reflects the wishes of the Russian electoral of the day' although pointing at irregularities in above mentioned regions and bias of the media (OSCE, final statement of the OSCE/ODIHR observer mission, p. 4).

7. An opinion poll conducted by Levada in the middle of August 2007 showed that Russians do not regard the failed coup attempt of August 1991 as a triumph for democracy. Only 10 per cent said it was a victory for the democratic revolution, 17 per cent said Yeltsin and the democrats were right while 8 per cent thought the coup plotters were right, 46 per cent said neither side was right (*Interfax*, 17 August 2007).

8. Stiglitz recalled 'how a smiling Gerashenko, the chairman of the Central Bank of Russia, told the president of the World Bank and me that it was simply market forces at work' when the IMF was confronted with the fact that the billions of dollars that it had given Russia was showing up in Cypriot and Swiss bank accounts just days after the loan was made, it claimed that these weren't their dollars. IMF policies led Russia into deeper debts, with nothing to show for it' (Stiglitz, 2002, p. 150).

9. It is reminiscent of reformists under tsarism. Billington (1970, p. 224) noticed that from Catherine, 'aristocratic thinkers ... learned to think in terms of sweeping reforms on abstract, rationalistic grounds rather than piecemeal changes rooted in concrete conditions and traditions'.

10. Berdyaev wrote 'Scientific positivism, and everything else Western, was accepted in its most extreme form and converted not only into a primitive metaphysic, but even into a special religion supplanting all previous religions' (as quoted in *The Times Literary Supplement*, 17 May 2006).

11. In July 1999, 35 per cent received salaries worth less than the then subsistence level of $36 a month (*Agence Press*, 24 November 2000).

12. According to the World Health Organization, in 2001 Russia had the second highest suicide rate at 41.5 per 100,000. Only Lithuania scored higher with 51.6 per 100,000. The WHO considers a suicide rate of more than 20 as critical. The suicide rate in France was 20, in the USA 13.9 and Canada 16.4. The suicide rate among Russian men reached an astonishing level of 106.7 per 100,000 (*Agence France Presse*, 11 August 2003). During 1993–2003 the number of people who became disabled as a result of psychiatric disorders increased by 50 per cent (*Interfax*, 4 January 2004).

13. About 3.8 million Russians were treated for psychological disorders in 2003. This figure has risen by more than one third since 1989, according to the Russian health ministry. Russia's rates are about 20 per cent higher than those of North America and Europe (*Chicago Tribune*, 1 January 2001). According to Interfax (4 January 2004), 10 per cent of Russians suffer from serious mental disorders and need psychiatric assistance. Mental disorders in children and teenagers increased by a factor of 2.5 in the last decade, this is related to the spread of family dislocation, leading to the loss of structured life patterns among youth.

14. Life expectancy in 2004 was 58.9 years for men and 72.3 years for women. High mortality of men is related to lifestyle, which includes heavy smoking and drinking. The annual alcohol consumption in Russia is about 15 litres per person annually. Related to alcoholism is the high rate of death from alcohol poisoning (22 per 100,000) and the extremely high homicide rate (19 per 100,000, i.e. 10 to 20 times higher than in Western Europe). Over 40 per cent of all deaths of working age males in the average Russian city are due to hazardous drinking (see Russia Analytical Report, Nr 35, 2008).

15. As a pretext for the war the bombing of apartment buildings was used in which terrorists from Chechnya were blamed but in which allegedly the FSB was involved. There is evidence that links the apartment bombings to the FSB (*Moscow News*, 14 January 2004 and 19 May 2005). Two members of an independent commission investigating the bombings, both Duma members, have been assassinated, another imprisoned while a fourth died in a car accident. An important witness, Mikhail Trepashkin, had been arrested and

imprisoned just before testifying as a witness to the above mentioned commission (*Moscow Times*, 8 February 2008, see also D. Satter, 'Terror in Russia: Myths and Facts', *The National Interest*, 27 January 2004).

16. Dmitry Medvedev, then First Deputy Prime Minister, was also chairman of Gazprom. Shkolov, a presidential aide, was on the board of directors of Transneft. Sobyanin, Putin's chief of staff, was also chairman of Tvel (a major producer of nuclear fuel).

17. See Volkov, 2005a. In the middle of 2002 there were 313,000 security agents in Russia. Half of the members of secret services were involved in private business during their working time, another 18–20 per cent in their free time. There are similarities with the reign of Tsar Alexander II under whom the highest echelons of the security services became involved in business and enriched themselves enormously (see the memories of Piotr Kropotkin, 1903, pp. 250–1).

18. For example, the international airport of Moscow, Sheremetevo, was under mafia control and a taxi to the town centre cost 40 to 100 dollars. After the mafia control had been broken, the tariff went to down to 20 dollars or less (Goldman, 2003, p. 191).

19. Nevertheless, there has been some progress with respect to the role of the judiciary. According to a new criminal code, accepted in 2002, a judge must approve arrest warrants, and the accused charged with a crime within two weeks, or released. Nationwide jury trials were introduced. Jury trials acquitted one out of six defendants while among those tried by judges just 3 per cent were acquitted in 2005 (*Moscow Times*, 1 June 2006). While the number of citizens turning to the courts for redress of their grievances was only 1 million under President Yeltsin, it shot up to 6 million under President Putin. Of cases brought against government authorities 71 per cent of plaintiffs have won the cases (ibid.). In 2003, 87 per cent of the court cases related to tax problems, in which a firm was the plaintiff, succeeded in the Moscow City Court (figures for the St Petersburg and Leningrad Oblast Court were 84.2 per cent) (Hendley, 2005, p. 22).

20. According to President Putin, in 2005, regional and local taxes constituted 12 per cent of the territories revenues (Itar-Tass, 7 June 2006).

21. For a number of regions this seemed justifiable as embezzlement of public funds was rife, especially in the Far East and Southern Russia.

22. In August 2000 Finance Minister Kudrin estimated that two-thirds of Moscow's enterprises did not report to the tax office (Ledeneva, 2006, p. 126).

23. Approximately one-sixth of families in 2005 could not pay rent and communal services (*Rossiyskaya Gazeta*, 28 April 2006).

24. From 1994 to 1998 the share of workers whose salaries were delayed increased from 38 to 64 per cent and the average sum owed increased by a quarter. By October 2005 the share reached 13 per cent (*Rossiyskaya Gazeta*, 28 April 2006).

25. During 2006 to 2007 the number of families with an annual income of more than $1 million doubled to 200,000 (*Kommersant*, 27 February 2008).

26. Asked about assessments of political leaders since Tsar Nicholas II, respondents in all age categories rated President Putin as the best leader while Boris Yeltsin received the worst ratings (Russlandanalysen 100, 2006, March

2006). Respondents in all age categories were also negative about President Gorbachev but positive about Brezhnev and Andropov.

27. A poll revealed that 36 per cent of respondents like their respective governor (17 per cent dislike) but 52 per cent of respondents are disappointed with the situation in their region. Almost half of respondents also believe that their governor breaks the law (*Vedomosti*, 11 August, 2006).

28. This should not create the illusion that the average Russian became twice as rich. First of all, increase of wealth went above all to the richer part of the population, second, real wage increases are exaggerated by official underestimation of inflation. Moreover, the gradual erosion of benefits in kind and the increase in informal payments for public services like education and health care makes the picture of income development less rosy.

29. This is confirmed by another survey (*Moscow Times*, 2 February 2007) of 1600 people which found that 38 per cent of respondents spend at least 74 per cent of their income on food while 20 per cent deny themselves basic staple food.

30. Russian life expectancy for males went down between 1991 and 1994 by over 6 years to 59 years. In 2007 it was 59 years, down from 62 years in 2000, remarkable for a period of robust economic growth. Russian life expectancy is 12 years less than in the United States (*RIA Novosti*, 8 December 2006).

31. It is telling that the first device that jams mobile phone connections during a theatre performance has been installed in Petersburg. Many visitors ignore calls to switch off mobile phones (*The Guardian*, 6 March 2007).

32. The arrogance of the upper class is exemplified by the fact that in Russia an estimated 5000 officials, and, reportedly, many wealthy businessmen, sport a blue flashing light with siren on their cars that entitles them to make up their own road rules. 'The unequal relationship between Russian citizens and their state can be seen most vividly on the roads' says Vyacheslav Lisakov of the Free Choice Motorists Movement which has approximately 5000 members (*Christian Science Monitor*, 12 June 2006).

4   National Character and Economy

1. A good description of Russian national character can be found in Sakharov (2006). Value change is best documented in Russian novels and films. Since the early 1980s a new genre has appeared, the 'black performance' (Tsjernuda), i.e. a genre that depicts in black colours values and value change in Russian society. A bright representative of this genre is Viktor Astanaviev, who described in *Petshalnii Detektiv* (The Sad Detective) life in a small provincial suburb, where moral rules are weak and where criminals are more appreciated than their victims. He described the cult of crime. The film *Zapomnite Menja Takoi* (Remember Me as I Was) describes how different value systems of different generations within one family clash.

2. Eckstein, as quoted by Fleron, 1998, p. 47. Shlapentokh (1996) distinguishes between a pragmatic layer and a mythological level in the thinking of Soviet citizens. The sharp distinction between those two levels eased the task of adapting to Soviet reality. In the new circumstances, the same phenomenon can be observed. Researchers in Donetsk observed market-oriented thinking while interviewing managers (Lyakh and Pankow, 1998). However, there

was incoherence between the diagnosis of the situation in their companies and their concrete behaviour. It seems that the managers only used the slogans of the new 'market-oriented thinking', without believing in it. Also, the situation in which they operate might have driven them to act in old ways.

3. Meyer (2006, p. 83), notices in this respect that in public opinion polls on political matters, usually between 10 and 40 per cent of Russians say they 'do not know' which stand to take.

4. Käänänien, 1997, p. 38. Other surveys, dealing in more detail with corruption, suggest another attitude towards corruption. In the research of Miller *et al.* (1999) in which people in the Czech Republic, Slovakia, Bulgaria and Ukraine were polled about corruption, Ukraine was singled out, not only for more frequent occurrence of corruption, but also for more tolerant attitudes towards corruption. We may assume that the situation with respect to corruption does not differ very much in Russia and Ukraine.

5. Russians spend an astounding $37 billion a year, roughly as much as the government's entire budget revenues, on bribes, according to INDEM, a Russian NGO. Ordinary citizens pay about $2.8 billion a year on bribes (Worldlink, July–August 2002).

6. In the corruption perception index 2007 of Transparency International, Russia ranked 143 out of 179 places, together with Indonesia, Gambia and Togo.

7. Haarland and Niessen (1997), quoted in Simon, 1998, p. 26.

8. Ibid.

9. Liberalism and constitutionalism traditionally had a negative connotation in Russia. In tsarist times liberals were often portrayed as English businessmen interested in purely formal liberties for the middle class (Billington, 1970, p. 378).

10. In the Baltic States 35 per cent of respondents consider their countries to be democratic, with 31 per cent of Byelorussians and 35 per cent of Ukrainians sharing the same opinion about their respective states (Interfax, 13 December 2005).

11. Schwarz compares seven cultural regions (Western Europe, Eastern Europe, Anglo-Saxon states, South Africa, South Asia and Confucian cultures) on the basis of three value preferences: autonomy/pertaining, equality/hierarchy and skill/harmony. It appears that the Anglo-Saxon culture is closest to the one of South Africa (cumulative difference of 0.39 points) while the Confucian cultures are much closer to the Anglo-Saxon states than Western Europe (0.61 against 1.74 points). See Yasin, 2007, p. 57.

12. See Rupnik, 1989, p. 236. It can be argued that literature, or the arts in general, assumed a civilizing role as this provided the only platform where all kind of ethical dilemmas could be discussed.

13. Schein (1969, in Guseva, 2001, p.19) distinguished three levels of culture: the upper and 'visible' level of artefact and behaviour, an underlying level of attitudes, and a deeper level of fundamental beliefs and assumptions about the world and the purpose of human existence.

14. The term is from Etkind and Gozmann, 1992.

15. This is also reflected in domestic violence that seems to occur in Russia more often than in Western countries. According to Amnesty International in its

report 'Nowhere to turn to', 70 per cent of married women in Russia have been subjected to physical, physiological or sexual violence at home and 9,000 Russian women are killed each year by their husband, partner or relative (2004). This number is in the USA between 2,000 and 3,500 each year although the population of the USA is almost 300 million while that of Russia 145 million (Radio Free Europe/Radio Liberty, 15 December 2005). Another survey shows that 52 per cent of women had been beaten at least once by their husbands, and 41 per cent said they had been beaten more than once (*Moscow Times*, 22 March 2006). Minister Nurgaliyev admitted that the level of domestic violence in Russia is one of the world's highest, calling for an effective system to tackle this problem (*Itar-Tass*, 20 February 2008).

16. Smith (1990) noticed that 'within the trusted tribal ring, the bonds are strong but outside it the frictions are abrasive and the mistrust corrosive' (p. 182). Trust in a small circle of family and friends is relative as there is almost an absence of delicacy with respect to matters of privacy. Usually, people have not learnt to be careful with personally entrusted information.

17. Only 5 per cent of Russians think they should solve their problems by themselves and not rely on the state (*Novaya Gazeta*, 17–19 July 2006, survey of Sociology Institute and Friedrich Ebert Foundation).

18. According to Dmitry Medvedev, 'Russia is a country of legal nihilism at the level that no European country can boast of' (*Agence Press*, 22 January 2008).

19. Dmitry Medvedev noticed with regard to increasing corruption that 'moral stimuli disappeared. Religious morals disappeared for a long eight decades. The only check was the (Communist) party membership card but then it disappeared too. That is why not just legal norms but also the raising of morals is needed to fight corruption' (*Itar-Tass*, 26 February 2008).

20. In his study 'Suicide, a study in sociology', Durkheim gave the classical description of anomie: 'In the case of economic disasters, indeed, something like a declassification occurs which suddenly casts certain individuals into a lower state than their previous one. Time is required for the public conscience to reclassify men and things. So long as the social forces thus freed have not regained equilibrium, their perspective values are unknown and so all regulations are locked for a time. The limits are unknown between the possible and the impossible, what is just and what is unjust, legitimate claims and hopes and those which are immoderate. Consequently, there is no restraint upon aspirations.' (1979, pp. 252–3).

21. The philosopher Berdyaev (1947) pointed to this. According to him, in Western Europe, the knight's honour has been replaced by the bookkeeper's honour, unlike in Russia (p. 63).

22. According to Berdyaev (1947) the slavophiles think 'there must be nothing formal, no juridical and no legal guarantees … Everything must be based upon reliance of good faith, upon love and upon freedom. Legalism, formalism, and aristocracy they ascribe to the spirit of Rome' (p. 51).

23. Many authors, among others Solzhenitsyn, noticed a similarity between the Soviet prison culture and the Soviet culture in general. In the Gulag the principle of *krugovaia poruka* was applied, that means that the prisoner brigade as a whole was responsible for its output target. If fulfilled each member was properly fed. It was in the interest of each brigade member to make sure that all the others worked harder. *Zeks* (prisoners) policed themselves. As Ivan

Denisovich, the hero of Solzhenitsyn's short labour camp novel, noticed, 'the zek is kept up to the mark not by his bosses but by the others in his gang' (Hosking, 2006, p. 127). The former Polish *zek* Gustaw Herling-Grudzinski confirms this: 'The most conscientious and fervent foremen were the prisoners themselves, for the norm was reckoned collectively by dividing the total output by the number of workers. Any feeling of mutual friendliness was completely abolished in favour of a race for percentages.... There was in all this something inhuman, merciless breaking of the only natural bond between prisoners – their solidarity in face of their persecutors' (ibid.). According to Hosking 'their economic life was the slave-like fulfilment of the NKVD output plan. Their psychological disposition was determined by their enforced way of life: fatalistic, cunning, parsimonious in word and gesture, energetic only in struggling for the essentials of life' (ibid). 'Some of the zeks' characteristics became those of an entire Soviet generation, having been taken up and developed in analogous conditions of privation and austerity outside the camps. Anyone who visited the Soviet Union up to the 1980s will recall how ferociously people would fight with their elbows to climb on to an already overcrowded bus or underground train, how they would jealously defend their hard-earned position in a line for defisitnye tovary (good in short supply)' (Hosking, 2006, p. 128).

24. Berdyaev (1937) described the uniqueness of the Russian intelligentsia, related to its marginal position in society. Berdyaev saw the Russian intelligentsia as sectarian, fundamentally disposed towards dogma while poorly understanding the meaning of relative and maximalist.

25. This is not only related to the Soviet legacy but also rooted in the anti-rationalistic culture of tsarist Russia that was supported by the Orthodox Church. In Russian Orthodoxy, all that is needed is 'right praising' (pravoslavie) and there was but one answer to any controversy.

26. According to Kon 'The monistic world view endemic to Soviet Marxism, – one party, one truth, one leader', – bred a rigid, authoritarian personality impervious to doubt and militated against the cognitive complexity and intellectual tolerance sorely needed in times of rapid change. No wonder that reforms plunged the average citizen into a state of confusion and made Perestroika seem a menace or, to use Zinoviev's word, katastroika' (Kon, 1996, p. 193).

27. Marquis de Custine (1975, p. 48) pointed to the deep intolerance he encountered in tsarist Russia (1839). Berdyaev (1947, p. 27) wrote that 'Russians are not sceptics, they are dogmatists ... they have little understanding of what is relative'.

28. Ledeneva (1998) argues that in everyday dealings with authorities lies come out almost automatically. 'One does not lie always blatantly or tell the uncomfortable truth. People have learned to mix the two into credible stories to resolve bureaucratic problems' (Ledeneva, 1998, p. 79). Ledeneva stresses that these lies should be perceived as practices of creating exceptional cases, rather than dishonesty, as an ability not only to live with the contradictions of their society, but also to manipulate them creatively (p. 79). Shlapentokh (1996) sees the lie as an institution of the privatization of the state. Lying is a means of survival. The Russian psychologist Smirnov speaks about dissociation. 'Other societies have it too. But with us it is taken to an absurd extreme. Dissociation. Everybody knows what is meant by the incongruity

between a word and an action. In our society we have made this into something ridiculous. It is not an exception to the rule, it is the rule. To say one thing and do another. That is the rule of life for the Soviet man. And you know what this is. It's schizophrenia. I mean this is in the symbolic sense. There is a split going on ... A man thinks that he's being governed by a bunch of monsters, but he'll still say, 'long live our Party and government'(quoted in Merridale, 2000, p. 360).
29. The (post-) Soviet socio-psychological syndrome should be understood in the context of specific social practices. The term 'social practice' captures attitudes and behaviour in a social context and points to the pervasive character of it.

5 How Russian Neo-Patrimonialism Works

1. Montesquieu (1689–1755) already noticed that institutions follow mental programmes and in the way they function they adapt to local culture (*L'Esprit des lois*) (Hofstede and Hofstede, 2005, p. 19). In this context it should be noticed that similar laws work differently in different countries as experienced in the EU. The US constitution was adopted by many Latin American countries in the nineteenth century but the results are, in Latin America, very different from the USA (see North, 1990, p. 101).
2. The Communist Parties of both Ukraine and Russia have been supported by leading businessmen and some among them bought parliament seats on a communist ticket. In Russia, since 1996 a large part of funding comes from the state budget (Wilson, 2005, p. 229). At critical moments the communist leadership supported those in power. For example, Zyuganov turned his back on the communist radicals in the Moscow White House in October 1993 (Wilson, 2005, p. 227). In Ukraine, communist party leader Symonenko supported President Kuchma during the Gongadze affair. When mistreated by those in power, the communist leadership did not protest. For example, the communists fulfilled the function of bogeymen for part of the electorate during important presidential elections while being easy accomplices in electoral fraud and challenging opposition politicians were kept at bay.
3. As part of an anti-black PR action in early 2001, a St Petersburg agency, Promaco PR, intentionally violated the Press Law by offering payment to 21 press outlets to publish commercial disinformation in an editorial format rather than as commercial advertising (introducing a non-existent company that opened a non-existent shop at an non-existent address). It appeared that 13 out of 21 outlets published the covert advertising in the form of an article on the condition of pre-payment, three recommended it for publication as advertising, four asked for additional information, and one published it free (Ledeneva, 2006, p. 35).
4. In 2006 'Just Russia' had been founded by the Kremlin in order to capture part of the electorate.
5. Here we should emphasize that a variety of polities is emerging in Russia, especially in the periphery. For example, in the Russian Republic of Sakha, the President is in control of the entire political system and all main economic assets of his republic (see Meyer, 2006, p. 61). He declared the Yakutian

language as the official state language alongside Russian and English. The hierarchy in the republic is based of kinship clans that are headed by a 'Tojun'. Even in Soviet times, the Communist Party had to rely heavily on the tojuns.

6. By 2000, Moscow counted 60,000 severely neglected children related to the low funding of child care (*Obshchaya Gazeta*, 1 March 2001). During 1988–2003 the number of Russian adolescents diagnosed with drug addiction increased by a factor of 15 (ibid.). Only 10–12 per cent of Russia's school children are healthy (Interfax, 7 September 2006). According to the Interior Ministry, there were in 2004 1,117,000 homeless children in Russia (the number was 200,000 in 1925 (*Novaya Gazeta*, 11 March 2000).

7. Here, Max Weber can be quoted (in Piirainen, 1997, p. 18) 'Two opposite attitudes towards activity that was oriented towards the acquisition of necessities appeared originally in immediate conjunction. First, in the inside, there was the attachment to tradition, a relation of mutual respect among the fellow members of the same tribe, family or house, and a corresponding restraint in the quest for unscrupulous acquisition inside this circle of fellow men, united by this relation of mutual respect: the inside morals. And second, in the relations with the outside, an absolute lack of restraint and consideration was predominant, whereby every stranger initially was an enemy, towards whom there were no ethical constraints: the outside morals'.

8. Although a clear trend under President Putin was to restore the 'vertical of power', to increase the role of the state in the economy, especially in the strategic sectors, there is no clear vision about how to tackle the major problems the country is faced with.

9. For example, police regulations require that all jewellery stores have bars on their windows. However, the fire laws require there be no bars on the windows.

10. Parallels with the tsarist bureaucracy are striking. Gatrell (1995) described how the bold reforms of Minister of Finance Bunge (1882–1886), aimed at creating new foundations for private enterprise, were obstructed by a bureaucratic economic culture, that was used to arbitrary administrative intervention and that proved to be very resistant.

11. According to various statistical sources, today's government apparatus is considerably smaller than the Soviet bureaucracy: 7 officials per 1000 citizens. Again, according to statistical data from the middle of the 1990s, the number of officials in Russia (per 1000 citizens) is lower than in any advanced European country (Lyubarsky, in *Social Reality*, 1, 2006).

12. The increase in the state bureaucracy was mainly at the local and regional levels (from 128,000 in 1996 to 464,000 in 2005 respectively from 446,000 in 1994 to 726,000 in 2005; www.gks;ru/kadr/tab1.htm) and also in the executive and judiciary (from 894,000 in 1994 to 1,236,000 in 2005 respectively from 103,000 in 1994 to 193,000 in 2005, www.gks;ru/kadr/tab1.htm).

13. Under President Yeltsin there were more presidential decrees than laws. Since 1998 the number of presidential decrees has waned while the overall volume of law making has remained relatively constant. The range of policy that can be decided by decree has gradually narrowed over time (see Haspel, Remington and Smith, 2006).

14. In 1997, according to official statistics, only 56.1 per cent of all court decisions were implemented (Ledeneva, 2006, p. 182).

15. Patrimonialism and feudalism are different kind of socio-economic formations. However, Russian neo-patrimonialism can be considered as a hybrid formation in which the patrimonial logic is dominant while feudal and legal-rational elements are also present.
16. Shiller *et al.* (1992) conducted a telephone based interview in Moscow only. In this survey Moscow is not fully representative of Russia and at the time only 25 per cent of Muscovites had a telephone (Goldman, 2003, p. 74).
17. The journal *Economic Development and Cultural Change*, founded in 1952, is one of the few economic periodicals that pay attention to the impact of cultural change upon economic development.
18. Raiser (1999) distinguishes three different types of trust. Transactions between members of a kinship group are based on 'ascribed trust'. The second type is that of 'process-based trust', existing between individuals who have known each other for a long time, without sharing the loyalty of a specific group. Transactions in this case are repeated. The third type of trust is 'extended trust', occurring between individuals who enter into a transaction with only limited information about the counterpart's specific attributes. Extended trust is a key element in modern economies. Central planning relied heavily on process-based trust, with enterprises, local and national government officials closely linked through informal networks.
19. Institutional trust should not be confused with interpersonal trust that is not particularly low in Russia. The European Values Survey showed that 10 other European countries, including France, Estonia and Slovenia, scored lower than Russia (http://www.atlasofeuropeanvalues.com/). However, the World Values Survey of 1990 showed that the sum of positive answers to the question 'Can a majority of people be trusted?' was in Russia 37.9 per cent while in Estonia it was 77.3 per cent and in France 57.5 per cent (Yasin, 2007, p. 39). Since 1990 the credibility level has been based on a more limited set of answers ('yes', 'no', 'don't know') shows the following dynamic of 'yes' answers in Russia: 1989 54 per cent; 1990 25 per cent; 1991 36 per cent; 1995 24 per cent; 1998 22 per cent; 2005 22 per cent; and in 2006 22 per cent. Surprising is that since 1998 the credibility level remained on the same low level (Yasin, 2007, p. 40).

    Taratko found that the youth was the least trustworthy (19 per cent against 22 per cent for all respondents, 2005). However, institutional trust was higher among the youth compared to all respondents (Taratko, 2007).
20. See for instance the scandal with defrauded apartments, Chapter 3.
21. Despite increasing corruption, since 1999 business activity has continued to boom. The business environment for Western business in Russia has also improved reflected in increased FDI and higher profit rates.
22. According to Kirill Kabanov, a member of the presidium of the National Anti-Corruption Committee, 'Corruption is only being fought in words, not in actions' (*RBC Daily*, 27 September 2007).
23. Prosecutor General Yury Chaika said that some 100,000 government officials had unlawfully been involved in commercial activities, holding shares and stakes and failing to submit tax declarations (*Interfax*, 19 February 2008).
24. A World Bank study (2004) on ownership concentration in Russia found that about two dozen oligarchic groups account for at least 35 per cent of sales, and in key sectors such as energy, chemicals, metallurgy and banking this

share is much higher. According to Boris Titov, head of the Business Russia Association, in 2000, 1,200 companies produced 80 per cent of GDP, while in 2007 fewer than 500 companies are producing 80 per cent of GDP (*Izvestia*, 12 July 2007).

25. The combined net worth of Russia's billionaires shot up from $90.6 billion in 2005 to $470 billion in 2007, i.e. more than twice the country's GDP, according to *Forbes* magazine. In 2007, 19 Russian billionaires were in the world's top 100, up from 5 in 2004 (*Moscow Times*, 7 March 2008).

6 Ukraine and the Russian Type of Neo-Patrimonialism

1. The Canadian ambassador in Ukraine has, since January 2004, coordinated secret meetings of Western ambassadors in order to organize support for Viktor Yushchenko. The youth movement Pora, a driving force behind the Orange Revolution, was supported financially and logistically. Deputy Chairman of the Central Election Commission Davydovych who refused to sign off the official election results, was promised safe passage before the elections took place. Western embassies invested in a controversial exit poll and organized an army of Western election observers who were sent, above all, to the Eastern and Southern provinces (*The Globe and Mail*, 14 April 2007). Pora has since 2001 organized around 75 cells across Ukraine and with a total of about 10,000 activists in the middle of 2004 (*Agence Press*, 11 December 2004). Western ambassadors warned President Kuchma that fraudulent elections would not be accepted. The US House of Representatives accepted an act (15 September 2004) according to which organizers of fraudulent elections in Ukraine would face denial of visas and freezing of accounts. An exit poll was financed with Western money. Interventions of Western governments were very important in avoiding violence. See also van Zon, 2005b.

2. Meyer (2006, p. 56) notices that 'in strongly personalized politics, politicians tend to overestimate themselves, to become arrogant and to pretend having personal charisma which they rarely actually have. Many at the top become unable to listen, hovering above society, in a relationship of mutual alienation.

3. According to the Blue Ribbon Report (November 2004) that sought to advise the Ukrainian government, the Ukrainian bureaucracy functioned not as an instrument of political power but rather as the sole subject of power (p. 13). The bureaucracy privatized functions of the state. According to the report, the state rules rather than serves society (p. 14), while the President and its administration have assumed the role previously played by the Central Committee of the Communist Party.

4. For example, the head of state-owned Naftogaz, the Ukrainian gas company, signed agreements with Russian Gazprom, not only about the delivery of gas for a specific price, but also agreements about giving over licenses to Gazprom-controlled companies to supply gas to industrial consumers in Ukraine and agreements about the ban of the re-export of gas etc. The government was not informed.

5. Presentation by Bohdan A. Futey, Washington DC, 16–17 October 2007 (Ronald Reagan Building).

6. According to *Corruption, Democracy and Investment in Ukraine* (Neutze and Karatnycky, 2007, p. 13) 'Raiders infiltrate the company of interest with agents who collect information. A small share of stock is purchased. Then, a usually frivolous lawsuit is filed with a lower-level court in a remote town. Armed with an often anomalous court injunction, raiders resort to force, sending a pseudo 'security firm' to take possession of the property (through forcible entry). Further, by bribing law enforcement agencies, they keep the object under their control – even in the face of a corrected court decision. Then, they try to re-sell property to themselves or to those who ordered the raid, to change the composition of charter capital (which requires changing the statute of the enterprise).
7. The Socialist Party defected after Our Ukraine broke its promise. Our Ukraine wanted Poroshenko as speaker of Parliament instead of Socialist Party leader Moroz.
8. The share of steel produced in Martin ovens is only slowly declining in Ukraine. It was 49 per cent in the middle of the 1990s and 46 per cent in 2003. Globally in 2004, 3.2 per cent of steel was produced in Martin ovens (6.6 per cent in 1996). The share of Ukrainian steel produced in electric furnaces has not increased since the middle of the 1990s (5.9 per cent in 1994, 5.4 per cent in 2003, 6.8 per cent in 2004).
9. From the first to the second round of the presidential elections, turnout in Donetsk increased by 40 per cent, up to 98.5 per cent, while many districts reported a vote count of more than 100 per cent (on a turnout of 127 per cent).
10. During 2005 Donetsk witnessed a sharp decline in industrial output. In the period January to May 2005, industrial output was 6.1 per cent lower that the same period in 2004 (Ukrainian Statistical Office; for Ukraine as a whole there was an increase of 6.2 per cent). Between January 2007 and April 2007 industrial output in Donetsk was 13.7 per cent higher than the same period in 2006 while in Ukraine it was 12.5 per cent higher. There is a remarkable correlation between Donetsk economic performance and the presence of the Donetsk clan in government.
11. President Yushchenko noticed that in September and October 2006 VAT arrears increased by 70 per cent compared with the same period in 2005, 42 per cent of these arrears were from enterprises in Donetsk (*Zerkalo Nedeli*, 21–27 May 2005). Between January and April 2007, the government reimbursed 40.3 per cent of the sum subject to VAT reimbursement in Ukraine overall, while in the Donetsk region it was 58.4 per cent, 52.1 per cent for Chernihivska region, 47.6 per cent for Cherkasy region, 46.8 per cent for Rivne region, 46.3 per cent for Zaporizhia region, and 45.5 per cent for Mykolaiv region (President of Ukraine, 26 May 2007, http://www.president.gov.ua/en/).

7 Path Creation: A Comparative Perspective

1. The absence of strict procedures and formal institutional arrangements does not mean that conflict and disorder are the norm. The preference for adaptability and fluidity usually harbours compromise politics within elites,

   while conflicts with the population at large remain limited given the docility of the population.

2. The concept of social capital became very popular during the second half of the 1990s. The concept has been criticized for being vague and chaotic (see Fine, 1999, pp. 1–14). Social capital is about the non-economic, or non-market factors that make the economy function better. Fine criticizes the concept as ignoring aspects of conflict and power. He quotes Evans as saying 'if a community is riven by conflicting interests, the nature of meaning of social capital becomes more complicated … if conflict codetermines the notion of social capital, why not take conflict and its theoretical underpinnings as the starting point rather than social capital which is rendered both ambiguous and redundant' (p. 14).

3. According to World Development Indicators 2005 (World Bank) domestic credit provided by the banking sector attained only 28 per cent of Russian GDP while in developed market economies it was on average 182 per cent of GDP and in low and middle income countries 79 per cent (2003).

4. In this respect the observations of Henry Kissinger (1979, p. 323) are interesting: 'Japan turned its feudal past into an asset by permeating its entire society with such a sense of shared respect that its internal differences could never mar the essential unity with which it faced foreigners'. Japan could 'adopt almost any system and still retain its Japanese character, which depended neither on form of government nor on methods of economics but on a complicated; imbued; shared set of social relationships. Far from being an obstacle to progress, tradition in Japan provided the emotional security and indeed the impetus to try the novel'.

5. China laid off 17,000 civil servants between 1996 and 2002 while 28,626 people resigned from public service, bringing the total to about 5 million civil servants compared to a population of more than 1.3 billion (*People's Daily*, 16 December 2003).

6. In December 2000, 891,000 small businesses were registered in Russia, less than in 1994. Poland, with a population of approximately one-quarter of that of Russia, counted about 2 million small enterprises. In Russia small businesses generated around 10 per cent of GDP, while in the West it generates approximately half (Goldman, 2003, p. 212). In Moscow, in order to open and register a business, it is necessary to comply with 50 different legal acts, visit between 20 and 30 government offices and obtain the agreement of 50 to 90 different officials (Goldman, 2003, p. 213).

7. This could, however, not prevent the emergence of deep social cleavages in China.

8. Whereas China has a much higher share of high tech exports than Russia, Russia has a much higher share of the population enrolled in tertiary education (72 versus 22 per cent; World Bank, Education at a Glance, 2006, www.worldbank.org).

9. First Deputy Prime Minister Ivanov said that 'if we exclude Russia's weapon's exports, the country's high technology exports are equivalent to one-third of those of the Philippines, to less than a quarter of those of Thailand, to one-tenth of those of Mexico and to one-eighteenth of those of South Korea' (*Interfax*, 18 March 2008).

10. High technology exports are often of low quality. That is why Algeria says it wants to return 15 jets purchased in Russia. (*The Economist*, 17 March 2001).
11. According to the Federal Budget Law federal expenditures on education will fall from 0.9 per cent of GDP during 2007 and 2008 to 0.8 per cent of GDP during 2008 and 2009 (World Bank, 2007b, p. 12).
12. 57.9 per cent of all foreign direct investment in 2005 went to extraction of mineral resources and 'coke and oil products' (World Bank, 2006a).
13. According to the Mergers.ru project, in the first three quarters of 2006, Russian companies acquired foreign companies worth a total of $4.2 billion (compared to $2.3 billion in the same period of 2005), while foreigners bought $5.8 billion worth of assets in Russia (compared to $6.7 billion in the same period of 2005) (World Bank, 2006b).
14. Although Russian oil production levels have become, in 2006, the highest in the world, new oil fields have not been taken into production. Private companies only recently started thinking about developing oil and gas fields that had been discovered in Soviet times. Rather than increasing production capacities, a crucial issue is how to reduce leaks from worn out oil pipelines. Many areas of Siberia have turned into oil swamps. It appeared that once oil companies were privatized, they preferred rent-seeking. Geological exploration is almost non-existent. Between 1991 and 2006 Russia had not built any new oil refineries (*Rodnaya Gazeta*, 25 August 2006; interview with Alexander Isayev, deputy director of the Oriental Studies Institute).
15. According to an opinion poll, 57 per cent of Russians disapprove of the performance of public services while 39 per cent have been faced with serious water and heating supply failures and outages (Jamestown Foundation Eurasia Daily Monitor, 10 January 2008). In another poll 40 per cent of respondents described their housing maintenance as bad or very bad (*Chicago Tribune*, 26 February 2008).
16. According to Dmitry Medvedev, 40 per cent of the meat consumed in Russia is imported (*Itar-Tass*, 11 January 2008).
17. The International Organization for Migration says that in early 2008 about two million Russians were working in Western countries. More than 50 per cent of certified graduates of medical colleges do not work in medicine. Instead, many graduates from former Soviet republics are employed in Russian health care (*Itar-Tass*, 31 March 2008).
18. Brazil has only 315 researchers per 1 million population, China 633 and India 112 (Cooper, 2006, p. 14)
19. World Bank, 2006b, p. 19, maintains that 'patents per capita are almost 10 times higher in Spain, 60 times higher in South Korea and 100 times higher in Germany'.
20. On 14 February 2008 President Putin pointed to this scenario when he said that 'the establishment of state corporations in certain sectors of the Russian economy does not mean a transition to state capitalism, and their IPOs will take place in the future, including their full privatization' (*Interfax*, 14 February 2008).

Bibliography

Ahrend, R. 'Russia's Post-Crisis Growth: Its Sources and Prospects for Continuation', *Europe-Asia Studies*, Vol. 58, January (2006).

Alexander, J. 'Surveying Attitudes in Russia', *Communist and Post-Communist Studies*, Vol. 30, June (1997) 107–27.

Anderson, P. 'Russia's Managed Democracy', *London Review of Books*, 25 January (2007).

Aron, L. 'The 'Mystery' of the Soviet Collapse', *Journal of Democracy*, Vol. 17, No.2, April (2006) 22–32.

Avdasheva, S. 'Business Groups in Russian Industries', in Oleinik, A.N. (2005), pp. 290–309.

Barner-Barry, C. and C; Hody, A. *The Politics of Change – The Transformation of the former Soviet Union.* (New York: St Martin's, 1995).

Barnes, A. *Owning Russia. The Struggle over Factories, Farms, and Power* (Ithaca, NY: Cornell University Press, 2006).

Belyayeva, N.Y. (ed.) *Publitsjnaya politika v sovremennoi Rossii-subjekti I institute* (Moscow: TEIS, 2006).

Berdyaev, N. *The Origin of Russian Communism* (London: The Centenary Press, 1937).

Berdyaev, N. *The Russian Idea* (London: The Centenary Press, 1947).

Berend, I.T., Ranki, G. *The European Periphery and Industrialization 1780–1914*, (Budapest: Akademiai Kiado, 1982).

Berend, I.T. 'From Regime Change to Sustained Growth in Central and Eastern Europe', *Economic Survey of Europe*, No. 2/3, Geneva: ECE/UN (2000) 47–59.

Bhaumik, S., Estrin, S. *How Transition Paths Differ: Enterprise Performance in Russia and China.* Discussion Paper Series, Nr 1484, IZA Bonn (2005).

Billington, J.H. *The Icon and the Axe. An Interpretative History of Russian Culture* (New York: Vintage Books, 1970).

Bonell, V., Gold, T. (eds) *The New Entrepreneurs of Europe and Asia* (Armonk, NY: M.E. Sharpe, 2002).

Bourdieu, P. *The Logic of Practice* (Cambridge: Polity Press, 1990).

Bremmer, I., Charap, S. 'The Siloviki in Putin's Russia. Who They Are and What They Want', *The Washington Quarterly*, Winter (2006–2007) 83–92.

Brown, A. *The Gorbachev Factor* (Oxford: Oxford University Press, 1996).

Carothers, Th. 'The end of the Transition Paradigm', *Journal of Democracy*, Vol. 13, No. 1 (2002), 5–21

Chen, I., Dzjenkov, S., Roland, G., Zhuravka, E. 'Predprinimatelstvo v Kitai, Rossii i Brazilii: sravnenie' , Conference presentation 'Economic Modernization and Social Development', Higher School of Economics, Moscow, 3–5 April 2007.

Cooper, J. 'Can Russia Compete in the Global Economy?', *Eurasian Geography and Economics*, 47, No. 4 (2006) 407–425.

Custine, Marquis de *Lettres de Russie* (Paris: Gallimard, 1975).

Dallago, B. 'The Importance of Small and Medium Sized Enterprises – Transitional Economies', *UN Chronicle*, December (2003).

Deutsche Bank. *The Soviet Union at the Crossroads, Facts and Figures on the Soviet Republic*. Economics Department, Deutsche Bank, Frankfurt (1990).

Durkheim, E. *Suicide – a study in sociology* (London: Routledge, 1979).

Easter, G.M. *Reconstructing the State, Personal Networks and Elite Identity in Soviet Russia*, (Cambridge: Cambridge University Press, 2000).

Eckstein, H., Fleron Jr, F.J., Hoffman, E.P., Revlinger, W.R. *Can Democracy Take Root in Post-Soviet Russia?* (Oxford: Rowman & Littlefield Publishers, 1998).

Elias, N. *Involvement and Detachment* (Oxford: Basil Blackwell, 1987).

Elias, N. 'Towards a theory of social processes', *British Journal of Sociology*, Vol. 48, Nr 3 (1997), 355–383.

Ellerman, D. 'On the Russian Privatization Debate', *Challenge*, May–June 2003, Vol. 36, Nr 3 (2003) 6–29.

Ellman, M., Kontorovich, V. (eds)*The Destruction of the Soviet Economic System – An Insiders View* (Armonk, New York: M.E. Sharpe,1998).

Elster, J., Offe, C., Preuss, U.K. *Institutional Design in Post-Communist Societies.* (Cambridge: Cambridge University Press, 1998).

Etkind, A., Gozmann, L. *The Psychology of Post-Totalitarianism* (London: Centre for Research into Communist Economies, 1992).

Evans, P. *Embedded Autonomy: States and Industrial Transformation* (Princeton: Princeton University Press, 1995).

Figes, O. *A People's Tragedy: The Russian Revolution* (London: Jonathan Cape, 1996).

Fine, B. 'The Developmental State is Dead – Long Live Social Capital', *Development and Change*, Vol. 30, No. 1, January (1999) 1–14.

Fishlow, A. 'Review of Alexander Gerschenkron, *Economic Backwardness in Historical Perspective: A Book of Essays*.' EH. Net Economic History Services, Feb 14 2003.

Fitzpatrick, S. *Everyday Stalinism – Ordinary Life in Extraordinary Times: Soviet Russia in the 1930s* (Oxford: Oxford University Press, 1999).

Fleron, Jr., F.J. 'Congruence Theory Applied: Democratization in Russia', in Eckstein *et al.* (1998) 35–69.

Frye, Th. (2007) 'Original Sin, Good Works and Property Rights in Russia. Survey Evidence from Economic Elites and the Mass Public', Conference presentation 'Economic Modernization and Social Development', Higher School of Economics, Moscow, 3–5 April 2007.

Gabrisch, H., Hoelscher, J. *The Successes and Failures of Economic Transition – the European Experience* (Basingstoke: Palgrave MacMillan, 2006).

Gatrell, P. 'Economic culture, economic policy and economic growth in Russia, 1861–1914', *Cahiers du Monde Russe*, January–June (1995).

Gerschenkron, A. *Economic Backwardness in Historical Perspective. A Book of Essays* (Cambridge MA: Belknap Press of Harvard University Press, 1962).

Goldman, M.I. *The Piratization of Russia* (London: Routledge, 2003).

Goldman, M.I. 'Political Graft: The Russian Way', *Current History*, Vol. 104, No. 684, October (2005) 314–18.

Gorzelak, G. *Regional and Local Potential for Transformation in Poland*, (Warsaw: European Institute for Regional and Local Development, 1998).

Grossman, V. *Life and Fate* (New York: Harper & Row, 1995).

Gudkov, L. 'Russlands Systemkrise. Negative Mobilisierung und kollektiver Zynismus', *Osteuropa*, 57, 1 (2007) 3–13.

Guseva, N. 'Cross-cultural Psychology as a method of scientific research', paper Management Research Centre, University of Wolverhampton, 2001.

Handelman, S. *Comrade Criminal: Russia's New Mafiya* (New Haven: Yale University Press, 1995).

Hanson, P. *The Rise and Fall of the Soviet Economy* (Harlow: Pearson Education, 2003).

Hanson, P., Teague, E. 'Big Business and the State in Russia', *Europe-Asia Studies*, Vol. 57, No. 5, July 2005, 657–681.

Haspel, M., Remington, Th.F., Smith, S.S. 'Law Making and Decree Making in the Russian Federation: Time, Space and Rules in Russian Policy Making', *Post-Soviet Affairs*, Vol. 22, July–September (2006) 249–275.

Havrylyshyn, O. *Divergent Paths in Post-Communist Transformation* (London/New York: Palgrave Macmillan, 2006).

Hedlund, S. *Russian Path Dependency: a people with a troubled history* (London: Routledge, 2005).

Heller, M. *A Cog and the Wheel: the development of Homo Sovieticus* (in Russian) (London: Overseas Publications Interchange Ltd, 1985).

Heller, M., Nekrich, A. *Utopia in Power, The History of the SU from 1917 to the Present* (London: Hutchinson, 1986).

Hellman, J.S. 'Winners Take All. The politics of partial reform in post-communist transitions', *World Politics*, 50, January (1998) 203–234.

Hellman, J.S., Jones, G., Kaufman, D. 'Seize the State, Seize the Day: state capture and influence in transition economies', *Journal of Comparative Economics* 31 (2003), pp. 751–777, December, Vol. 31, No. 4.

Hendley, K. 'Accelerated Procedures in the Russian Arbitrazh Courts. A case study of unintended consequences', *Problems of Post-Communism*, November–December (2005).

Hirszowicz, M. *The Bureaucratic Leviathan. A Study in the Sociology of Communism* (Oxford: M. Robertson, 1980).

Hodgson, G.M. *Economics and Utopia. Why the learning economy is not the end of history* (London: Routledge, 1999).

Hoffmann, D.L. *Peasant Metropolis. Social Identities in Moscow, 1929–1941.* (London/Ithaca NY: Cornell University Press, 1994).

Hofstede, G. *Culture's Consequences – International Differences in Work-Related Values* (London: Sage Publishers, 1984).

Hofstede, G., Hofstede, G.-J. *Cultures and Organizations. Software of the Mind* (New York: McGraw-Hill, 2005).

Hosking, G. *Rulers and Victims: The Russians in the Soviet Union* (Cambridge MA: Belknap Press, 2006).

Hough, J.F. *The Logic of Economic Reform in Russia* (Washington, DC: Brookings Institution Press, 2001).

Huntington, S. 'The Clash of Civilizations?', *Foreign Affairs* Summer (1993) 22–50.

Inglehart, R. *Modernization and Postmodernization: Cultural, economic and political change in 43 societies* (Princeton, NJ: Princeton University Press, 1997).

International Monetary Fund, OECD, EBRD *The Economy of the USSR* (Washington, DC: World Bank, 1990).

Ioffe, G. 'Understanding Belarus: Economy and Political Landscape', *Europe-Asia Studies*, Vol. 56, Nr 1, January (2004) 86–118.

Ioffe, G. 'Downsizing Russian Agriculture', *Europe-Asia Studies*, Vol. 57, No. 2, March (2005) 179–208.

Jensen, D.D. 'The Boss: How Yuri Luzhkov Runs Moscow', Conflict Studies Research Centre, December 1999.

Jowitt, K. *New World Disorder: The Leninist Extinction* (Berkeley: University of California Press, 1992).

Kääriänen, K. 'Moral Crisis or Immoral Society? Russian Values after the Collapse of Communism', *Berichte des Bundesinstituts für ostwissenschaftliche und internationale Studien*, No. 26 (1997).

Kagarlitsky, B. *The Dialectic of Change* (New York/London: Verso, 1990).

Kang, D. *Crony Capitalism. Corruption as Development in South Korea and the Philippines* (Cambridge: Cambridge University Press, 2002).

Karklins, R. *The System Made Me Do It. Corruption in Post-Communist Societies* (Armonk, New York/London: M.E. Sharpe, 2005).

Kapuscinski, R. *Imperium* (London: Granta Books, 1994).

Katchanovski, I. 'Divergence in Growth in Post-Communist Countries,' *Journal of Public Policy*, Vol. 20, No. 1 (2000) 55–81.

Katchanovski, I. 'Regional Political Divisions in Ukraine in 1991–2006', *Nationalities Papers*, Vol. 34, No. 5 (2006) 507–533.

Kissinger, H. *The White House Years* (London: Weidenfeld & Nicolson and Michael Joseph, 1979).

Koestler, A. *Darkness at Noon* (New York: Bantam Books, 1975).

Kon, I.S. 'Moral Culture', in Shalin, D.N. (ed.) (1996) 191–206.

Kosals, L. 'Essay on Clan Capitalism in Russia', *Acta Oeconomica*, Vol. 57, No. 1 (2007) 67–85.

Kropotkin, P. *Autour d'une Vie* (Paris: P.-V. Stock, 1903).

Kryshtanovskaya, O., White, S. 'Putin's Militocracy', *Post-Soviet Affairs*, Vol. 19, No. 4 (2003) 289–306.

Kuklinski, A., Lusinski, C., Pawlowski, K. *Towards a New Creative and Innovative Europe* (Warsaw: Wyzsza Szkola Biznesu – National Louis University, Nowy Sacz, 2006) 187–91.

Landes, D. *The Wealth and Poverty of Nations. Why Some Are So Rich and Some So Poor* (London: Abacus, 1999).

Lapin, N.I. 'Bazovie tsenosti, sotsialnoie samotsjustvie: doverie institutam vlasti', Conference presentation 'Economic Modernization and Social Development', Higher School of Economics, Moscow, 3–5 April (2007).

Latov, Y.V. 'Regionalnaya differentiatsia i perspektivi izmenenia rossiiskii khoziastvenii kulturi', Conference presentation 'Economic Modernization and Social Development', Higher School of Economics, Moscow, 3–5 April (2007).

Leach, J.A (ed.). Russian Money Laundering: Congressional Hearings, Diana Publishing (2000).

Ledeneva, A. *Russia's Economy of Favours. Blat, Networking and Informal System of Favours.* (Cambridge: Cambridge University Press, 1998).

Ledeneva, A. *How Russia Really Works* (Ithaca, New York: Cornell University Press, 2006).

Lewin, M. 'The Social Background of Stalinism', in Tucker, R.C. (ed.), (1977), pp. 111–37.

Lewin, M. *The Soviet Century* (London/New York: Verso, 2005).

Lyakh, A. and Pankow, W. (eds) *The Future of Old Industrial Regions in Europe. The Case of Donetsk Region in Ukraine* (Warsaw: Foundation for Economic Education, 1998).

Maddison, A. *L'Economie Mondiale, Une Perspective Millénaire* (Paris: OECD, 2001).

Mandelstam, N. *Hope Against Hope. A Memoir* (Harmondsworth: Penguin, 1970).

Milosz, C. *The Captive Mind* (New York: Alfred Knopf, 1953).

Menshikov, S. 'The Anatomy of Russian Capitalism', *Challenge*, March/April (2005).

Mendras, M. 'How Regional Élites Preserve Their Power', *Post-Soviet Affairs*, Vol. 15, October–December (1999) 295–312.

Merridale, C. *Night of Stone. Death and Memory in Russia* (London: Granta Books, 2000).

Messner, D. *The Network Society. Economic Development and International Competitiveness as Problems of Social Governance* (London, Portland: Frank Cass, 1997).

Meyer, G. (ed.) *Formal Institutions and Informal Politics in Central and Eastern Europe* (Opladen: Barbara Budrich Publishers, 2006).

Millar, J.R., Wolchik, S. *The Social Legacy of Communism* (Cambridge: Cambridge University Press, 1994).

Milosz, C. *The Captive Mind*. New York: Alfred Knopf, 1953).

Mohacsi, P. *The Meltdown of the Russian State* (Cheltenham: Edward Elgar, 2000).

Moshra, A. (ed.) *The Economics of Corruption* (Oxford: Oxford University Press, 2005).

Murrell, P. 'Evolutionary and radical approaches to economic reform', in Poznanski, K. (ed.) (1993) 219–21.

Myrdal, G. 'Corruption, its causes and effects', in Moshra, A. (ed.) (2005) 37–63.

North, D.C. *Institutions, Institutional Change and Economic Performance* (Cambridge: Cambridge University Press, 1990).

Neutze, J., Karatnycky, A. 'Corruption, Democracy and Investment in Ukraine', The Atlantic Council of the US, Policy Paper, October 2007.

Oleinik, A.N. *Organized Crime, Prison and Post-Soviet Societies* (Aldershot, Ashgate, 2003).

Oleinik, A.N. (ed.) *The Institutional Economics of Russia's Transformation* (Ashgate: Aldershot, 2005).

Owen, T.C. *Capitalism and Politics in Russia: A Social History of the Moscow Merchants, 1855–1905* (New York: Cambridge University Press, 1981).

Peregudov, S.P. 'Biznes i burokratia: evolutsia otnosenii', in Belyayeva, N.Y. (ed.) *Publitsjnaya politika v sovremennoi Rossii- subjekti I institute* (Moscow: TEIS, 2006). 87–96.

Piirainen, T. *Towards a New Social Order in Russia – Transforming Structures and Everyday Life* (Aldershot: Dartmouth, 1997).

Pijl, K. van der *Global Rivalries. From the Cold War to Iraq* (London: Pluto Press, 2006).

Pipes, R. *Russia under the Old Regime* (New York: Charles Scribner's Sons, 1974).

Pipes, R. 'Flight from Freedom', *Foreign Affairs*, May/June, Vol. 83, No. 3 (2004) 45–65.

Pleines, H. *Ukrainische Seilschaften. Informelle Einflussnahme in der Ukrainischen Wirtschaftspolitik 1992–2004* (Muenchen: Lit Verlag, 2005).

Polanyi, K. The Great Transformation. The Political and Economic Origins of Our Time. (Boston: Beacon, 1957).

Poznanski, K. (ed.) Stabilization and Privatization in Poland: An Economic Evaluation of the Shock Therapy Program (Boston: Kluwer Academic Press, 1993).

Primakov, E. *Au Coeur du pouvoir. Mémoires politiques* (Paris: Éditions des Syrtes, 2001)

Putnam, R. *Making Democracy Work: Civic Traditions in Modern Italy* (Princeton NY: Princeton University Press, 1993).

Radaev, V. 'Entrepreneurship strategies and the structure of transaction costs in Russian business', in Bonell and Gold (eds) (2002), 191–213.

Raiser, M. 'Trust in transition', *Working Paper*, No. 39 (April) (London: European Bank for Reconstruction and Development, 1999).

Raspopov, N.P. 'Krupnie finansovo-promislenije korporatsii v pole regionalnoi publitsjnoi politiki: novie modeli otnosjenii s vlastju (na primere Nizjegorod-skoi oblasti', in Belyayeva, N.Y. (ed.) *Publitsjnaya politika v sovremennoi Rossii-subjekti I institute* (Moscow: TEIS, 2006) 107–131.

Renz, B. 'Putin's Militocracy? An Alternative Interpretation of Siloviki in Contemporary Russian Politics', *Europe-Asia Studies*, Vol. 58, No. 6 (2006) 903–924.

Rifkin, J. *The European Dream. How Europe's Vision of the Future is Quietly Eclipsing the American Dream* (New York: Tarcher/Penguin, 2005).

Rose, R. *Getting Real: Social Capital in Post-Communist Societies.* Studies in Public Policy, No. 278, Glasgow (1997).

Rose, R. *Getting Things Done with Social Capital: NRB VII*, Studies in Public Policy, Nr 303, Glasgow (1998).

Rose, R., Munro, N., Mishler, W. 'Resigned Acceptance of an Incomplete Democracy: Russia's Political Equilibrium', in *Post-Soviet Affairs*, Vol. 20, July/September, No. 3 (2004) 195–218.

Rossiiskii Statistisheshkii Ezhegodnik, 2006 (Moscow: Federalnaya Sluzhba Gosudarstvennoi Statistiki, 2006).

Runciman, W.G. (ed.) *Weber. Selections in translation* (Cambridge: Cambridge University Press, 1978).

Rupnik, J. *The Other Europe* (London: Weidenfeld & Nicolson, 1989).

Sakharov, N.L. *Biznes v Rossii, Specifika Upravlenije* (Moscow, St Petersburg: Vershina, 2006).

Sandholtz, W., Taagepera, R. 'Corruption, Culture and Communism', *International Review of Sociology*, Vol. 15, No. 1, January (2005) 109–31.

Schienstock, G. 'Path Dependency and Path Creation in Finland', in Kuklinski, A., Lusinski, C., Pawlowski, K. (2006) 187–191.

Shalin, D.N. (ed.) *Russian Culture at the Crossroads: paradoxes of post-communist consciousness* (Oxford: Westview Press, 1996).

Shevtsova, L. 'Imitation Russia, Democracy or Dictatorship? Friend or Foe?', *The American Interest*, Vol. 2, Nr 2, November/December (2006).

Shiller, R.J., Boycko, M., Korobov, V. 'Hunting for Homo Sovieticus: Situational versus Attitudinal Factors in Economic Behavior', *Brookings Papers on Economic Activity*, Vol. 1 (1992).

Shlapentokh, V. *Public and Private Life of the Soviet People* (New York and Oxford: Oxford University Press, 1989).

Shlapentokh, V. 'Early Feudalism – The Best Parallel for Contemporary Russia', *Europe-Asia Studies*, Vol. 48, No. 3 (1996) 393–411.

Shlapentokh, V. 'The USSR in the mid-1980s : structural factors', in Ellman, M. and Kontorovich, V. (eds) (1998) 30–40.

Shlapentokh, V. 'The SU: A Normal Totalitarian Society', *Journal of Communist Studies and Transition Politics*, Vol. 15, No. 4, December (1999).

Shlapentokh, V. 'The Short Time Horizon in the Russian Mind', paper published in David Johnson Russian newsletter, 21 August 2004.

Shleifer, A. *A Normal Country: Russia after Communism* (Cambridge, Massachusetts, London: Harvard University Press, 2005).

Simon, G. Welchen Raum läßt die Geschichte für die Modernisierung Rußlands? *Berichte des Bundesinstituts für ostwissenschaftliche und internationale Studien*, No. 19 (1998).

Smith, H. *The New Russians* (New York: Random House, 1990).

Solnick, S.L. 'The Breakdown of Hierarchies in the Soviet Union and China: A Neoinstitutional Perspective', *World Politics, Vol.* 48, January (1996) 449–57)

Sowell, T. *Race and Culture* (New York: Basic Books, 1994).

Sowell, T. *Conquests and Cultures. An International History* (New York: Basic Books, 1998).

Spulber, N. *Russia's Economic Transitions. From Late Tsarism to the New Millenium* (Cambridge: Cambridge University Press, 2003).

Srubar, I. 'War der reale Sozialismus modern? Versuch einer strukturellen Bestimmung', *Kölner Zeitschrift fur Soziologie und Sozialpsychologie*, Vol. 43, No. 3 (1999) 415–32.

Stiglitz, J. *Globalization and Its Discontents* (London: Penguin Books, 2002).

Stoner-Weiss, *Resisting the State: Reform and Retrenchment in Post-Soviet Russia*, (Cambridge: Cambridge University Press, 2006).

Suhara, M. 'Corruption in Russia: A Historical Perspective', Slavic Research Centre (2004), 383–402.

Taratko, A.N. 'Psichologitsjetskie isledovania sotsialnogo kapitala v sovremenie Rossii' Conference presentation 'Economic Modernization and Social Development', Higher School of Economics, Moscow, 3–5 April 2007.

Tichonova, N. 'Russlands Sozialstruktur nach acht Jahren Reformen', *Berichte des Bundesinstituts für ostwissenschaftliche und internationale Studien*, No. 31 (1999).

Tucker, R.C. (Ed.) *Stalinism - Essays in Historical Interpretation* (New York: W.W. Norton & Company, 1977).

Unger, J., Chan, A. 'China, Corporatism, and the East Asian Model' *The Australian Journal of Chinese Affairs*, No. 33, January (1995) 29–53.

United Nations Development Programme (UNDP) *Russia's Regions: Goals, Challenges, and Achievements* (Moscow, 2007).

Veblen, T. *The Theory of the Leisure Class* (London: Prometheus Books, 1998).

Visnevskii, A.G. Russkii ili Prusskii- razmislenia perekhodnogo vremeni, Moskva (Izdatelstva dom GU VSE, 2005).

Voigt, P. 'Russia's Way From Planning toward Market: A Success Story? A Review of Economic Trajectories. Transition Progress and Putin's Merits', *Post-Communist Economies*, Vol. 18, June (2006) 123–39.

Volkov, V. *Silovoe Predprinimatelstvo – ekonomiko-sotsiologitestkii analyz* (Moscow: Izdatelskii Dom GU VSE, 2005a).

Volkov, V. 'Po tu storonu sudebnoi siltami potsjemu zakoni rabotaiut ne tak, kak dolzni' *Neprikosnovenii Zapas*, No. 42 (2005b).

Voslensky, M. *La Nomenklatura* (Paris: P. Belfond, 1980).

Weber, M., Wittich, C., Roth, G. (eds) *Economy and Society. An Outline of Interpretive Sociology* (University of California Press, 1979).

Wells, G.C., Baehr, P. (eds) *Max Weber. The Russian Revolutions* (Ithaca, NY: Cornell University Press, 1995, originally published 1917).

Wilson, A. *Virtual Politics. Faking Democracy in the Post-Soviet World* (New Haven: Yale University Press, 2005).

Winiecki, J. 'Determinants of Catching Up or Falling Behind: interaction of formal and informal institutions', *Post-Communist Economies*, Vol. 16, No. 2, June (2004) 137–52.

Wischnewskij, A. 'Die Modernisierung der UdSSR als konservative Revolution', *Berichte des Bundesinstituts für ostwissenschaftliche und internationale Studien*, No. 49 (1998).

Wittfogel, K. *Oriental Despotism. A Comparative Study of Total Power* (New Haven: Yale University Press, 1957).

Wolferen, K.G. van *Japan. De Onzichtbare Drijfveren van een Wereldmacht* (Amsterdam: Uitgeverij Balans, 1989).

Wood, T. 'Contours of the Putin Era. A Response to Vladimir Popov', *New Left Review*. March–April (2007) 53–68.

World Bank *From Transition to Development. A Country Economic Memorandum for the Russian Federation* (Moscow, 2005a).

World Bank *Growth, Poverty and Inequality. Eastern Europe and the former Soviet Union* (Washington, 2005b).

World Bank, 'Russian Economic Report, April 2006' (www.worldbank.org.ru) (World Bank, 2006a).

World Bank, 'Russian Economic Report, December 2006' (www.worldbank.org.ru) (World Bank, 2006b).

World Bank, 'Russian Economic Report, June 2007' (www.worldbank.org.ru) (World Bank, 2007a).

World Bank, 'Russian Economic Report, November 2007' (www.worldbank.org.ru) (World Bank, 2007b).

Yasin, E. (2007) 'Modernization and Society', Conference presentation 'Economic Modernization and Social Development', Higher School of Economics, Moscow, 3–5 April 2007.

Zimmer, K. 'Formal Institutions and Informal Politics in Ukraine', in Meyer, G. (ed.) (2006) 274–322.

Zon, H. van, Kreslavska, A. *Neizvestnaya Tragediya Zaparozhya*, (Saint Petersburg: Amadeus 2001).

Zon, H. van *The Political Economy of Independent Ukraine* (London: Macmillan, 2000).

Zon, H. van 'Neo-patrimonial practices in Ukraine: implications for economic development', *Journal of Communist Studies and Transition Politics*, Vol. 17, No. 3, September (2001) 71–95.

Zon, H. van 'Political Culture and Neo-Patrimonialism under Leonid Kuchma', *Problems of Post-Communism*, Vol. 52, No. 5, September/October (2005a) 58–65.

Zon, H. van 'Why the Orange Revolution Succeeded', *Perspectives on European Politics and Society*, Vol. 6, No. 3 (2005b), 373–403.

Zudin, A.Y. 'Polititsjeskie rezjim v Rossii v predverii novoi transformatsii' Conference presentation 'Economic Modernization and Social Development', Higher School of Economics, Moscow, 3–5 April 2007.

Index